THE ACADEMIC MIND
AND REFORM

The
ACADEMIC MIND
AND REFORM

The Influence of Richard T. Ely
in American Life

BENJAMIN G. RADER

UNIVERSITY OF KENTUCKY PRESS

PREFACE

FOR OVER TWO generations economist Richard T. Ely (1854-1943) popularized a wide spectrum of significant social ideas and mirrored many of the dilemmas, frustrations, and successes of the academician engaged in reform. He was both a participant in formulating, and a recipient of, the powerful ideas that agitated American reform circles in the late nineteenth and early twentieth centuries. He repudiated the older ideas that had blocked effective reform and lent an air of respectability to even radical proposals, while constantly appealing to traditional ethics. He infected a host of students and a large public audience with the need of applying human intelligence to social problems. With a fresh perspective to political economy Ely pioneered in new research and concluded his career by founding a new discipline, land economics. The story of Richard T. Ely lends itself especially well to exploring the role of the professor as both a contributor to reform ideology and as an activist in reform movements.

It is pleasant to have the opportunity to acknowledge my indebtedness to individuals who have been of particular assistance to me. Above all I want to thank my wife, Barbara, who has viewed the manuscript with a perceptive eye for stylistic improvement and handled much of the arduous task of typing. To her I owe an inestimable debt. Professor Paul K. Conkin provided searching criticisms and encouragement at each step of the manuscript's progress; my appreciation to him extends far beyond this book. I am obligated to Professors Edwin R. Bingham and Horace S. Merrill for several suggestions. In writing about the latter years of Ely's life I especially benefited from a critical reading of the manuscript by Dr. Allan Nevins, Dr. Edward W. Morehouse, son-in-law of Ely and onetime member of Ely's Institute for Research in Land Economics and Public Utilities, and Dr. Henry C. Taylor, another longtime Ely associate. All of these men should be absolved from responsibility for the final results. Librarians at the Johns Hopkins University, the Library of Congress, the University of Montana, and especially the State Historical Society of Wisconsin were always courteous and helpful. The Graduate Council of the University of Montana generously extended me a grant for microfilming costs and typing.

B.G.R.

CONTENTS

Preface   PAGE V

ONE   *Finding His Mission*   1

TWO   *His Message: The New Economics*   28

THREE   *His Message: Class Warfare*   54

FOUR   *"The Golden Mean"*   83

FIVE   *New Vistas in the West*   106

SIX   *Retreat from Reform*   130

SEVEN   *A Barometer of Wisconsin Progressivism*   159

EIGHT   *"Under All, the Land"*   192

NINE   *His Final Years*   223

Appendix: The Works of Richard T. Ely   237

Bibliographical Note   255

Index   259

Chapter One

FINDING HIS MISSION

WAVES OF HEAT danced from the New York sidewalks on a sultry midsummer day in 1880. Richard Theodore Ely, a short, pink-cheeked young man had just returned from Europe, walked along the streets in search of temporary work. Before him lay broken pavement and little children playing in dirty, treeless streets. On every side evidence of ugly corruption, of municipal incompetence, of an improper conception of the role of government met his sensitive eyes. His heart sank. What a "painful contrast," he reflected, with the sweeping breadth, the beauty, and the cleanliness of the streets of Berlin and Liverpool. Nostalgia, a momentary desire to return to Europe, the Europe which had opened his eyes to a brave new world that lay ahead, welled up within him. "Is this my America?" he asked himself. He then quietly resolved to "use every opportunity to benefit those who suffer."[1]

The young man's resolution came as no sudden impulse. From the time of his youth he had determined to find the

first principles by which men might improve their worldly
lot; he wished to identify and articulate the methods by which
his understanding of the Christian message could become a
reality. He was a missionary and an evangelist to the American public. His insatiable ambition propelled him to face and
overcome new challenges, but he was never able to find
complete personal satisfaction. The failure of the public to
respond instantly to his mission and of his fellow professors
to perceive the righteousness of his cause often led to personal
bitterness and an attitude of moral superiority. Frequently he
confused criticism of his methods with a personal challenge to
his sincerity; such criticism almost always meant a ruptured
friendship. But he harnessed his ambition and zeal to the
reform movement of the late nineteenth and early twentieth
centuries.

Richard Theodore Ely, born at Ripley, New York, on
April 13, 1854, was the first child of Ezra Sterling and Harriet
Gardner Mason Ely. Shortly after Richard's birth, his father
purchased a ninety-acre farm near Fredonia, New York, where
Richard spent his first sixteen years. Richard took pride in his
rise from rural origins. He remembered with some bitterness
the rocky, thin topsoil and the long, cold winters of western
New York State. Overcoming the stinginess of nature and the
increasing competition of the vast staple-producing Midwest
taxed the wits of the most skilled farmer. And father Ezra
lacked both the talents and the initiative for success. Sadly
deficient in farming experience, he relied on popular, and
often misleading, farm magazines for the intricate knowledge
needed to master the arts of plowing, planting, harvesting, and
restoring fertility to the soil. His religious beliefs interfered
with intelligent farm practices. Unlike many other Yankee

[1] Richard T. Ely, *Ground Under Our Feet: An Autobiography* (New
York: Macmillan, 1938), p. 65; Ely to Joseph A. Labadie, Aug. 14, 1885,
in Sidney Fine, ed., "The Ely-Labadie Letters," *Michigan History*,
XXXVI (March, 1952), 17.

farmers, the elder Ely allowed his hay to be ruined rather
than bring it in on Sunday. He stoutly refused to raise barley,
a crop eminently suited for the Ely farm, because he knew it
would be used for brewing beer. His farming operations
suffered from incredibly bad luck. After he finished the back-
breaking chore of clearing a fertile piece of ground for corn,
the crows ate the seed. Once, when the elder Ely "finally"
raised a bumper crop of potatoes, the bottom fell out of the
market.[2]

Despite hardship, farm life instilled in young Ely many
of the qualities that he held dear for his entire life. Assigned
a long list of jobs as a young boy, he learned the discipline
and duties of the typical farm youth. Wood had to be carried
in, butter churned, and, much to his chagrin, dishes washed.
His father had to be helped with the haying and rocks had
to be picked off the farm. Later he was responsible for seeing
that the cows were milked, even when it meant rising before
dawn and facing the cold wind and snow that whipped down
the plain lying between the Chautauqua County hills and
Lake Erie. On one occasion, Richard, without being told
and without consulting his father, decided to clear a thirty-
acre meadow which was strewn with stones, making the
mowing of hay so difficult. He hitched up the old team of
horses to the lumber wagon, enlisted the support of his
younger brother George and sister Frances, and picked up
the stones from the field. Impatient to remake the world,
young Richard assumed the role of a man at an age when
many boys seek escape from decisions and responsibility.

Years later, when Richard attempted self-analysis, he
became keenly aware of the "powerful influence of heredity"
in shaping his personality. On his father's side he proudly
traced his origins back to Cromwellian England to the first

---

[2] Ely, *Ground Under Our Feet,* p. 8; Frances Mason Ely, "Story and
Life of Harriet Gardner Ely," pp. 61, 65, typewritten manuscript in Ely
MSS, State Historical Society of Wisconsin, Madison.

Richard Ely, an ardent Puritan, who had hurriedly fled the mother country during the Restoration of the 1660's for the more friendly shores of New England. Settling temporarily in Boston, he had soon moved to Lyme, Connecticut, where, through marriage, he inherited a large farm. Lyme remained the home of his descendants for the next two centuries. The Elys followed a typical pattern for the lower gentry of Connecticut. A few farmed; several obtained college educations and served as ministers in the Congregational or Presbyterian churches. Few of the family earned more than local reputations. But one of his relatives, the Reverend Ezra Stiles Ely, pastor of the Third Presbyterian Church in Philadelphia, became something of a pamphleteer and aroused a furor in the Jacksonian era by advocating a united Christian party to purify Pennsylvania politics.[3]

Richard's father, Ezra Sterling Ely, had been appropriately named after the illustrious Philadelphia minister. Ezra wanted to follow in the footsteps of his ancestors by obtaining a college degree and perhaps preaching, but the poverty of his parents forced him to limit his educational ambitions to two academies of the "superior" type. Nonetheless, Ezra became a talented civil engineer, working on several railroads, but, because a regular job would have required traveling and Sunday work, his employment was sporadic. Stern-faced Ezra's true interests lay in theology and more abstract learning. He amazed friends by his capacity to read the most difficult Latin for pleasure.[4] He kept one of the finest libraries in the

[3] Ely, *Ground Under Our Feet*, pp. 1-3, 14; Moses E. Beach and William Ely, *The Ely Ancestry* (New York: Calumet, 1902), pp. 65, 515; John R. Bodo, *The Protestant Clergy and Public Issues, 1812-1848* (Princeton, N.J.: Princeton University Press, 1954), pp. 46-47; Elizabeth M. Geffen, "Philadelphia Protestantism Reacts to Social Reform Movements before the Civil War," *Pennsylvania History*, XXX (April, 1963), 208.

[4] Ezra Sterling Ely to R. T. Ely, Nov. 21, 1896, Dec. 3, 1896, in Frances Mason Ely, "In Memoriam, Ezra Sterling Ely, 1825-1899," pp. 139, 153, typewritten manuscript in Ely MSS.

vicinity of Fredonia, admired beauty, and deeply loved poetry, sometimes scratching out a few lines himself. Young Richard's inclination toward an academic way of life surprised no one; in fact, his younger brother, George, also was a teacher for a time.

While religious life was central to the history of Fredonia, Ezra took his faith far more seriously than his neighbors. Richard remembered that the Presbyterian ministers preached about an angry and jealous God, drawn directly from the Old Testament. Eternal damnation in a pit of fire faced those who had no conversion experience. Bitter sectarianism frequently flared at community gatherings, with the discussion invariably turning to such theological questions as predestination and the proper means of baptism, sprinkling or immersion. But, while many Fredonians apparently took part in the controversies as a means of escape from the impoverished social life of the community, Ezra took them seriously. His dedication made him a "gloomy," brooding, introspective Christian. Tobacco he considered a filthy habit; he never used liquors and wines. The awe and respect with which Richard viewed his father concealed any overt hostility. But close affection between father and son was impossible, for Ezra attempted to mold the family to a demanding perfection. He prohibited the reading of secular books and playing on the Sabbath. Unable to play marbles for "keeps," Richard felt ostracized by the boys in the neighborhood and found easy familiarity with them difficult.

Anxiety beclouded Richard's youth. Despite conscientious effort he failed to have a conversion experience. Richard later explained that he could never accept the inconsistency of a good God damning a large part of men to eternal torment. Ezra constantly worried about his son's unorthodoxy. "I should feel much more at ease and settled about you," his father wrote in 1876, "were I satisfied that you had given yourself . . . to the service of Christ and His church. I never shall feel satisfied with anything else."[5] When Richard went to Columbia, he again tried "to become a good Presbyterian." But he soon gave up and, for a short time and to the consternation of his father, considered becoming a Universalist minister. Before completing his studies in New York, he joined the Protestant Episcopal church, where he found the theology and maintenance of the spirit of Christian love more congenial. He participated actively as a layman in church affairs for the rest of his life.[6]

Despite differences of theology between father and son, Ezra shaped Richard's determination to live according to high ideals and to convey them to others. Ezra's ardent faith included a strong belief in equalitarianism and social reform. Once, to the dismay of the family, he appeared in church in his farm overalls to demonstrate the principle that both the rich and the poor were equal in the sight of God. He felt that a mirror should be used only for shaving lest it cultivate vanity. In every family prayer he emphasized the obligation of a Christian to improve the condition of his fellow man. On one occasion he published an article condemning the practices of the Chautauqua County jail. The purpose of detention should be to reform criminals as well as to protect society, Ezra insisted. Since boyhood, Richard recalled, he had felt the same desire as his father to "set the world on fire." Not surprisingly, Richard's early hero was Horace Greeley, perpetual sponsor of reform movements.[7]

Richard's mother tempered the ascetic quality of Ezra's faith. Harriet Gardner Ely, born somewhat lower in the social order than Ezra, extended "boundless love" to the children. Richard felt much more at ease with her and always sought her out for advice on matters of crucial personal concern. Over Ezra's long resistance she insisted that the Ely family

---

[5] Ezra Sterling Ely to R. T. Ely, April 27, 1876, *ibid.*, p. 121.
[6] See J. M. Pullman to R. T. Ely, Feb. 6, 1886, Ely MSS.
[7] See Ely, *Ground Under Our Feet*, pp. 24, 286.

celebrate the "papish" practice of Christmas. Small, fragile, and often in poor health, she nonetheless had tremendous vitality and a wide versatility. Though she had no formal training in painting, she took most of the prizes at the Chautauqua County fair and even supplemented the family's meager income by selling her paintings and teaching art at the Fredonia Normal School. She never seemed to grow old. Richard believed that he inherited his own "abundant energy" and lifelong youthful zeal from her.[8]

Richard remained intimate with the immediate family throughout his life. Almost every summer, while his parents were alive, he returned to Fredonia for extended visits and lectured to the nearby Chautauqua Summer School. When he moved to Baltimore to assume a post at the Johns Hopkins University and later to the University of Wisconsin, he and his parents frequently exchanged visits. During the 1880's, his father lost heavily on some speculative investments and the family faced financial ruin. Richard, despite his own modest income, lent regular assistance in both the eighties and nineties. Richard's outward admiration for his father never diminished. He sent him manuscripts for books, asked his advice on professional matters, and, most important, attempted to live up to the Christian principles set by his father.

Richard's dedication to principle and his relentless personal drive found their source in the matrix of his family and religious background. Physically, he stood only five feet and five inches tall; he had a slight build, close-set ears, and a rather boyish face. But his piercing eyes revealed a boundless energy, a restless desire to set the world aright. The demands he placed upon himself were high, almost unbearably so. When he failed to obtain an academic post upon his return

[8] Apart from Richard's autobiography, see F. M. Ely, "Story and Life of Harriet Gardner Ely," for an intimate account of the nature of family relations.

Ely's favorite instructor. The training under Nairne was "part of the reason," Ely later recalled, "why I decided to go to Germany to study philosophy and find the 'absolute truth.' "[12] Nairne had high praise for Ely, judging him "as one of the best metaphysicians he had had under his training in the College."[13] Under Nairne's guidance he prepared an essay on Oliver Goldsmith that was judged the best in the graduating class. In all his many publications, Ely attempted to write in "a plain, straight-forward style," making Oliver Goldsmith and Washington Irving his "masters," and he advised his students to do likewise.[14]

At Columbia Ely met and shared the company of the wealthy sons of the New York City gentility. Because of his own modest financial means, he found that fellow students never asked him to contribute to the athletic events, yet they always invited him to their social functions. The action of one wealthy classmate, Eugene Seligman, in refusing to try for a fellowship awarded by the college because it should go to a more needy student, impressed Ely. When Ely returned from Germany without work, Seligman loaned him money. Despite Ely's harsh criticism of the competitive order in later years, he continued to admire wealthy men who assumed wide social responsibilities. And he viewed himself as something of an intellectual aristocrat who should lead and direct from above the social order in the interest of all classes.

In his senior year Ely decided to work for the $500 fellowship awarded by the college for three years of study abroad. In 1876, with the support of Nairne and the Goldsmith essay, he received the fellowship, only the second to be awarded in letters by Columbia. His mother wrote enthusiastically to his sister about the fellowship: "The President spoke of the

---

[12] *Ibid.*, p. 34.
[13] Henry Drisler to William McVikar, April 20, 1887, Ely MSS.
[14] See Ely, "Oliver Goldsmith," *Acta Columbiana*, Nov., 1876, pp. 23-36; Ely to Edward A. Ross, Dec. 9, 1904, Ross MSS, State Historical Society of Wisconsin, Madison.

extreme difficulty in getting it and gave him great honor for his success. When it was announced the class gave cheer after cheer—stamping and clapping, I mean, and then when he went up again, cheering, and when he came down they made the house ring and everyone it seems to me grasped his hand as he passed on to his seat. It was delightful to see their interest in him."[15]

With the coveted fellowship in hand Ely sought suggestions for his study of philosophy in Germany. The Columbia faculty could make no recommendations, but, in a chance meeting, a New York University professor suggested that he contact the president of Yale University, Noah Porter. When Ely arrived in New Haven, Porter, who was preoccupied, offhandedly advised him to study under Ulrici of the University of Halle. With this scanty information Ely, now a young man of twenty-three, sailed for Germany and landed in Hamburg in June of 1877. Upon his arrival he became suspicious of Porter's advice, for his new German friends had never heard of Ulrici. In order to learn to speak the language more fluently, Ely stayed with a German family in Kiel. Having taken second prize in German at Columbia, he quickly became proficient, and by the end of the summer he was ready to search for Ulrici. In September Ely went to Halle but discovered that Ulrici was very old and had retired from teaching.

At Halle Ely fortunately met Simon N. Patten, a "gawky, rural mannered" youth from the Midwest who became a lifelong friend. Patten, along with two other Americans, Edmund J. James and Joseph F. Johnson, had been at the University of Halle for some time. Patten immediately took Ely under his care and found him a place to live. It was Patten who introduced Ely to Professor Johannes Conrad, a disciple of the German Historical School of economics and a specialist in

[15] Harriet Ely to F. M. Ely, June 28, 1876, in F. M. Ely, "Story and Life of Harriet Gardner Ely," pp. 182-183.

agrarian policy.[16] Initially Ely continued his study of philosophy, but he soon found Conrad's course in economics more
exciting. He also found the skepticism of Professor Rudolph
Haym in philosophy disillusioning. Ely later wrote: Haym
"did a great deal to influence me to abandon my youthful
idealistic purpose of seeking the absolute truth."[17] He also
found that his training in Scottish "commonsense" philosophy
was inadequate for the advanced study of the more technical
German philosophy of Hegel and Kant. Economics, he
decided, "where I could keep my feet on the ground," provided ample room for speculative capacities.

Discouraged with his work in philosophy and encouraged
by friends to join them in the study of economics and political
science at the University of Heidelberg, he left Halle in April,
1878. At Heidelberg he discovered a "delightful" cosmopolitan atmosphere, with students from all parts of the world.
Each day he studied and listened to lectures until five o'clock,
then took a walk in the beautiful streets and sometimes into
the countryside. Far away from the restrictive influence of
home Ely enjoyed the freer manner of living he found in
Germany. Undoubtedly his father was a bit shocked when
Richard wrote home: "In America we would undoubtedly be
healthier and handsomer if we knew how to live. If we could
ever learn that when God gave us a faculty for enjoyment,
pleasure and means of gratifying it, He meant we should
enjoy ourselves, that we honored Him not only in church-
going and long prayers, but also in laughing, jumping, dancing
and being happy in this world! So long as we continue above
all people in the world, to neglect this truth in our lives, we
will continue to suffer for it."[18]

While escaping the orthodoxy imposed by his father,

[16] See Ely, "Recollections of the Life and Work of Professor Simon
N. Patten," *Papers and Proceedings of the American Economic Association*, 4th ser., XIII (1923), 259.
[17] Ely, *Ground Under Our Feet*, p. 40.
[18] Quoted *ibid.*, pp. 54-55.

Richard also escaped the dry educational methods so typical of the American colleges of the period. Instead of the American recitation system based on a text containing established truths, the German professors treated the students as fellow colleagues in the pursuit of new knowledge. "They are very different from American professors in this respect," he wrote home. "It is that which makes studying in Germany such a pleasure to every real student. You learn here, and only here, how to do independent, real scientific work."[19] The idea of seeking new knowledge through research thrilled Ely, for now he felt that he could contribute something original and worthwhile to posterity.

Ely soon chose Karl Knies, aging economist at Heidelberg, as his major professor. Knies, along with Wilhelm Roscher and Bruno Hildebrand, had developed the approach of the German Historical School of economics. The sad-eyed, lonely, old professor felt that his contribution to the school had been underrated, an opinion which Ely shared. While other American students at Heidelberg, such as John Bates Clark, seemed little impressed with Knies, Ely acknowledged him as "my *meister.*"[20] Knies presented to Ely immense new possibilities for the crusading heart. Man, Knies insisted, rather than the abstract mechanical laws of the classicists, should stand at the center of all economic study. Economic science should attempt to prescribe formulas which allowed man to square his ethics with reality. These were the sort of ideas which Ely had been seeking, a message worth living and working for.

After taking the Doctor of Philosophy degree *summa cum laude* at Heidelberg, Ely briefly toured Switzerland, where he took courses in economics and French literature at the University of Geneva. In five "not very profitable" months

[19] Quoted *ibid.*, p. 43.
[20] Ely, *The World War and Leadership in a Democracy* (New York: Macmillan, 1918), p. 30. Knies wrote Ely a fine letter of recommendation; Nov. 26, 1878, Ely MSS.

he produced one article, "The Scaffold in Switzerland,"[21] and then returned to Berlin for the third year of the fellowship. At Berlin he tutored private students, attended sessions of the Reichstag and meetings of German socialists, observed the Berlin Congress of 1878, and presumptuously predicted the German domination of Russia.[22] He became a member of the Royal Statistical Bureau, directed by Dr. Ernst Engel, and at the famous Round Table of the bureau he heard lectures from Engel and Professor Adolf Wagner, the leading "professorial" socialist in Germany. He was introduced to Engel's law of consumption and may have been the first person to expound the theory in the United States. He also wrote a few nondescript articles for the New York *Evening Post* as well as one article on German universities and American colleges for *Harper's New Monthly Magazine.*[23]

In Berlin Ely met President Andrew D. White of Cornell, who was acting American minister to Germany. White took Ely under his tutelage, as he had many other young American scholars, and Ely became a devoted admirer. Dedicating his first book-length publication to White, Ely wrote: "The publication of this volume is due to the friendly counsel of the Honorable Andrew D. White, . . . a gentleman tireless in his efforts to encourage young men, and alive to every opportunity to speak fitting words of hope and cheer. . . . I am indebted to him more than I can say."[24] White impressed upon Ely that too many scholars wasted valuable time revising their work, whereas the important thing was to present one's ideas

[21] New York *Evening Post,* June 11, 1879.
[22] [Ely], "Germany and Russia," New York *Evening Post,* Nov. 1, 1879.
[23] [Ely], "Germany's Burdens," New York *Evening Post,* March 24, 1880; [Ely], "Street Cleaning in Berlin," *ibid.,* April 6, 1881; Ely, "American Colleges and German Universities," *Harper's New Monthly Magazine,* LXI (July, 1880), 253-260; Ely and Frank Bohn, *The Great Change* (New York: Nelson, 1935), p. 146.
[24] Ely, *French and German Socialism in Modern Times* (New York: Harper, 1883), p. 1.

to the public.[25] Errors if made would be corrected later. This advice Ely consistently followed throughout his life. "I recognized this as good counsel," he later wrote, "and I followed it. Some may say that I followed it too unreservedly, but, at any rate, I transformed my various ideas into numerous books and articles. They have been criticized, and justly so. . . . But I believe that in writing them I have served, even if in small measure, as a clarifying influence on economic thought."[26]

At the solicitation of White, Ely studied the administration of the city of Berlin and the purchase of private railroads by Prussia. The State Department published the latter report at the suggestion of White, and it aided Ely in securing a position at the Johns Hopkins University. Perhaps fortunately for Ely, White did not read the article on the administration of Berlin until 1885. Although on the whole favorably disposed toward his analysis, White believed Ely had made a serious mistake in presenting the German bureaucracy as the ideal. White maintained that the existence of the bureaucracy demanded a "general surrender of individualism."[27]

At the expiration of his fellowship in 1880 Ely returned to America, but his admiration for German scholarship never diminished. He published a series of articles over the years testifying to his belief in the superiority of German educational methods. As a matter of course he expected his superior graduate students to study in Germany. His return trips in 1891 and in 1911 stimulated his zest for tackling the economic

25 Ely to Edwin R. A. Seligman, June 23, 1885, in Joseph Dorfman, ed., "The Seligman Correspondence, II," *Political Science Quarterly*, LVI (June, 1941), 280.

26 Ely, *Ground Under Our Feet*, p. 59.

27 [Ely], "Administration of the City of Berlin," *Nation*, XXXIV (March 23, 30, 1882), 245-246, 267-269; Ely, "A Brief Sketch of the Railway History of Germany," in *Papers Relating to the Foreign Relations of the United States, Transmitted to Congress with the Annual Message of the President, December 6, 1880*, pp. 408-422; Andrew D. White to Ely, July 6, 1885, Ely MSS.

problems that beset America. Germany served as an enviable benchmark from which American achievements in reform and research could be measured.

Upon his return to New York, Ely's first task was to find a suitable academic post. Openings were scarce, for only a few American colleges offered full-time work in political economy. He was forced to wait a year, "tramping the streets of New York city looking for work," producing a few articles for popular periodicals, and tutoring students in German for a livelihood. But, after a favorable editorial by Carl Schurz in the New York *Evening Post* and the *Nation* on his report on Prussian railroads, he learned of an opening at the Johns Hopkins University in Baltimore, Maryland. Originally he received an appointment as an instructor at $600 for a half year beginning in 1881 but won an extension to a full year with an additional $500. Now young Ely was ready to fulfill the pledge which he had made that hot summer day, to "use every opportunity to benefit those who suffer."[28]

Johns Hopkins had already acquired an international reputation for the quality of its graduate work. By placing emphasis on research, the institution produced many of the leaders of academic thought in the late nineteenth century. Original research and innovations in teaching methods took precedence over formal lectures. Ideally, both student and professor were engaged in the joint pursuit of truth. The Hopkins president, Daniel C. Gilman, had employed six full professors of worldwide reputations but was unable to obtain a renowned scholar for history and the social sciences. Consequently, Herbert Baxter Adams, a graduate of Hopkins, was appointed as an associate in history. He also offered the first course of lectures in political economy. Later, Henry C.

28 Ely, *Ground Under Our Feet*, pp. 164-165; Ely to Charles McCarthy, April 6, 1912, Ely to Theodore Ely Hamilton, Sept. 25, 1899, Ely MSS; Hugh Hawkins, *Pioneer: A History of the Johns Hopkins University, 1874-1889* (Ithaca, N.Y.: Cornell University Press, 1960), p. 178.

Adams taught political economy for one year but proved unsatisfactory for a permanent position.[29] Ely had no outstanding credentials for the Johns Hopkins post. As E. L. Godkin, editor of the *Nation* and close adviser of Gilman, explained, Ely had "only written one thing for the *Nation*, an account of the municipal Government of Berlin, and though this was careful and well done, it was simply descriptive and did not furnish materials for an opinion of any value as to his general equipment as an economist."[30] On the other hand, Ely was young, could be obtained for a low salary, and had the recommendation of President White of Cornell. Regent George W. Brown summarized the feeling of Hopkins officials when he wrote Gilman that "in Political Economy we must rely on young men of promise and Ely strikes me as one who ought to be tried."[31]

When hired, Ely assured Gilman that he planned no radical breaks with traditionalism in economics. "I should not endeavor so much to teach or enforce any specific economic doctrines as to explain the various theories actually maintained by those who have contributed one way or another to the growth of the science. I should seek to explain the origin of various economic schools, and their relations . . . to point out to my hearers the sources to economic information and to put them as far as possible in a position to conduct original investigations on special economic topics."[32] Only the last objective gave any indication of the Ely approach to economics which was to help foment a revolution against orthodox classical doctrines.

Although the salary was low and the appointment on an annual basis, Ely had probably obtained the best possible position for exercising a decisive influence on economic

---

[29] See Hawkins, *Pioneer*, pp. 177-178.
[30] Godkin to Gilman, June 17, 1882, Gilman MSS, Johns Hopkins University Library, Baltimore.
[31] Brown to Gilman, Aug. 11, 1881, Gilman MSS.
[32] Ely to Gilman, Sept. 23, 1881, Gilman MSS.

thought and public opinion. Working in a loose arrangement
under Herbert Baxter Adams, he came into contact with the
history and political science as well as the economics students
through the famous Seminary which met each Friday night.
Gathering around a long green table, Adams, Ely, and later
J. Franklin Jameson (in 1882) led the reading and critical
examination of scholarly research papers. The Seminary, in
the mind of the staff, was analogous to the research laboratory
of the biological scientist. Here conclusions were subjected
to detailed criticism. As an additional inducement to quality
research, the University published the "Johns Hopkins University Studies in Historical and Political Science" under the
editorial direction of Adams. The best graduate theses and
writings of both Ely and Adams appeared in the famous
studies.

In 1881 Ely assumed his temporary appointment as
lecturer of political economy and moved into a rooming house
at 156 Biddle Street in Baltimore. "Homely and insignificant"
in appearance, the twenty-seven-year-old bachelor had not
completely outgrown his childhood shyness. Although not
adept at informal conversation, he relished serious discussion
in his own field. On occasion he invited the "boys," which
often included his brother George, who received a fellowship
in mathematics at Hopkins in 1881, to his home for light
refreshments and conversation. He led student devotional
meetings for the university Young Men's Christian Association
and even drafted a bill for the students' "House of Commons."
No older than many of his graduate students, Ely enjoyed a
comradeship with them which was lacking between the
older professors and students.[33]

[33] *Johns Hopkins University Circulars,* I (Dec., 1881), 156; J.
Franklin Jameson Diary, Oct. 7, 1881, Dec. 4, 1881, Jameson MSS,
Library of Congress; Edward A. Ross, *Seventy Years of It: An Autobiog-
raphy* (New York: Appleton-Century, 1936), p. 42; *Johns Hopkins Uni-
versity Circulars,* VII (April, 1888), 80, IX (Dec., 1889), 23; Hawkins,
Pioneer, pp. 278-279.

While vacationing in the summer of 1883 he met Anna Morris Anderson at a Virginia Military Institute ball in Lexington and immediately fell in love with the charming southern girl whose personality contrasted markedly with his own. By December of 1883 he was writing to his mother in ecstatic terms. "I wish I could give you some idea of what she is, but it is impossible, because I am certain no one ever like her ever lived. . . . I am glad our natures are as diverse as they are, since they supplement each other so admirably."[34] After their marriage on June 25, 1884, they honeymooned at the Pullman village near Chicago, Illinois. Characteristically, Ely spent part of his honeymoon studying the company town for a magazine article—an early indication that his family life would remain largely subordinate to his work. In the early years of their marriage, Richard's mother warned him repeatedly to spend more time with Anna and less with his work. But Ely ignored her advice and apparently Anna gracefully accepted her secondary role. Being of the First Families of Virginia, she proved a superb hostess to faculty wives, visiting reformers, and students. With the low cost of living in Baltimore and Richard's writing income, the Elys were able to afford part-time servants for cooking and cleaning. When a son, Richard Sterling, was born in 1887, they built a three-story brick house at 2400 Calvert Street, next to Goucher College.[35]

Ely's first year as a teacher was inauspicious. Although he obtained an extension of his one-term contract for the full academic year of 1881-1882 and was invited to return for the 1882-1883 academic year at a $1,250 salary, President Gilman and Herbert Baxter Adams initially had some doubts as to his permanency. His public lecture series on civil service in

[34] Ely to Harriet Mason Ely, Dec. 30, 1883, in Ely, *Ground Under Our Feet*, pp. 165-166.

[35] Harriet Mason Ely to Ely, Oct. 24, 1884, in F. M. Ely, "Story and Life of Harriet Gardner Ely," p. 257; Ely, *Ground Under Our Feet*, pp. 166, 174-175; E. A. Ross to Ely, Sept. 30, 1896, Ely MSS; Jameson Diary, Dec. 20, 1884, Nov. 23, 1886, April 28, 1888; photostatic copy of Ely family record contained in family Bible, Ely MSS.

Hopkins Hall failed dismally, attracting the smallest crowds of any in the year. Two of the seasoned graduate students, J. Franklin Jameson and Thorstein Veblen, thought that Ely was no improvement over Henry C. Adams, their former instructor. According to Jameson, Ely was impossible to take notes from, repetitious, temperamental, and infatuated with the German Historical School of economics. After one term Veblen left for Yale, and Jameson felt that Veblen had "undoubtedly" chosen a better place to study economics. Veblen indicated, however, that he would return to Hopkins if offered a fellowship and, further, that he appreciated Ely's encouragement to publish a paper that he had prepared for Ely's class.[36]

In spite of Ely's modest beginning, the enrollment of students in his courses grew steadily. While only five or six took his courses in his first year, by 1885 he averaged over thirty and by 1890 over forty students. More important, he attracted high quality graduate students. They came for different reasons, some because of the reputation of the university and Ely, others because Ely was a controversial figure dedicated to reform. After reading a scathing review of Ely's *Labor Movement* in the *Nation*, John R. Commons determined to make Ely his master. When enrolled at Hopkins he wrote his mother letters flaming with enthusiasm for Ely and the new economics taught by him.[37] Albion Small passed up a $750 fellowship at Harvard and went to Ely "because I knew," he explained, "that your writings had done more than any other influence to attract to the Hopkins the best men who were in the Political department when I was there."[38]

[36] Jameson Diary, Dec. 17, 1881; Ely to D. C. Gilman, Aug. 2, 1882, Gilman MSS; Jameson Diary, Nov. 1, 1881, Feb. 4, 1882; Veblen to Jameson, Feb. 12, 1883, Jameson MSS.

[37] John R. Commons, *Myself* (New York: Macmillan, 1934), pp. 40, 44.

[38] Small to Ely, Nov. 20, 1899, April 11, 1891, Ely MSS. See also Ross to Theodore Herfurth, Feb. 2, 1946, Herfurth MSS, State Historical Society of Wisconsin, Madison.

The personal encouragement that Ely gave Veblen illustrated an important trait which all of his students profoundly appreciated. Recognizing the potential of Edward A. Ross, he praised him for his superior achievement. "Last Wednesday Dr. Ely called me into his office and told me," Ross wrote to his foster mother, that "he was very much pleased with my paper and that I would undoubtedly make an economist. . . . Then on Thursday in his lecture Dr. Ely quotes an opinion 'as Mr. Ross showed in his paper.'" Again on a different note he wrote: "I read the rest of my paper at Dr. Ely's Seminary. At the conclusion Dr. Ely commended it highly before the rest of the boys."[39]

Ely encouraged his students to publish their best work, even writing letters of introduction to publishers commending their papers. He sponsored several cooperative works with his students, such as a joint history of American economic ideas with Woodrow Wilson and Davis R. Dewey. Although never completed, even the impatient Wilson became intensely involved in the work. As secretary of the American Economic Association, Ely helped to obtain publishers for Albert Shaw, Edward Bemis, and Amos G. Warner, all on some phase of cooperation. He credited another student, John H. Finley, with joint authorship of *Taxation in American States and Cities*. And time after time he acknowledged the work of his students in prefaces, footnotes, the body of his work, and in personal correspondence. A human dynamo, Ely devoted an amazing amount of attention to his students while maintaining numerous personal projects.[40]

[39] Ross to M. D. Beach, April 13, May 2, 1890, Ross MSS. See also L. P. Powell to Ross, Nov. 24, 1891, Ross MSS.
[40] Ross to M. D. Beach, Nov. 11, 1890, Ross MSS; *Johns Hopkins University Circulars*, V (July, 1886), 132; Ray Stannard Baker, ed., *Woodrow Wilson, Life and Letters: Youth, 1856-1890* (Garden City, N.Y.: Doubleday, Page, 1927), pp. 180-181; Ely, *Ground Under Our Feet*, p. 113; Ely, "The American Economic Association, 1885-1909," *Publications of the American Economic Association*, 3d ser., XI (1910), 75.

Ely took a special interest in Japanese students at both Johns Hopkins and Wisconsin, even making them personal loans. They returned to their mother country as dedicated disciples of Ely's brand of social ethics. Five of his books, including his popular *Introduction to Political Economy*, were translated and used as texts in Japanese schools. Shosuke Sato, a former Ely student, wrote upon completing the translation of the *Introduction* that "the work is the very kind we need in Japan. I have no doubt that it will do a great deal of good in Japan." He explained later that the Japanese public was "tired to hear the dry explanations of the Manchester School for vital economic problems of to-day" and welcomed the approach of the new school.[41] Another Ely student, Charles Meriwether, when he arrived in Japan as a missionary, found Ely had "a wide reputation here in Japan."[42] In 1920, President Charles S. Reifseirder of St. Paul's College, Tokyo, claimed that in Japan Ely's works were "probably more widely read than all the other works on Political Economy put together."[43]

Ely's primary appeal as a teacher and an economist lay in his strong ethical commitments. His high Christian idealism and open sympathies with the underprivileged contrasted quite markedly with the majority of academicians. "I think we all have you to thank that you disclosed to us the whole forest rather than a few trees which constituted the science of political economy in the past, and that man is something more than a mere covetous machine and that the science which deals with him in society has larger aims than the study of rent, interest, wages and value," wrote Frederic C. Howe, an Ely student who became a significant municipal reformer, progressive, and New Dealer.[44] Not surprisingly, after train-

[41] Sato to Ely, Jan. 7, 1890, Nov. 5, 1891, Ely MSS.
[42] Meriwether to L. P. Powell, April 22, 1892, Ely MSS. For a similar conclusion, see T. Sasaki to Ely, Aug. 11, 1899, Ely MSS.
[43] Reifseirder to Ely, Oct. 8, 1920, Ely MSS.
[44] Howe to Ely, Aug. 1, 1894, Ely MSS.

ing in economics under Ely, several of his students entered
the ministry. George P. Morris, later editor of the *Congregationalist*, and George Gates, later editor of the *Kingdom*, became influential leaders in the social gospel movement. John
R. Commons became an important lay spokesman for the
Christian sociology movement. Other students went into
social work. Charles D. Warner wrote the first basic text on
charities, and Philip W. Ayres later headed the Associated
Charities in Cincinnati, Chicago, and New York.[45]

Ely encouraged his students to "look and see" what
economic conditions were rather than concentrating their
studies in economic theory. He himself set the pace. When
Johann Most, a violent anarchist who had just been chased
from Europe, spoke in Baltimore, Ely took a seat next to the
workingmen of the city. "I considered it of weight that I
should hear for myself an exposition of the ideas of a man
who was conducting an agitation which aimed at the abolition
of existing social institutions," he reported to the Seminary.
The students listened intently to his description of Most as a
man whose "mind has become diseased. He is fanatical and
bloodthirsty." But "the socialism of a man like Wagner
[a professorial socialist]," Ely told them, ". . . differs from that
of Most as black and white. Indeed, men of the stamp of
Most reject the professorial socialist from the start as timid
and reactionary."[46]

Unlike other academic economists who disdained popular
social movements, Ely felt they were of crucial importance.
He lectured and wrote on Henry George, the single-tax
advocate. When George spoke at a mass rally in Baltimore
in 1888, Ely and his students were conspicuously present. In

[45] See the *Johns Hopkins University Circulars*, 1881-1892, for lists
of Ely students.

[46] Ely, "Herr Most in Baltimore," March 2, 1882, typewritten manuscript in Ely MSS. Even the sarcastic Jameson recorded that "we had
a big crowd; Ely read a very good paper on 'Herr Most in Baltimore.'"
Jameson Diary, March 2, 1883.

1887 Ely addressed the American Federation of Labor at Baltimore and thereby became the first academic economist to speak before a national convention of a labor organization.[47] When the Baltimore streetcar workers held a rally for a twelve-hour day law in 1886, Ely wrote an open letter of sympathy to them which appeared on the front page of the Baltimore *Sun*. While a scholar must retain a cool, objective judgment, Ely wrote, "I do not hesitate to condemn in severe terms the treatment street-car employees have received from their employers. In future years it will inevitably be described as a blot on our much-vaunted nineteenth-century civilization, that in all large American cities men worked from fourteen to nineteen hours a day in the sight of public, and that the moral sense of the community was not sufficiently elevated to revolt against this barbarity." Ely expressed his "hearty approval" of a suitable twelve-hour law and maintained that it was "a popular fallacy that legislation can have no influence on these matters. The experience of all modern nations refutes this."[48] He typically concluded his letter with a plea for the municipal ownership of the street railways. Other high-minded men, including ministers, joined in support of the streetcar workers and the Maryland legislature passed a twelve-hour law.[49]

Ely's commitment to an ethical ideal in economic life meshed with his insistence that the facts be examined. "Merely to know what is in all its bearings itself often shows what ought to be, as in the case of the evils of child labor, and itself suggests a remedy for evils."[50] Edward A. Ross in 1946

[47] Baltimore *Sun*, Feb. 6, 1888; Ely, "Address before the Annual Meeting of the American Federation of Labor," *Christian Union*, XXXVII (Feb. 9, 1888), 170. For a concise summary of Ely's views on George, see Ely, "The Single Tax," *Christian Advocate*, LXV (Dec. 25, 1890), 856.

[48] Baltimore *Sun*, March 9, 1886.

[49] Ely, "How to Prevent Strikes," *Christian Union*, XXXIX (Feb. 21, 1889), 231; Ely, *Ground Under Our Feet*, p. 78.

[50] Ely, *An Introduction to Political Economy* (New York: Chautauqua, 1889), pp. 102-103.

explained this side of the Ely approach. "Constantly he incited us to examine the facts—all the facts available—and see what they appeared to add up to. More than any other scholar he deserves the credit of the inductive, realistic trend that has dominated American political economy of the last forty years."[51] But Ross exaggerated one side of the Ely approach, for Ely's profound faith in progress through human manipulation of the environment left an equally important impression on his students. Facts did not stand alone, Ely thought, but in the context of a plastic human nature and an ethical ideal. The new starting point for economic investigations set by Ely gave his work an air of contagious excitement and purpose.

The research topics chosen by Ely's students ignored highly theoretical subjects. Ely advised Ross that "the proper subjects [for theses] are those which are largely historical and description."[52] He usually suggested topics denoting the ultimate direction of economic evolution as he saw it. Popular subjects, for example, were cooperatives and communal societies. Some papers took quite restricted forms, such as M. A. Mikkelson's "Bishop Hill: A Religious Communistic Society in Henry County, Illinois." Other students examined subjects more attractive to the immediate demands of nineteenth-century reformers. They did extensive research on cities which owned their gas, water, and electric works. They compared private railway ownership in the United States with the state ownership in Prussia and Australia, inevitably concluding in favor of the latter. John R. Commons even prepared a topic for Ely on "How to Obtain a Home in Baltimore," and Amos G. Warner wrote on organized charities in Baltimore.[53]

51 Ross to Theodore Herfurth, Feb. 2, 1946, Herfurth MSS.
52 Ely to Ross, June 23, 1891, Ross MSS.
53 See *Johns Hopkins University Circulars*, IV (Nov., 1884), 209, IV (July, 1885), 105, VI (April, 1887), 86, VII (Sept., 1889), 105, X (April, 1891), 80; Bemis to Ely, Sept. 29, 1886, Ely MSS; Albert Shaw, *Icaria: A Chapter in the History of Communism* (New York: Putnam, 1884).

The concrete nature of the research subjects selected by Ely appealed to the idealism of his students, for they felt they were contributing significantly to the improvement of human welfare. Ely left an incalculable impression on such undergraduates as Newton D. Baker, who later served as a reform mayor of Cleveland and secretary of war under President Wilson. The interest of Wilson, Albert Shaw, and William Willoughby in public administration stemmed from their training under Ely and Adams. Both attended Ely's weekly lectures on administration. Shaw, who later edited the *Review of Reviews,* led in the movement for better municipal government and was an adviser to President Theodore Roosevelt. And it followed for Roosevelt to claim that Ely had made him "sane" in his economic radicalism.[54]

The eleven years that Ely spent at the Johns Hopkins University were the most productive of his life. He could well describe them as his "golden years," for during that period he published over fifty journal articles and seven important monographs, served on the Baltimore and the Maryland tax commissions, and advised and influenced reformers of all varieties across the country. He also played the primary role in the founding of the American Economic Association and as secretary assured its success in the early years. But his most enduring personal monument probably rested in the accomplishments of his students. No professor of political economy in the country directed or helped to direct so many of the future leaders in the social sciences. To name a few, Davis R. Dewey, John R. Commons, Edward A. Ross, Albion Small, Albert Shaw, Edward H. Bemis, Thomas Nixon Carver, and Frederic C. Howe did their major work under Ely; and

[54] C. H. Cramer, *Newton D. Baker: A Biography* (Cleveland: World, 1961), p. 23; Ely, "Request that Mr. Henry D. Gardner be allowed to offer administration as a minor for the degree of Ph.D." [1885?], in Herbert Baxter Adams MSS, Johns Hopkins University Library, Baltimore; Ely to Lucy Washburn, Feb. 17, 1919, Ely MSS; Ely, *Ground Under Our Feet,* pp. 278-279.

Frederick Jackson Turner, Charles Haskins, W. W. and W. F. Willoughby, Woodrow Wilson, and J. Franklin Jameson took a minor under him. His association with Hopkins also revealed the inner workings of the university during a crucial period of experimentation, the period that formed the mold for future higher education in America.

Chapter Two

HIS MESSAGE:
THE NEW ECONOMICS

RAIN DAMPENED the gray Adirondacks as a group of approximately fifty men gathered at the Bethesda Parish Building at Saratoga, New York, on September 8, 1885. Richard T. Ely, the thirty-one-year-old Johns Hopkins University professor, arose and addressed the assemblage of economists, ministers, and a few businessmen. They should organize for the purpose of issuing a "proclamation of emancipation" from classical economics, the pugnacious little professor declared. Like the Hebrew prophets of old they should cry out against the sins of their society and replace the dogma which "deified a monstrosity known as economic man." They should sponsor scientific investigations that would project man to the forefront of all economic studies.[1] In launching the American Economic Association that day, Ely sounded the tocsin not only for a revolt against classical economics but for the coming revolution in the social sciences.

By this time Ely had already established himself as the

most influential member of the "new school" of economics in the United States. The new school, a counterpart of the German Historical School, claimed that classical economic theory no longer represented a true science. The major premises of the older political economy as well as its practical guides to policy had been shown to be inadequate by the Germans. Ely and most progressive reformers thought that the new scientific insights released economics from a strait-jacket of ideas that hampered reform efforts. The new economists attempted to construct an economics which permitted and promoted reform.

J. Franklin Jameson, one of Ely's first students and an acid critic of all his Johns Hopkins professors, found Ely to be obsessed with the contrasts between the two schools of economics. In recording for his diary an appearance by Ely before the Historical and Political Science Seminary, Jameson wrote: "Was late to Dr. Ely's paper, but didn't miss much, for what I heard was the same as he said over and over again in his lectures of last year. He fought his man of straw, the *à priori* economist over again, and demolished him much as usual." On another occasion he despairingly wrote: "His [Ely's] narrow little mind has become so steeped in German prejudices, that he can't see any good in the English economists." The only English economist, according to Jameson, whom Ely thought worth reading was T. E. Cliffe-Leslie, a close ally of the new school. On one occasion Ely loaned Jameson a copy of Leslie's essays which was marked with "dispraises" of the classicist John Stuart Mill. And at times Ely lost his temper when students implied criticism of his treatment of the subject. Jameson finally despaired of ques-

1 Ely, *Ground Under Our Feet: An Autobiography* (New York: Macmillan, 1938), p. 138; Ely, "Report of the Organization of the American Economic Association," *Publications of the American Economic Association,* I (1887), 13; Ely, "The American Economic Association, 1885-1909," *Publications of the American Economic Association,* 3d ser., XI (1910), 62.

tioning him; he did not want to "rile" the "little pill."[2] But other students found his dedication to the new economics and criticism of classical economy a very appealing feature of his teaching.

Jameson's criticism of Ely's one-sidedness was somewhat exaggerated, for Ely, throughout most of his stay at Hopkins, taught a graduate course on Mill and used his famous *Principles* as one of the texts in the basic course on political economy. Apparently the course Ely offered on Mill was in part designed to criticize Mill's acceptance of the basic premises of classicism. Ely saw Mill as a "trimmer" between the old and new schools of economics; Mill, although he retained the basic premises of classicism, had come to recognize the importance of the humanitarian impulse in man.[3]

In his survey course Ely usually included as required reading, in addition to Mill, the works of Émile de Lavéléye, a Belgian of the Historical School, and General Francis A. Walker, an American of the new school. During the first term he critically examined classical theory. In the second term he took up the economic history of various countries and assigned special research topics. The student papers generally dealt with either some historical phase of economics or a criticism of some of the classical tenets. The upper-division course always included works by members of the German Historical School such as Karl Knies, Wilhelm Roscher, Adolph Wagner, and Gustav Schönberg.

In his early publications Ely enthusiastically presented the

[2] Jameson Diary, Oct. 20, May 2, 5, April 26, 27, 1882, Dec. 10, 1886, Jameson MSS, Library of Congress. For a similar expression by Woodrow Wilson, see Ray Stannard Baker, ed., *Woodrow Wilson, Life and Letters: Youth, 1856-1890* (Garden City, N. Y.: Doubleday, Page, 1927), p. 179.

[3] Ely, "The Past and the Present of Political Economy," in Herbert B. Adams, ed., *Johns Hopkins University Studies in Historical and Political Science*, II (Baltimore: Johns Hopkins Press, 1884), p. 42. For the class offerings of Ely and the course descriptions, see *Johns Hopkins University Circulars*, I-XII (1879-1892).

distinctions between his own and the classical school of economics. In his second year at Hopkins he delivered a polemic to the Seminary entitled "The Past and the Present of Political Economy" in which he violently attacked the "leading assumptions" of the classical school as being "largely false." In 1884 he published an expanded version under the same title in the *Johns Hopkins University Studies* and for the first time received substantial public recognition of his heretical views. The economically orthodox *Nation* led the attack in the first of a long series of scathing reviews of Ely's works. With tongue in cheek the anonymous reviewer wrote: "Dr. Ely is an enthusiastic disciple of the modern German school, and the simplicity with which he reproduces the lucubrations of its professors renders his pamphlet entertaining reading. He maintains, with evident sincerity, that the system developed by the English economists is quite out of date, and, to judge from the account of it given in his pages, it should be a matter of surprise that it ever came into existence."[4] Fortunately for Ely a powerful regent of the university, George W. Brown, felt that the *Nation's* review "hardly" did the young professor justice. To Gilman, who was apparently upset by the review, Brown wrote reassuringly: "The critique represents the school of laissez-faire, to which I incline myself very strongly, but Political Economy is not a completed science and the Historical School has something to say for itself."[5]

Ely's views soon drew fire within the university from a more formidable antagonist, the highly respected professor of mathematics, Simon Newcomb. Although Newcomb was associated with the Nautical Office of the Navy Department and specialized in mathematics and physics, he had given a lecture series on economics at Harvard in 1879-1880 and had

[4] "Notes," *Nation*, XXXVIII (July 24, 1884), 74.
[5] Brown to Gilman, Aug. 12 [1884?], Gilman MSS, Johns Hopkins University Library, Baltimore.

published in the field. A follower of Stanley Jevons, Newcomb wanted to introduce more mathematics and the concept of marginal utility into economics.[6] After reading Ely's account of the contrasts between the new school and classical economists, Newcomb was, as he put it, "stirred up." He went directly to President Gilman. "It looks a little incongruous," he wrote, "to see so sweeping and wholesale [an] attack upon the introduction of any rational or scientific method in economics come from a university whose other specialities have tended in the opposite direction." Newcomb then submitted a paper to Gilman presenting his own views of the new school and asking the president for criticism and suggestions. At the same time he attempted to persuade Gilman that he and Ely should get together and discuss their differences. "You will notice," he wrote Gilman, "that my paper is founded on the fact that I have never been able to see any essential difference between the objections raised against political economy from the new school point of view and the general objections of the public against the value of theoretical science."[7]

During 1885 the antagonism between Ely and Newcomb grew. Newcomb began to attack Ely in private conversations and read a paper in February before the Scientific Association "On the Possibility of Applying Mathematics to Political Economy." One of Ely's students, Charles H. Levermore, responded two days later with a discussion before the Seminary on "Newcomb on Mathematical Economy." The personal strife between the two men frightened Ely and his students. They feared that Newcomb would force Ely's resignation much as William Graham Sumner, conservative Yale professor, had pressured General Francis A. Walker out of Yale.[8]

[6] Joseph Dorfman, *The Economic Mind in American Civilization*, III (New York: Viking, 1949), pp. 83-87.

[7] Newcomb to Gilman, May 3, 14, June 4, 1884, Gilman MSS.

[8] Ely to E. R. A. Seligman, June 23, 1885, in Joseph Dorfman, ed., "The Seligman Correspondence, II," *Political Science Quarterly*, LVI (June, 1941), 281; Albert Shaw, "Recollections," Gilman MSS; *Johns Hopkins University Circulars*, IV (March, 1885), 66; Ely to Shaw, May

When Newcomb published his *Principles of Political
Economy* in 1885, Ely "severely reviewed" it before the
Seminary,[9] and Albert Shaw assaulted it in *Dial* magazine.
"I reviewed it with the irreverent scorn of a confirmed Elyite,"
Shaw later wrote, "and called it an essay in logic that under-
took to treat the law of supply and demand as the analogy in
social science of the law of gravitation in physics."[10] But in
fact Ely had urged Shaw to write an even harsher review.
In a detailed and self-righteous letter, Ely pointed out a long
list of "errors" in Newcomb's work and assured Shaw that
Newcomb was "an ignoramus as regards the investigations of
scholars during the past generation."[11] Ely and Newcomb
continued their battle in 1886 through a series of articles in
Science magazine, Ely preparing one on "Ethics and Economics" and Newcomb one on "Can Economists Agree upon
the Basis of Their Teaching?"[12]

The controversy helped inspire Ely to organize the
American Economic Association in 1885 in order to combat
"the Sumner, Newcomb crowd" and to propagate the new
economics. Among several of the younger economists who
had, along with Ely, made the trek to Germany, the idea of
forming an organization modeled after the German Society for
Social Policy had been in the air for some time. Upon their
return to America they met stout resistence to the German
economic ideas in academic circles and in the popular mind.
In particular, William Graham Sumner, the professorial inter-
preter of Herbert Spencer, seemed to be winning converts
among the young people to a classical economics buttressed
by Darwinism. On the other hand, the opportunity for

7, 1885, in Hugh Hawkins, *Pioneer: A History of the Johns Hopkins University, 1874-1889* (Ithaca, N. Y.: Cornell University Press, 1960), p.
181.
9 Jameson Diary, Oct. 31, 1885.
10 Shaw, "Recollections."
11 Ely to Shaw, Nov. 19, 1885, in Hawkins, *Pioneer*, pp. 181-182.
12 The series was published under Ely's editorial supervision as a
book, *Science-Economic Discussion* (New York: Science, 1887).

disseminating the ideas of the Historical School appeared to be propitious, for increasingly many Americans were coming to realize that their earlier agrarian, individualistic values somehow failed to assure justice during the machine age. The feeling especially infected members of the urban clergy and those who were not benefiting from the fruits of rapid industrialization.

The conservative economists organized first, forming the Political Economy Club at Delmonico's in New York City in November of 1883. Although such new economists as Ely, H. C. Adams, and Edmund J. James were among the first members of the organization, the club was dominated by the Sumner-Newcomb group, with Newcomb as its president and J. Laurence Laughlin its secretary-treasurer. The roster of membership included Charles Francis Adams, Edward Atkinson, E. L. Godkin, Charles Dunbar, Sumner, Henry Farnam, and Arthur Perry, all conservative on fundamental economic questions.[13] The next year, 1884, Simon N. Patten and Edmund J. James proposed a countersociety that would promote extensive government action for social welfare programs. The platform for the "Society for the Study of National Economy" called the state "a positive factor in material production" which had "legitimate claims to a share of the product." The public interest could be best served "by the States' appropriating and applying this share to promote public ends."[14] However, the frankly "socialistic" platform of the Patten-James venture apparently alienated even the sympathetic allies of the new school.

[13] Laughlin to Ely, Jan. 20, 1910, Ely MSS, State Historical Society of Wisconsin, Madison. The Political Economy Club continued to meet semiannually until 1897. Most of their members initially refused to join the American Economic Association.

[14] Original draft of the platform is in Ely, comp., "Scrapbook . . . of the American Economic Association, 1885-1910," State Historical Society of Wisconsin, Madison; a later draft is cited in full in Ely, "The American Economic Association, 1885-1909," pp. 51-54; and Ely, *Ground Under Our Feet*, pp. 296-299.

Although Ely also had proposed an organization as early
as 1884, he deferred concrete action until the Patten-James
proposal had failed.[15] In the summer of 1885 he sent out a
prospectus to a selected group of young, mostly German-
trained economists, ministers, and sympathetic businessmen.
The Ely proposal did not substantially alter the tone of the
Patten-James platform. "We regard the State," Ely declared,
"as an educational and ethical agency whose positive aid is
an indispensable condition of human progress. While we
recognize the necessity of individual initiative in industrial
life, we hold that the doctrine of *laissez-faire* is unsafe in
politics and unsound in morals; and that it suggests an inadequate explanation of the relation between the State and
citizens." Further, "we do not accept the final statements
which characterized the political economy of the past generation; for we believe that political economy is still in the first
stages of its scientific development, and we look not so much
to speculation as to an impartial study of actual conditions of
economic life for the satisfactory accomplishment of that
development." The proposed platform concluded: "We hold
that the conflict of labor and capital has brought to the front
a vast number of social problems whose solution is impossible
without the united efforts of Church, State, and Science."[16]

Obviously Ely desired much more than a scholarly society
for the mutual interchange of economic ideas. He wanted
an organization that would come to grips with publicizing
and implementing a social reform program. Not every economist was invited to join. As Ely frankly admitted, the society
"had an inclusive as well as exclusive aim."[17] He wanted, he
wrote to Edwin R. A. Seligman of Columbia, an "association
of the younger progressive elements and the platform must

15 Francis A. Walker to Ely, April 30, 1884, Ely MSS.
16 Original copy in Ely, comp., "Scrapbook . . . of the American
Economic Association"; Ely, "Report of the Organization of the American
Economic Association," pp. 6-7; Ely, *Ground Under Our Feet*, p. 136.
17 Ely, "The American Economic Association, 1885-1909," p. 52.

be broad yet it must not include men of the Sumner type."[18] Newcomb put it more sarcastically. He claimed that the association, as visualized by Ely, was "intended to be sort of a Church requiring for admission to its full communion a renunciation of ancient errors, and an adhesion to the supposed new creed."[19]

Unlike Patten and James, Ely took concrete steps to insure the success of his proposed organization. He received the support of his colleague, Herbert Baxter Adams, who had already demonstrated organizational skill in founding the American Historical Association in the previous year. Adams agreed to the expediency of forming the economic society at the next regular meeting of the historical association, a group to which many economists belonged, and lined up most of the prominent historians in support of the Ely plan. Ely also sought the support of influential college presidents: Daniel C. Gilman of Johns Hopkins, Andrew D. White of Cornell, Charles K. Adams of Michigan, and W. W. Folwell of Minnesota. Ely, in sending the prospectus to Gilman, explained: "It has been submitted to a large number of the younger economists of the country and favorable replies have been received in every case with one exception." To organize the economists with varying views had been difficult, Ely wrote, but "has brought me to appreciate—if you will allow me to say it—better than ever before the work which has been done at the Johns Hopkins." Ely further explained the purpose of the association to Gilman as an effort to form "an influential movement which will help in the diffusion of a sound, Christian political economy."[20]

With favorable responses to his prospectus Ely scheduled

[18] Ely to Seligman, June 23, 1885, in Dorfman, ed., "The Seligman Correspondence, II," p. 281.

[19] Newcomb, review of Ely's "Outlines of Economics," *Journal of Political Economy*, III (Dec., 1894), 106. See also Newcomb to the Editor, July 3, 1891, in *Nation*, LIII (July 9, 1891), 27.

[20] Ely to Gilman, July 11, 1885, Gilman MSS.

the first organizational meeting for September 8, 1885, at Saratoga Springs, New York, in conjunction with the American Historical Association. Ely began the meeting with a strong defense of his proposed platform. Only through an explicitly worded statement of principles could the association insure its own vitality and influence public opinion, he declared to his fellow economists. The association should recognize that economic thought must no longer be encased in the *laissez faire* doctrine. Economic behavior cannot be explained by rigid laws like chemistry and physics, Ely said. Although "no one . . . contemplates a form of pure socialism," the economists should firmly resist any rigid deterministic approach and recognize the beneficent qualities of the state. Christian moral responsibility should be emphasized rather than the search for mechanistic laws. "All have duties as well as rights," Ely appealed; "it is time we heard more about duties and less about rights."[21]

Ely, however, exaggerated the spirit of rebellion felt by most of the group. After Ely's opening speech it soon became evident that they objected to the provocative wording of the statement of principles. In general, they supported a shift in methodology but hesitated to support a platform aimed directly at reform. Modern economics had not yet achieved enough certainty, Seligman said, to authorize wide-scale public activity. A formal denial of classical economics might mean, Henry C. Adams of Michigan added, that the public would assume the association accepted entirely the "German view of social relations." Others added similar objections. Only Ely was left to defend the entire statement.[22]

When no agreement could be reached in the plenary session on the wording of the platform, Herbert Baxter Adams

[21] Ely, "Report of the Organization of the American Economic Association," pp. 15-17.
[22] *Ibid.*, p. 21. Also see Seligman to Ely, June 29, 1889, Ely MSS; Ely to Seligman, June 23, 1885, H. C. Adams to Seligman, April 27, 1887, in Dorfman, ed., "Seligman Correspondence, II," pp. 281, 271.

finally suggested the appointment of a special committee to draw up a new statement of principles. Further, the organizational meeting stipulated that, whatever the principles formulated, they would in no way be binding on the individual members of the association. This disclaimer was to be printed with the platform. Ely served with Henry C. Adams, Alexander Johnston, John Bates Clark, and Washington Gladden on the special platform committee. Although the special committee's statement fell short of all that Ely regarded as necessary, the state was still to be regarded "as an agency whose positive assistance is one of the indispensable conditions of human progress."[23] Ely thereby salvaged the essence of his demands and he alone could probably claim credit for the association's retaining even a watered-down platform.

The association awarded the presidency to General Francis A. Walker, the secretarial post to Ely, and the treasurership to Seligman. These three officers served from 1885 to 1892, the critical period of the organization's history. Ely, more than any single individual, insured the early success of the association. He superbly handled the publicity of the association, flooding the newspapers and periodicals with notices and articles.[24] With his amazing capacity for pursuing several arduous tasks simultaneously, he scheduled meetings, set up programs for the conventions, and approved expenditures. As Ely explained the post to his successor Edward A. Ross: "You will find that you never make any headway if you submit minor matters . . . to the Executive committee. You must go ahead and do a great many things on your own responsibility,

[23] Ely, "Report of the Organization of the American Economic Association," p. 35. The new platform is also cited in full in Ely, *Ground Under Our Feet,* p. 140.
[24] See "American Economic Association," *Annals of the American Academy of Political and Social Science,* I (Jan., 1891), 527; Ely, "The American Economic Association," *Independent,* XXXIX (June 2, 1887), 681-682; Ely, "Political Economy in America," *North American Review,* CXLIV (Feb., 1887), 113-119; Ely, *Social Aspects of Christianity and Other Essays* (New York: Crowell, 1889), pp. 25, 47; Ely, *An Introduction to Political Economy* (New York: Chautauqua, 1889), p. 326.

that is what I did, and what I think every one does who is successful in such positions."[25] Ely also handled all of the editorial and financial problems concerned with the various publications of the association.

Ely took the initiative in gaining new members and raising funds. He vigorously encouraged the sale of the society's publications through book dealers and personally arranged sales to many libraries and individuals. He also successfully urged wealthy businessmen to enlist for $35.00 life memberships in the association. When Ely left his post in 1892, the association showed a balance of over $2,000 and a membership of over 700. Ely helped organize branch societies in Springfield, Massachusetts; Buffalo, New York; Galesburg and Geneseo, Illinois; Orange, New Jersey; Kansas City, Kansas; Canton, Ohio; Austin, Texas; and Washington, D. C. Clergymen played a leading role in the branch organizations, giving some basis for the belief that the society was quasi-reform in nature.[26] Ely induced the association to offer prizes for quality essays. He personally raised over $1,000 for prize money and most frequently selected topics typical of his reform interest. For example, the association awarded $250 for the best essay on women wage earners. Other prizes went for papers on state and local taxation, evils of unrestricted immigration, housing of the poor in American cities, and accidents to employees of steam railways.[27]

Through the work of Ely the association was also influential abroad. A former Ely student organized an association

[25] Ely to Ross, Sept. 15, 1892, Ross MSS, State Historical Society of Wisconsin, Madison.

[26] Ely, comp., "Scrapbook . . . of the American Economic Association"; Ely to John H. Finley, July 3, 1899, Ely MSS; Ely, "American Economic Association, 1885-1909," pp. 87n-88n; George P. Garrison to Ely, Dec. 24, 1888, Jan. 28, 1889, Howard MacQueary to Ely, Dec. 6, 1890, John B. Daish to Ely, Nov. 6, 1888, Ely MSS.

[27] Ely, "American Economic Association, 1885-1909," p. 29n; Ely, comp., "Scrapbook . . . of the American Economic Association"; Fred G. Sherman to Ely, Dec. 12, 1889, Francis A. Walker to Ely, Dec. 12, 1889, Andrew Carnegie to Ely, March 26, 1890, Ely MSS.

in Japan after the American model. The success of the American society led to emulation in England by the formation of the British Economic Association. Ely, moreover, obtained authorization to present honorary memberships to most of the leading European economists. From Sidney Webb, a leading Fabian socialist, he secured for the American association a widely discussed article on socialism.[28]

While secretary, Ely served as a clearinghouse for information on economic subjects. In this capacity he had an inestimable influence on public opinion and policy. No request was too small to receive a prompt response. Each year at least a hundred letters poured into Baltimore from unknown people requesting information on such subjects as the gas rates in Rochester, New York, and the best works on the labor question. Ely answered even trivial requests with long letters requiring tedious work and time.

Only his dedication to the principles of his reform program and his strong personal ambition can explain the impressive quantity of his work. During his tenure of office he published seven books and over fifty journal articles. Thomas Y. Crowell, the publisher for most of Ely's early works, expressed the typical astonishment of his contemporaries at his capacity for work. "You must allow me to say once more," Crowell wrote in 1889, "you are taking on too much and you will surely kill yourself with overwork if you continue this way."[29] Crowell conservatively estimated that Ely would not reach the age of fifty at his current pace of work. "The marvel is," Andrew Carnegie wrote, "how so small a man can be so big a man."[30]

Ely's fervent productivity and his rebellion against classical economists sprang in part from his sense of mission and a new sense of intellectual freedom. The rigidity and deter-

[28] Ely, comp., "Scrapbook . . . of the American Economic Association"; Webb to Ely, Feb. 1, March 19, 1889, Ely MSS.
[29] Crowell to Ely, April 13, 1889, Ely MSS.
[30] Carnegie to Ely, Nov. 19, 1890, Ely MSS.

minism of classicism reminded young Ely of orthodox Presbyterianism. He had escaped the theological orthodoxy of
rural New York by going to the city; he escaped the economic
orthodoxy of Columbia College by his trip to Germany. Ely
had listened intently as his German masters explained that no
ironclad principles of economics existed. A whole new world
came before his eyes, one in which man in his capacity as a
social being played an essential part in the progress of society.
For him, personally, the new economics supplied the higher
purpose and the meaning of life that he had so vainly sought.
It provided a basis for a new science of economics that would
assist him in accomplishing the vow he made upon his return
from Germany, to work for the underprivileged in American
society.[31]

Economic science, Ely explained in his 1884 essay, "The
Past and the Present of Political Economy," was on the thresh-
old of demolishing the ideas which had barred the development of the humane impulse of man and a truly scientific
analysis of economic phenomena. In America classicism had
"acquired the reputation of orthodoxy," Ely wrote, "and to
be a heretic in political economy became worse than to be an
apostate in religion."[32] By reducing a complex maze of economic facts to a few simple and alluring propositions, the
classicists "appealed irresistibly to the vanity of the average
man." Any social problems that arose, past or present, could
be solved simply by reference to these tenets. Ely cited several
popular classicists to the effect that all the necessary natural
laws of economics had been ascertained. Nothing further
remained to be discovered. Privileged classes, especially the
captains of industry, found in classicism a rationale for their
exploitation and freedom from regulation. According to
orthodox canons, assistance to economic unfortunates inter-

[31] See Ely to Joseph A. Labadie, Aug. 14, 1885, in Sidney Fine,
ed., "The Ely-Labadie Letters," *Michigan History*, XXXVI (March,
1952), 17.
[32] Ely, "The Past and the Present," p. 10.

fered with natural law. The laborer received exactly what he deserved.

Even the academic success of political economists often depended upon their capacity to reiterate classical principles in their strongest form. Earlier, Ely claimed, a "small clique of men" formed a conspiracy against the scientific approach to economics. These men, "not without newspaper influence, constituted themselves its special guardians and, still maintaining that position, even now attempt to exercise a sort of terrorism over the intellect of the country."[33] But an irresistible tide had developed for a revaluation of classical tenets.

Jameson correctly surmised that Ely deliberately posited the classical economists as vulnerable "straw men." For Ely did not bother to analyze the thought of any one economist as a representative figure of the older school. He simply eliminated Adam Smith from consideration by claiming that all economists traced their inspiration to him. According to Ely, Thomas Malthus, David Ricardo, Nassau Senior, and James and John Stuart Mill all contributed an essential part to the economic system which Americans contemplated with awe and admiration. Although the principles of these six figures differed in a few minor respects, Ely claimed, the passage of time had produced a "form commonly acceptable." If pressed, Ely might well have admitted that the "commonly acceptable" principles he ascribed to the older political economy would not have been totally acceptable to any of the six figures. For Ely's man of straw was largely the popular conception of economics held by Americans who wanted to protect a special interest. Ely was rebelling more against the crude practical guides to policy that followed from the popular conception than against the analyses of the classical economists, although he claimed to be attacking both.

Ely's man of straw had built his theory on a few simple hypotheses concerning human nature and the external world.

[33] Ely, "Political Economy in America," p. 114.

While accepting a set or given human nature, the older school theorized that man's most important motivating force was self-interest. Universal self-interest "was the animating and overwhelmingly preponderating cause of economic phenomena." Ely defined the self-interest concept merely in terms of wealth pursuit, not other possible satisfactions. Although in a footnote he distinguished between "self-interest" and "selfishness," he sometimes deliberately used the terms interchangeably and apparently failed to comprehend any basic distinction between them.[34]

The second hypothesis of the older school, Ely admitted, had been presented in several widely varied forms. Stated in its least objectional form, man possessed the intellectual power of judging the "efficacy of means to an end, along with the inclination to reach our ends by the easiest and shortest means."[35] In other words, needless exertion would not be expended in order to attain wealth. Any addition in wealth must be balanced against a sacrifice of pleasure and ease.

Finally, Ely's straw man perceived that the free play of the first two motives brought the best good for all of society. It brought economic growth, employment, and wealth. The basic requirement for achieving an unending pageant of progress was for the state to practice laissez faire, laissez passer, let alone—"the oft-repeated maxim of *à priori* economists." The classicists argued that in a competitive economy unfettered by the intervention of the state, the organization of labor, or a monopoly of capital, the supply of goods always tended to balance the demand. When men wanted more of a particular good, entrepreneurs, pursuing their self-interest,

[34] Ely, "The Past and the Present," pp. 10, 10n. In a paper prepared in 1887 on labor organizations Ely accused the classicists of glorifying "selfishness as the only true principle of industrial and economic action." Henry C. Adams, in a penciled-in criticism, questioned Ely's failure to make the distinction. The original paper and criticism are in Ely, comp., "Personal Scrapbooks, 1873-1908," XVIII, 5, State Historical Society of Wisconsin, Madison.

[35] Ely, "The Past and the Present," p. 12.

responded automatically with improved technology, more capital, and an increased supply of labor, with the end result being greater production. According to "Say's Law," the increased production provided even more demand, thus reestablishing an equilibrium at a higher level of sustained economic activity. Labor functioned in exactly the same way as a commodity. Thus the marketplace served as a wonderful "invisible hand" to guide resources, labor, capital, and energies to their highest productivity. Admittedly wealth had increased historically, but its growth always rested on the same set of eternal principles. Ely confessed that not all classicists accepted the harmony of economic interests by various groups. Yet, even when they were pessimistic about the pageant of progress, as for example Ricardo was, they still insisted that the natural laws of political economy could not be escaped.

Thus, according to Ely, the classicists had conferred the dignity of natural law on this inspiring edifice. They felt that economics now had achieved the certainty of a physical science, that they had accomplished for economics what Newton had for physics. The principles of self-interest, of adjudging ends by a pleasure-pain calculus, of the free marketplace as the mechanism for bringing the best good to all, held true for all times and all places. Not only were underlying conceptions universal and immutable in the mind of the classicists, Ely wrote, but also the deductions that flowed from their precepts.

To Ely the forces of history and new scientific insights, particularly those provided by the idea of evolution, accounted for the decline and imminent fall of the older school. In the late eighteenth and early nineteenth centuries, classicism had played a meritorious role, for it had assisted in the destruction of obstacles to economic growth, especially the outmoded institutions of the Middle Ages. Like the French Revolution it had cleared the way for the growth of new institutions. Ely explained that from the standpoint of science, classicism had laid the foundation for scientific economic study by separating the concept of wealth and its pursuit from other social phenomena. Equally important, the theory of self-interest threw such a flood of light on economic motives that it could not be ignored by any economist.

However, classicism proved valuable only for a given time and place. From a practical standpoint, Ely believed, historical experience had eroded its claim to lasting value. Since the only advice of the classical economists to the statesman was purely negative—that is, hands off by the state —they furnished no solutions to fresh new problems arising from industrial progress. Even historically, Ely wrote, "it never held at any time in any country, and no maxim ever made a more complete fiasco when the attempt was seriously made to apply it in the state."[36] The unfettered play of supply and demand had allowed the forests to be plundered, women and children to be victimized, and class war to erupt. The harmony of economic interests had become a chimera. Strangely enough the politicians were the first to recognize the irrelevancy of classicism to the new environment. The stern requirements of representing the people had forced them, usually apologetically, to abandon one bastion after another of the older political economy.

Science, Ely believed, was to deliver the final blow to the classical edifice. The method of the older school was largely deductive, whereas the new school's was more inductive. Although Ely admitted that both methods were necessary to a scientific economics, the crux of the difference between the two schools lay in the origin of their premises. He accused the classicists of being "idealistic," for they found their "chief premises ready-made in the mind." They were utopian in that they assumed man had set motives, unaffected by society or tradition. On the other hand, the new economists, or the

36 *Ibid.*, pp. 23-24.

"realistic school," continuously looked "to the outside world for premises."[37] They took into account tradition, mores, and institutions.

With the new scientific insights drawn from Darwin and the German economists, Ely claimed we could now confidently assert that natural laws for economics did not exist. To Ely the meaning of Darwin was change, growth, and novelty. Herbert Spencer erred by assuming that man was completely subject to physical evolution. Man stood outside of physical evolution, acting not only upon animal instinct but, more important, upon the accumulated knowledge of the past. Unlike other animals who were born into a natural environment, man was born into a society formed by history. Thus the context of time and place, based on growth and development, meant a continually changing economic theory. "In every stage of its progress," Ely quoted his master, Karl Knies, "the theory of political economy is the generalization of truths recognized up to a certain point of time, and this theory cannot be declared complete either as respects its form or substance."[38] History made economics always an incomplete science, changing with society. History had released the straitjacket of ideas.

Turning to various premises of the classicists, Ely explained their weaknesses in the light of history. Because of the shaping force of society and traditions, Ely stated, man could not be abstracted as an atomistic individual apart from his social context. "It is impossible to separate the individual from his surroundings in state and society," Ely wrote. Man was "inextricable and organically bound up in state and society." Individual self-interest was subject to the same shaping force—society as historically formed. Thus, more basic than an abstract concept of self-interest in understanding men's motives were *"social considerations which are the first*

37 *Ibid.*, pp. 7, 7n.
38 *Ibid.*, pp. 46-47.

and foremost factor in economic life in modern times."[39] Only the expression of self-interest bore significance. It might induce individuals to smuggle. But what if the duties on imports were lowered? "Lo! the proportion between smugglers and non-smugglers has changed."[40] Or consider the able German civil servant who passed up opportunities for lucrative salaries in private industry. He had become a civil servant for the social esteem attached to such a position, an esteem resulting from historical causes. Admittedly he pursued what he considered to be his self-interest, but his motive was conditioned by society and consequently bore little resemblance to the classical abstraction of an individual's pursuing self-interest only for wealth.

The German Historical School of Knies, Bruno Hildebrand, and Wilhelm Roscher rejected the abstractions of the classical school and allied themselves with reformers in politics, jurisprudence, and theology. They cast aside all *à priori* assumptions, postponing even tentative hypotheses until ample facts could be observed. "The first thing is to gather facts," Ely wrote. "It has, indeed, been claimed that for an entire generation no attempt should be made to discover laws, but this is an extreme position."[41] The new school gathered, classified, and compared facts from various lands; they gathered statistics; they noted that economics was analogous to physiology in that it called attention to the social body. Above all, political economy under the German influence became only one branch of the social sciences, dealing with social phenomena from the economic standpoint. Economics "is not regarded as something fixed and unalterable, but as a growth and development, changing with society," Ely repeatedly emphasized. "The political economy of to-day is not the political economy of yesterday; while the political economy of

[39] *Ibid.*, pp. 35-36.
[40] Ely, *An Introduction to Political Economy*, p. 125.
[41] Ely, "The Past and the Present," p. 47.

Germany is not identical with that of England or America."[42]
Ely had thus arrived at a dilemma unconsciously shared by his
generation of reformers. Did this mean that each generation
wrote its own political economy without any reference to
an objective good or truth? Had the new economist not
affirmed the moral neutrality of the universe?

Ely confidently answered these questions by claiming that
science attested to a moral attribute—the ideal of brotherhood
—in man's basic nature. Admittedly, history as commonly
observed—that is, the chronicle of the rise and fall of civiliza-
tions—defied any ultimate explanation and provided no moral
absolutes. But a second history, the history of the ideal of
brotherhood, was constantly progressive and was ascertainable
to the scientist. Current anthropological studies showed that
the most primitive men, Ely wrote, viewed the members of
their village as brothers. Consequently they refrained from
sharp practices. "There is within man an ethical feeling . . .
which has been clarified by religion, telling us that in our
economic life as well as elsewhere we must seek to promote
the welfare of our neighbor and brother."[43] Brotherly love
was an integral part of man's basic nature, Ely concluded.

Quite obviously the ideal of brotherhood had not always
been practiced. When trade began between two villages, the
ethical ideal of brotherly love frequently broke down, although
in principle it was never sacrificed. With the industrial
revolution the ideal faced a tremendous challenge. Industrialism destroyed family and village ties which had earlier
furnished the social basis of brotherhood, but it provided the

42 *Ibid.*, pp. 45-46.
43 Ely, *An Introduction to Political Economy*, pp. 67-68. The theme
of a progressive historical development of the ideal of brotherhood finds
expression in most of Ely's works. See especially the following: Ely, *The
Social Law of Service* (New York: Eaton & Mains, 1896); Ely, *Social
Aspects of Christianity and Other Essays*; Ely, "Suggestions for Social
Topics: VII—The Widening and Deepening Range of Ethical Obligations," *Christian Advocate*, LXVI (Aug. 13, 1891), 538; Ely, "Christianity as a Social Force," in John H. Barrows, ed., *The World's Parliament
of Religions* (Chicago: Parliament, 1893), II, 1056-1061.

opportunity to extend the range of ethical obligation until it embraced all of humanity. The ideal then progressed beyond the exclusive character of village brotherhood. "There has been, then, an extension of brotherhood which is simply immense, placing us in the modern world indefinitely in advance of the closely related but exclusive groups of the ancient world."[44] While the ethical ideal of brotherhood had widened, the work of deepening the feeling moved more slowly forward.

Modern science and the ethical ideal supported each other. "The widening and deepening range of ethical obligation rests upon a basis of solid facts."[45] The evolution of man both ethically and practically was toward a potential perfectibility. The responsibility of the economic scientist was to expose and to assist in correcting those practices, customs, and institutions which blocked eventual perfection. In short, the economists had to study economic phenomena in the light of what ought to be, for this was the inevitable direction of the evolution of the ethical ideal and its practice. Thus Ely shared the common assumption of his generation of reformers—a profound faith in progress.

Modern economic science, in Ely's estimation, had already, after rejecting classical premises, discovered a great deal concerning the application of the ideal of brotherhood. The new school conceived of society as organic in nature, as the first society had been. "The nation in its economic life is an organism, of which individuals, families, groups, and even towns, cities, provinces, etc., in their economic life form parts. This is strictly and literally true, as is shown conclusively by comparing the facts of economic life with the ideas embraced in the conception, organism."[46] Ely's proof of an

44 Ely, *Studies in the Evolution of an Industrial Society* (New York: Macmillan, 1903), p. 429. See Ely, *An Introduction to Political Economy*, pp. 45, 67-69.
45 Ely, *Studies in the Evolution of an Industrial Society*, p. 437.
46 Ely, "The Past and the Present," p. 49.

organic society rested on the principle of economic interdependence. Man had always been dependent upon the activities of his fellow man. "Men form more truly than ever before a social and industrial organism, whose numberless parts are in infinite variety of manner interdependent. Infinite interrelations! infinite interdependences!"[47] The phenomena of exchange and division of labor, which made man dependent on the activities of others, increased with industrialization. The growth of interdependence also, of course, provided new opportunities for the practice of brotherhood.

To Ely, the state was the most important instrument of the social organism. Americans had mistakenly accepted the Lockean view that the state was an artificial creation of rational men to protect their natural rights. But Ely, again returning to the ancient community, asserted that the state was an attribute of the ethical ideal. The first men had been born into a society that included some form of a state. The state, like the principle of brotherhood, the family, and religious worship, came into existence simultaneously with society. Since the state could be used as a tool for achieving brotherhood, the economist had to define the possible roles of state activity.

In his essay comparing the new school and classicism Ely hardly attempted to answer the Spencerian charge that state action led men into slavery. The individual would not be absorbed by the state, Ely argued at that time, because each individual is a separate organism "of which each has its own ends and is in turn composed of parts, performing their own functions, essential to the existence of the whole."[48] He added that the "interests of the state-organism" diverged only in the case of a state action which benefited society as a whole but restricted the liberty of the individual. Ely later pub-

[47] Ely, "Social Studies: I—The Nature of the Railway Problem," *Harper's New Monthly Magazine*, LXXIII (July, 1886), 251. For this paragraph also see, Ely, *An Introduction to Political Economy*, pp. 26-29.
[48] Ely, "The Past and the Present," p. 51.

lished an essay, "Industrial Liberty," that developed a more adequate answer to Spencer's charge. The Founding Fathers, Ely explained, conceived of liberty in negative terms. If all restrictions and restraints on the individual were stripped away, liberty would assert itself as a benign force. For men, by pursuing their own interests, guarantee not only their individual interests but the interests of society. Ely believed that the new economic science disclosed other restrictions besides the state that infringed more seriously on individual liberties. The forces that curtailed liberty were only to a limited extent political; they were mostly economic. Man soon found himself bargaining with a huge corporation rather than another individual. Spencer's "absence of all social regulations means the unrestricted tyranny of the strong."[49]

The modern conception of liberty must be positive, Ely wrote. "True liberty means the expression of positive powers of the individual, and . . . it can be reached only as a result of a long and arduous constructive process."[50] In other words, opportunity must be found for the individual to develop to his fullest potential talents. The state could promote positive liberty by regulating the conditions of contract between a large corporation and the individual, or even by setting up a public school system. It might pass a law regulating the hours of work for women. Though admittedly such regulation restricted the liberty of the employer of women, this social action added to the liberty of the women and assisted in the establishment of the ethical ideal.

The new economist, Ely concluded, had breathed new life into what had become a dead science to the public. Now economists studied those subjects with which the man on the street felt a real concern. The new economist "tacitly assumed that the economist who studies and examines eco-

[49] Ely, *Studies in the Evolution of an Industrial Society*, p. 420. For this paragraph also see Ely, "Heredity and Circumstances," *Outlook,* XLVIII (Sept. 16, 1893), 505.

[50] Ely, *Studies in the Evolution of an Industrial Society,* p. 402.

nomic life will not neglect to advise and to prescribe norms for the most satisfactory economic organism." Now the younger Americans were joining the German, the French, the Italian, and most recently the English economists "in abandoning the dry bones of orthodox English political economy for the live methods of the German school."[51]

Ely felt the entire change in the spirit of political economy was an event worthy of "rejoicing." The historical method made it impossible for economics to become enmeshed in "*doctrinaire* extremes." Even if a new economist believed in socialism as the ultimate forms of society, he would advocate a slow approach and, if experience showed him that his ideas were leading to harm, call it to a halt. The new economics would object to allowing the "greedy and avaricious" to use political economy as a tool of oppression. "It does not acknowledge *laissez-faire* as an excuse for doing nothing while people starve, nor allow the all-sufficiency of competition as a plea for grinding the poor." The new economics searched for the key to unlock the secrets which would allow man to practice his true nature. "It denotes a return to the grand principle of common sense and Christian precept. Love, generosity, nobility of character, self-sacrifice, and all that is best and truest in *our nature* have their place in economic life."[52] In short, it would encourage a return to the Golden Rule, "As ye would that men should do to you, do ye also to them likewise."

The new economics, Richard T. Ely believed, destroyed an older system of ideas which had prevented the development of a scientific basis for reform. Ely denied the existence of natural laws and emphasized that man was born primarily into history, a history that shaped his instincts, and not into a purely physical environment. Principles of political economy had to be sufficiently flexible to adjust to changing conditions.

[51] Ely, "The Past and the Present," pp. 58, 64. See also Ely, *An Introduction to Political Economy*, pp. 99-100.
[52] Ely, "The Past and the Present," p. 64 (emphasis added).

But at any one point of development, a society had an enduring structure that provided a factual basis for relating the brotherhood of man to the universe.

Although as a distinctive school the new economics was short-lived, its disciples influenced the social sciences on two fronts. First, their insistence on the examination of facts in a historical context continued to shape American economic thought. Like the new economics, the next generation of institutional economists, such as Thorstein Veblen, Wesley Clair Mitchell, and John R. Commons, rejected the static model of classicism and was impressed by the importance of auxiliary disciplines. Less emphasis was given to theory and more to the institutional framework within which economic decisions were made. The institutional tradition remains a strong force in American economic thought, as is evident in the studies of Gardner C. Means and A. A. Berle, Jr., on the modern corporation and private property in the thirties and in the work of John Kenneth Galbraith in the fifties.

Second, on a broader and perhaps more important front, the new economists anticipated the viewpoint that would soon prevail in both philosophy and the social sciences in America. Admittedly, there was a tremendous growth in logical grasp, in clarity of expression, in precision of terms, and in historical understanding between Ely and many of his successors. But Ely saw quite clearly the role of the social sciences in normative terms, that is, as a method of resolving social problems. To him, the social sciences had no other value. Since, unlike the classicists, the new economists rejected any simple or permanent economic principles for resolving actual policy issues, research and experimentation became absolutely imperative. If an idea such as a communal society had been tested for its consistency with the principle of brotherhood and could be applied to a larger society, then it should be tried. The future evolution of an industrial society was subject to teleological action.

Chapter Three

HIS MESSAGE:
CLASS WARFARE

LATE IN JUNE of 1884 Richard T. Ely and his young bride, Anna, arrived at the Hotel Florence in Pullman, Illinois. Youthful and optimistic, they not only looked forward to their honeymoon but also to studying the Pullman village, a planned and presumably model community. H. M. Alden, editor of *Harper's New Monthly Magazine,* had already promised to publish the results. The paternalistic village sponsored by George M. Pullman, owner of the Pullman Palace Car Company, was in Ely's opinion a miniature social experiment. As a disciple of the new economics, he planned to put the community to the acid test, to "look and see" if, in actual practice, it fulfilled the requirements of practical brotherhood. The couple visited the local church, went to a town picnic, and watched torchlight parades for Blaine and Cleveland, the respective candidates for the presidency in 1884. At first they were favorably impressed with the "unity of design and an unexpected variety" in the buildings. Green and neatly trimmed lawns contrasted markedly with the dirty barren yards of the worker's districts in most American cities. Low rents, excellent municipal services, and central planning gave the community the surface appearance of an ideal village.[1]

But after a few days of careful investigation Ely found ugly examples of tyranny beneath the veneer. A pervasive veil of "needless secrecy" hung over the village. Residents felt that they were constantly watched by company spies and were afraid to talk freely, Ely wrote. Only with skill and patience did the Elys discover the exact nature of life in Pullman. A cobbler proved loquacious, and so Mrs. Ely's shoes frequently fell in need of repair. The couple accompanied the local Presbyterian pastor on his house calls and learned that the village was far from the idyllic. Favoritism and nepotism led to a "bad administration" with respect to steady employment and promotion. The workers owned no property and could be evicted with ten days' notice. Everyone in the village sensed an "all-pervading feeling of insecurity," and nobody regarded Pullman as a permanent home.

Although Ely admitted Pullman was probably better to his employees than most of the other captains of industry, he concluded that the social experiment repressed the instincts of self-help and individual liberty. "The power of Bismarck in Germany is utterly insignificant when compared with the power of the ruling authority of the Pullman Palace Car Company," he wrote. Pullman owned the single church building in which all services were held, the theater, the marketplace, the hotel, the homes, everything in the village. The town had no newspapers as an outlet to air grievances, and when an individual complained, he was forced to leave. "In looking over the facts of the case," Ely wrote, "the con-

[1] Ely, *Ground Under Our Feet: An Autobiography* (New York: Macmillan, 1938), pp. 166-168; Ely, "Pullman: A Social Study," *Harper's New Monthly Magazine*, LXX (Feb., 1885), 453-459.

clusion is unavoidable that the idea of Pullman is un-American." Copying such experiments would lead to "the most absolute power of capital, and the repression of all freedom."[2] In private correspondence on the subject he was even more biting. "It makes me indignant to see a thoroughly selfish man, who is attempting to enslave labor, pose as a philanthropist," Ely wrote to Albert Shaw.[3]

Ely's conclusions on the Pullman experiment predictably followed his earlier articles concerning class antagonism. Along with a host of concerned observers of the decade, Ely felt that the United States faced a "spectacular crisis" resulting from the increased polarization of labor and capital. He particularly asked the churchmen and men of means to give due consideration to the claims of socialist and labor spokesmen. While the church might suffer a setback by participating in the struggle, the crisis afforded unparalleled opportunities for it to guide future evolution along ethical lines. "The Church must gain leadership," Ely insisted. "The spirit of Christ should be infused into the social movement under consideration and the social forces which are producing this upheaval should become mighty ethical forces."[4] Blind opposition to the labor movement was futile; only ethical control and direction could avert violent bloodshed and bring about a beneficent revolution. His mission was to cement the loyalty of the working class to a society organically bound by the spirit of brotherhood. This required concessions from both labor and capital.

During his second year at Johns Hopkins Ely gave six public lectures on French and German socialism at Hopkins Hall. The enthusiastic reception of crowds averaging over a hundred led to an invitation by President White to deliver the

[2] Ely, "Pullman," pp. 463, 465.
[3] Ely to Shaw, Jan. 10, 1885, in Hugh Hawkins, *Pioneer: A History of John Hopkins University, 1874-1889* (Ithaca, N.Y.: Cornell University Press, 1960), p. 179.
[4] Ely, *Social Aspects of Christianity and Other Essays* (New York: Crowell, 1889), p. 147.

same lectures at Cornell University. The next year Harper & Brothers accepted them for publication under the title *French and German Socialism in Modern Times.* The book went through a second edition with a British reprint.[5] Although Ely competently traced a brief historical background of the rise of European socialism and presented the views of various socialist leaders, the distinctive quality of his book lay in his sympathetic treatment of such a controversial subject. Anticipating criticism, he claimed to present a "perfectly fair and impartial account." On the other hand, he insisted that a proper analysis could be made only if the "supporters themselves could not find fault" with it. In short, he wrote, "to obtain an adequate idea of socialism and the justice of its claims, we must imagine ourselves for the time being laborers, with all their trials and sufferings."[6]

Socialists from across America praised his "sympathy" for the movement. Christian socialist Reverend R. Heber Newton of the Protestant Episcopal church noted the rarity of finding a professor of political economy who treated socialism with such a "calm and just spirit." Lawrence Gronlund, equally enthusiastic about Ely's book, sent him a draft of his own, *Cooperative Commonwealth,* for criticism. But secular socialists felt that Ely's personal commitment was unclear and confusing.[7] S. Robert Wilnn, editor of the revolutionary socialist newspaper, the *Truth,* admitted that Ely was the first man of his class not to "lose his head" when treating socialism. But he told Ely that compromise was impossible. Christianity and socialism did not mix, Wilnn

[5] Ely to Daniel C. Gilman, Oct. 10, Nov. 25, 1882, Gilman MSS, Johns Hopkins University Library, Baltimore; *Johns Hopkins University Circulars,* II (June, 1883), 135; "The Labor Problem," *Critic,* VI (July 10, 1886), 15-16.

[6] Ely, *French and German Socialism in Modern Times* (New York: Harper, 1883), p. 15.

[7] Newton to Ely, Sept. 24, 1883, Gronlund to Ely, Sept. 28, 1883, Ely MSS, State Historical Society of Wisconsin, Madison; Ely to Joseph A. Labadie, June 30, 1885, in Sidney Fine, ed., "The Ely-Labadie Letters," *Michigan History,* XXXVI (March, 1952), 8.

wrote, and Ely must decide when "the Conflict comes" on which side he would be fighting—"in the ranks of the oppressor or the oppressed, on the side of Socialism or Capitalism."[8]

Ely believed there was a middle way, that the best of socialism and the best of capitalism could be mixed. To be sure, the church had to meet the labor leader and the captain of industry on common ground. Admittedly, churches favored the employer, failed to condemn blatant oppression, and were hypocritical in their pretensions of brotherhood. In 1889 the secretary of the Journeymen Baker's National Union reported to Ely a universal lack of sympathy by the clergy in New York City. The Baker's union sent out 500 circulars to the clergy of New York and Brooklyn asking support for enforcement of Sabbath laws and a proposed ten-hour day law. Only a half dozen bothered to answer. "You will have a hard time Prof.," the secretary wrote Ely, "to convince the toilers of this country that the clergy will ever do anything for them—there is no money in it—you know."[9] While the working class found no solace in organized religion, they still professed to be followers of Jesus. They demanded that the church take a position on questions of social justice.

By 1884 Ely had begun to contribute significantly to the ethical position of the churches with respect to the labor problem. The Reverend H. A. Schauffler of the American Home Missionary Society requested that Ely send him his ideas and views on the labor movement for their next annual meeting. The Reverend Samuel H. Virgin then constructed a sermon around Ely's letter. The labor problem had reached a crisis, Ely had written, for the movement was increasingly coming under the leadership of revolutionary socialists. "It is an undoubted fact that modern Socialism of the worst type

[8] Wilnn to Ely, Nov. 1, 1883, Ely MSS.
[9] G. Black to Ely, June 4, 1889, Ely MSS. Also see Ely and Seth Low, "A Programme for Labor Reform," *Century Magazine*, XXXIX (April, 1890), 944.

is spreading to an alarming extent among our working classes, both foreign and native." Christians must throw themselves into the breach in order to restore the brotherhood of all classes. "What is needed is Christianity, and the Christian Church can do far more than political economists towards a reconciliation of social classes." It was not socialism per se that was to be feared, but socialism without an infusion of Christian principles. The working class had become alienated from the church "because the Church has forgotten her mission," Ely wrote; "she has got on to a wrong track; she has gone so far out of the way that through her instrumentalities it is harder for a poor man to be saved, than for a camel to pass through the eye of a needle."[10]

Ely's letter "made a deep impression on the audience of from 12 to 1400 of the most intelligent people that can be brought together, from all parts of the country," the Reverend H. A. Schauffler wrote. Ely's opinions were given "emphatic endorsement" by President Seelye of Amherst College, who was also president of the Home Missionary Society. Seelye especially valued "testimony coming from one who is such an authority on social quetion [*sic*]" as Ely.[11] Upon his return to Amherst, Seelye based his baccalaureate sermon on Ely's ideas. The Home Missionary Society appointed a special committee to take up the evangelization of the foreign element in big cities. And Dr. Lyman Abbott requested Ely's letter for publication in the *Christian Union*.[12]

In the same year, 1884, Ely published "Recent American Socialism," which also struck an alarmist note from beginning to end. The International Working People's Associa-

[10] Ely to Schauffler as quoted in "Address of Rev. Samuel H. Virgin," *Home Missionary*, LVII (Oct., 1884), 227-228. Also see Ely, "Socialism," *Andover Review*, V (Feb., 1886), 150-163.

[11] Schauffler to Ely, June 12, 1884, Ely MSS.

[12] H. B. Adams to D. C. Gilman, July 21, 1884, Gilman MSS; Schauffler to Ely, June 12, 1884, Ely MSS. The letter was published as "Christianity the Remedy for Socialism," *Christian Union*, XXXI (June 26, 1884), 605, and "Modern Socialism" in the Springfield, Mass., *Daily Union*, July 26, 1884.

tion, or the "anarchists," Ely wrote, planned to overthrow the existing society by violence. Instead of advocating the necessary class harmony, they preached discontent, bitterness, and hate. Using dynamite and assassination as their weapons, these "mad souls" awaited the opportune moment to plunge the country into a nationwide blood bath. Companies of no fewer than 1,500 men, Ely reported, were drilling in Chicago, armed with rifles for the coming revolution. If actual class warfare erupted, the anarchists could count on the support of many mild socialists as well as members of the Knights of Labor. Over 14 percent of the labor force appeared to be unemployed and might be expected to join forces with the revolutionaries.[13] The present leaders of society blinded themselves to the danger by burying their heads in the sand. These philistines, Ely stated, "and the greater majority of the ruling middle class are Philistines," ignored the warnings and prophesies which they wished to avoid. Ely compared his position with the unpopular prophet Jeremiah. "But thoroughly persuaded that serious dangers are in store for us, that calamities are ahead of us which it will be impossible for us to escape entirely, . . . the writer feels compelled to speak his honest opinion and incur the risk of both ridicule and blame."[14] Although the complete overthrow of the existing social arrangements did not appear likely in the immediate future, immense bloodshed, destruction of property, and increased class antagonism sufficient to check American economic growth for years was a certainty unless reforms were made.

After 1884 Ely became increasingly effective in reaching churchmen with his message for resolving class conflict. He wrote *The Social Aspects of Christianity and Other Es-*

[13] See also Ely, "Herr Most in Baltimore," March 2, 1882, typewritten manuscript in Ely MSS.

[14] Ely, "Recent American Socialism," in Herbert B. Adams, ed., *Johns Hopkins University Studies in Historical and Political Science,* III (Baltimore: Johns Hopkins Press, 1885), p. 61.

says (1889) and *The Social Law of Service* (1896), which
became standard texts for Protestant social reformers. For
more than twenty years every minister entering the Methodist Episcopal church was required to read *Social Aspects*
as well as Ely's *An Introduction to Political Economy* (1889).
The Social Law of Service became part of the required reading course of the Epworth Youth League of the Methodist
church in both the United States and Canada. Ely's works
also were on the required reading list for theological students
in the United Brethren of Christ church. Almost all branches
of the Christian Social Union of the Anglican and Protestant
Episcopal churches in Canada and the United States studied
the works of Ely. Seminaries used them as texts, and theology professors such as George Herron of Iowa College
sent their advanced ministerial candidates directly to Ely for
training in the social sciences.[15] "Unto whom should I send
them if not to you?" Herron once asked Ely rhetorically.[16]
Ministers across the country used Ely's writing as a basis for
sermons and led special classes of young people in the study
of his works.[17]

Ely's influence extended to Catholic reformers as well.
James Cardinal Gibbons, the most influential reform figure
in the Catholic church in America, found his writings "most
suggestive." In 1886 Ely and the cardinal worked hand in
hand to avert a strike of streetcar workers in Baltimore and
helped to secure the passage of a twelve-hour day law by the
Maryland state legislature. The Right Reverend Monsignor
John A. Ryan read Ely's *Socialism and Social Reform* (1894)

[15] See Hunt & Eaton to Ely, Aug. 26, 1892, Nov. 30, 1895, J.
Fred Heisse to Ely, Sept. 28, 1892, A. C. Crews to Ely, May 7, 1897,
Henry W. Brown to Ely, July 21, 1892, John Mockridge to Ely, May
30, 1892, J. Macbride Sterrett to Ely, March 16, 1890, May 30, 1892,
Barton O. Aylisworth to Ely, Dec., 1889, all in Ely MSS; James Dom-
browski, *The Early Days of Christian Socialism in America* (New York:
Columbia University Press, 1936), pp. 50, 53.

[16] Herron to Ely, Nov. 7, 1893, Ely MSS.

[17] The Ely MSS abound with letters from ministers testifying to
the use of Ely's works for special classes and sermons.

as a seminary student and was struck by Ely's suggestion that
reformers and socialists could agree on programs even though
they completely disagreed on premises. In 1906 Ryan sent
his influential work, *A Living Wage,* to Ely, who found a
publisher for it and wrote a glowing introduction.[18]

In the 1880's and 1890's Ely spoke before religious groups
throughout the country. He gave lectures and lay sermons
before seminaries, divinity classes, and church conferences,
including the Evangelical Alliance in Boston, Baptist Pastor's
Conference of New York, the Interdenominational Conference
in Cincinnati, the World's Parliament of Religions in Chicago,
the Carew Lectures at the Hartford Divinity School, the
Protestant Episcopal Divinity School in Philadelphia, and a
host of lesser engagements. He counted almost every prominent minister of a social gospel inclination as a personal
friend, including Washington Gladden, Lyman Abbott, T.
Edwin Brown, H. Heber Newton, Josiah Strong, Leighton
Williams, Bishop J. O. S. Huntington, George Herron, Bishop
John H. Vincent, Walter Rauschenbusch, and William D. P.
Bliss.

Ely also actively participated in the international interchange of inspiration and ideas relevant to a social Christianity. He was particularly inspired by the English Christian socialists. In 1883 he met the Reverend Thomas Hughes,
who was visiting the United States. He maintained a steady
correspondence with Hughes and the Reverends Frederick
D. Maurice and Vansittart Neale, the three leading English
Christian socialists. Ely, perhaps more than any other American, popularized the ideas of the movement in the United
States. He wrote the introduction to Bishop Canon Fremantle's *The World as the Subject of Redemption* and contributed to the *Economic Review,* a publication of the Chris-

[18] James Cardinal Gibbons, "Wealth and Its Obligations," *North
American Review,* CLII (April, 1891), 388; Ely, *Ground Under Our
Feet,* pp. 78-79; Francis L. Broderick, *Right Reverend New Dealer
John A. Ryan* (New York: Macmillan, 1963), pp. 21, 45.

tian Social Union of the Church of England. And Ely, while
secretary of the American and Canadian branch of the Christian Social Union in the early 1890's, frequently exchanged
ideas with the Reverend John Carter, president of the English
branch.[19]
Ely's books were important not only for their analysis
of class conflict but also in the history of academic sociology.
The approach of his *Introduction to Political Economy* was
"sharply" distinctive because of its "Sociological standpoint,
and the Historical method, also the generally human spirit
in it," economist John Bates Clark felt.[20] For the second
edition Ely seriously considered the more appropriate title,
"Social Ethics." At one time, while at Hopkins, he toyed
with the idea of obtaining an endowed chair of "advanced
sociology" for himself. When he went to Wisconsin in 1892,
he taught courses listed under sociology and established a
separate division of sociology in 1894.[21] Albion Small, an

[19] See *Johns Hopkins University Circulars*, III (Nov., 1883), 4;
Ely and L. S. Merriam, "Report on Social Legislation in the United
States for 1889-1890," *Economic Review*, I (April, 1891), 234-256.
Apart from his numerous publications on various phases of socialism and
the labor movement in which he almost always discussed English Chris-
tian socialism, Ely wrote three articles specifically on the subject:
"Christian Socialism in England," *Christian Union*, XXXI (May 28,
June 4, 11, 1885), 7-8, 7-8, 7-8. Also see his "The Progress of Cooperation in England," *Congregationalist*, XXXVII (March 12, 1885), 87,
and "Important New Social Movements in England," *Christian Union*,
XLII (Nov. 6, 1890), 593-594. For Ely's appreciation of French social
movements see his "The French Protestant Association for the Practical
Study of Social Questions," *Virginia Seminary Magazine*, V (June,
1892), 373-378.
[20] Clark to Ely, April 20, 1889, Ely MSS.
[21] Ely to John H. Vincent, Jan. 20, 1891, Lyman Abbott to Ely,
Nov. 24, 1890, Ely MSS; "School of Economics, Political Science, and
History, Announcement for 1895-6," *Annual Catalogue of the University of Wisconsin, 1894-5*, p. 116. The following courses under "Sociology" are listed for Ely: "American Charities and Crime," "Social
Ethics," and "Socialism." Also see Ely and Edward D. Jones, "Instruction in Charities and Correction in the University of Wisconsin,"
Lend-a-Hand, XIV (June, 1895), 406-411; Ely, "The Proper Aims
of Schools of Economics and Politics," *Independent*, XLIV (May 19,
1892), 682-683.

Ely student and a sociologist, described Ely as the "founder of the 'Christian Sociology' movement."[22]

Apart from ministers and laymen intimately connected with the social gospel movement, Ely reached a larger public audience for his Christian sociology through the Chautauqua movement. When he accepted an invitation from Dr. William Rainey Harper, principal of the College of Liberal Arts of the Chautauqua, in 1887,[23] the Summer School and the Literary and Scientific Circle of Chautauqua had already become household words for most Americans. Inaugurated in 1874 by Bishop John H. Vincent for the training of Methodist Sunday school teachers, the movement rapidly became the most important national instrument for adult education. By the mid-1880's course offerings had been expanded to include all of the elementary subjects taught in American colleges. Each summer several hundred students of all ages, of various backgrounds, and of both sexes, gathered on the shores of Lake Chautauqua, New York, for the Summer School. And up to 400,000 participated yearly in the Literary and Scientific Circle, the extension division of Chautauqua.[24]

Ely's courses at the Summer School primarily attracted college graduates, many of them ministerial candidates and graduate students at various universities. Almost all of his offerings were more sociological in approach than the ones he taught at Johns Hopkins. He frequently gave lectures on English social movements, the labor movement, socialism, and cooperatives, many of which were published in either the

[22] Small to Ely, June 5, 1894, Ely MSS.

[23] Ely recalled in his autobiography that his association with Chautauqua began in 1884 at the invitation of Bishop Vincent and lasted for seven years. The Ely correspondence indicates, however, that his association began in 1887 at the invitation of Harper and ended in 1894. See Ely, *Ground Under Our Feet*, p. 81; Harper to Ely, Feb. 23, 1895, Ely to John H. Vincent, Feb. 8, 1895, Vincent to Ely, Feb. 16, 1895, Ely MSS.

[24] Ely, *Social Aspects of Christianity*, p. 36.

Chautauquan magazine or the *Chautauqua Assembly Herald.*
Although Ely failed to attract huge classes, as did popular
lecturers such as evangelist Sam Jones, the Reverend Washington Gladden, or Bishop Vincent, he had a devoted coterie
of students ranging from future muckraker Ida Tarbell to
future academicians Charles J. Bullock and David Kinley.[25]

Through the Chautauqua Literary and Scientific Circle,
Ely reached an even larger audience than he did through the
Summer School. His *Introduction to Political Economy* was
originally written for the circle as part of the required reading course and was printed by the Methodist printing concern,
Hunt & Eaton. The *Introduction* soon became, in the words
of Bishop Vincent, "the book of the course."[26] Revised seven
times over the next fifty years under a new title, *Outlines of
Economics,* it became the largest selling economics textbook
in the United States. Though the revised editions were more
conservative in tone than the original work, they continued to
present a blend of ethics and economics.[27]

Besides the Chautauqua, Ely during the 1890's extended
his message of Christian sociology to several other organizations. For the summer of 1893 he served as principal of the
Bay View Summer School at Flint, Michigan, an imitation of
the parent Chautauqua. He also lectured two summers, 1894
and 1895, at the Colorado Summer School, Colorado Springs.
During 1893 and 1894 he served as president of the American Institute of Christian Sociology, a short-lived society
composed of academicians and ministers, including John R.
Commons and George Herron. And in 1891 he helped to

25 Ely, "Higher Educational Work of Chautauqua," *Christian
Union,* XLI (June, 1890), 896; T. H. Vincent to Ely, Jan. 4, 1888,
Ely MSS; H. B. Adams to D. C. Gilman [1888?], Gilman MSS; Tarbell
to Ely, Oct. 9, 1896, Ely MSS; Tarbell, *All in a Day's Work: An Autobiography* (New York: Macmillan, 1939), p. 76; Ely, *Ground Under
Our Feet,* p. 83.
26 Vincent to Ely, Oct. 19, 1888, Jan. 28, 1890, Ely MSS.
27 Joseph Dorfman, *The Economic Mind in American Civilization,*
IV-V (New York: Viking, 1959), p. 211.

organize the Christian Social Union of the Protestant Episcopal church. As secretary of the union from 1891 to 1894, he worked hand in hand with the Reverend William D. P. Bliss, chief organizer of the union. Under Ely's editorial direction, one number of the *Bulletin of the Christian Social Union in the United States and Canada* appeared in March of 1893. The union published, also under Ely's supervision, several pamphlets on social problems, and many of the branches studied his works.[28]

After 1884 Ely diverted his attention from revolutionary socialism to the more peaceful Knights of Labor. Never before in American history had a labor organization so captured the fancy of millions of Americans from every walk of life. When Ely returned from Germany in 1880, organized labor had started an upward climb which reached an apex in 1886. He had little hope that the crafts unions would ever promote the evolution of modern society toward the ethical ideal of brotherhood, but he became highly enamored of the Knights of Labor. By 1885 the Knights had increased their membership to nearly 111,000 members. After a successful strike against Jay Gould's railroad lines in the Southwest, their prestige increased rapidly. Benefiting in addition from a revival of interest in eight-hour day legislation, membership leaped from 111,000 in July, 1885, to over 700,000 a year later.

The mushroom growth of the Knights led Ely to believe that a new order based on the principles of brotherhood was much nearer achievement than he had thought. The platform of the Knights squared with Ely's hope for industrial evolution. Instead of the exclusive character of the crafts unions, the Knights were industrywide, inviting membership from all

[28] See John Neal to Ely, March 26, 1892, Josiah Strong to Ely, Jan. 24, 1894, Commons to Ely, Jan. 30, 1894, William L. Bull to Ely, May 25, 1894, John Carter to Holland, Jan. 1, 1891, Carter to Ely, Feb. 7, 1891, Ely MSS; Ely, "The Christian Social Union: A Social University," *Churchman*, LV (April 2, 1892), 414-415.

workingmen, even ministers and teachers. They asked for the eventual substitution of cooperation for the wage system. They wanted to settle disputes by peaceful means, by bringing employer and employee together. In unqualified terms Ely declared that the Knights were "the most powerful and the most remarkable organization of modern times." They were "established on truly scientific principles, which involved either an intuitive perception of the nature of industrial progress, or a wonderful acquaintance with the laws of economic society."[29]

Unfortunately most Americans misunderstood the grand mission of the Knights. The newspapers lost "all regard for truth" when labor questions were discussed, businessmen were violently partisan, and those with traditional prejudices exaggerated the evil side of labor activities. But most of the opposition to labor unions rested on public ignorance. Ely claimed that he too once regarded labor unions with suspicion, but long intensive study had convinced him of their beneficence. He had yet to find an opponent of the labor movement among those who had given it thorough study.[30] "Among political economists it is no longer necessary to vindicate their usefulness, for they almost unanimously favor them," he wrote in gross overstatement.[31]

In the summer of 1885, one year after his visit to Pullman, Ely began research for his *Labor Movement in America.* Thomas Y. Crowell, his publisher, wanted a work which covered "the present condition of the Labor Question in this

[29] Ely, *The Labor Movement in America* (New York: Crowell, 1886), p. 75. Also see Ely, "American Labor Organizations: Their Probable Future," *Congregationalist,* XXXIX (Jan. 20, 1887), 20, and Ely, *Problems of To-Day: A Discussion of Protective Tariffs, Taxation, and Monopolies* (New York: Crowell, 1888), p. 47.

[30] See Ely, "Conditions of Industrial Peace," *Forum,* III (Aug., 1887), 643; Ely, "Labor Organizations," *Forum,* III (March, 1887), 50-51; Ely, "Arbitration," *North American Review,* CXLIII (Oct., 1886), 324; Ely, ed., *Science-Economic Discussion* (New York: Science, 1887), p. viii.

[31] Ely, *Labor Movement,* p. 154.

country—the various Trades Union. Knights of Labor." And
he suggested that Ely describe the views and grievances of
the working class. Ely went busily to work, interviewing
major labor leaders Terrence V. Powderly and Samuel Gompers, and visiting Chicago and Pittsburgh, the centers of labor
agitation.[32] "At the time I was full of enthusiasm and was
fired with the thought that I was fulfilling a mission," Ely
later wrote. And to his mother he wrote: "Woe is me if I
preach not this gospel!"[33]

And preach the gospel he did. From the first to the last
page of the *Labor Movement* he mixed superficial and fragmentary research with strong moral expletives. He preached
to both the worker and the employer. He warned the workingman that he must put away the pervasive and pernicious
American belief in the myth of the self-made man. "Let us,
then, begin any treatment of the labor question, or any other
social problem, with a frank recognition of the fact that we
have to deal with the ninety-nine out of a hundred who by
no human possibility can ascend to the 'upper story.'"[34] In
order to make the best of his position, the worker should attempt to raise the stature of the entire working class by
recognizing superior leadership. "Christ and all Christly
people are with you," Ely explained.[35] Although he maintained that violence resulted from a lack of organization, it
was to be eschewed at all times. "It is only necessary to
restrain a comparatively few hot-headed and vicious capitalists, and a comparatively few hot-headed and vicious labor-

[32] Crowell to Ely, March 20, 27, 1885, Powderly to Ely, June 6,
1885, Ely MSS; Ely to Joseph A. Labadie, Aug. 14, 1885, in Fine, ed.,
"The Ely-Labadie Letters," p. 17.
[33] Ely, *Ground Under Our Feet*, p. 172.
[34] Ely, *Labor Movement*, p. 93. Also see Ely, "Fundamental Beliefs in My Social Philosophy," *Forum*, XVIII (Oct., 1894), 182. Examples of Ely's fragmentary research are revealed in his letters with
Joseph A. Labadie, a member of the Knights of Labor and friend of
many labor leaders. Many of Labadie's letters were used verbatim.
See Fine, ed., "The Ely-Labadie Letters," pp. 26n-27n.
[35] Ely, *Labor Movement*, p. xi.

ers, to ensure a peaceful evolution of industrial society."[36] Ely encouraged men of wealth to make a conscientious effort at understanding labor and to apply Christian ethics to the labor problem. Rather than repress the labor movement, they should assume positions of leadership.[37]

Such undisguised sympathy for the Knights brought down the howls of both conservatives and genteel reformers. Ely had gone too far to suit the major organ of genteel reform, the *Nation*, which favored only clean government through a civil service system. The *Nation*, behind its anonymous pages, invited Ely's old antagonist Simon Newcomb to put an end to the young upstart professor. "The author of this book enjoys the double distinction of being the leading professor of his subject in the Johns Hopkins University and, for the moment, the most voluminous writer in the country on economic topics," Newcomb wrote. But, he quickly implied, Ely was hardly qualified for such a distinction. When discussing social movements, Newcomb wrote, Ely on the whole "shows a lack of logical acumen and narrowness of view which, in a university teacher, are most remarkable." Further, the book's "worst defect" was "an intensity of bias, and a bitterness toward all classes of society except one." He accused Ely of intellectual confusion, "puerility of tone and treatment, a scrappiness of narrative, and the absence of everything like strength of touch, mental grasp, or logical unity." Newcomb concluded by noting that Ely was "seriously out of place in a university chair."[38]

Little wonder that Ely and his friends feared the worst —his dismissal from the university. Henry C. Adams was under attack at Cornell and the next year was fired for holding similar views. However, H. B. Adams and Ely's

[36] Ely, "Labor Organizations," p. 58.
[37] See Ely and Low, "A Programme for Labor Reform," p. 951; Ely to Amos P. Wilder, July 27, 1894, Ely MSS.
[38] [Newcomb], "Dr. Ely on the Labor Movement," *Nation*, XLIII (Oct. 7, 1886), 293-294.

former students proved to be loyal friends.[39]   Albert Shaw reviewed the *Labor Movement* for *Dial*, calling it "conservative in the truest sense of the word." And in the same review he attacked another book by Newcomb, *A Plain Man's Talk on the Labor Question*, on the basis of suggestions sent to him by Ely. The religious leaders rallied to Ely's defense and Lyman Abbott, at Ely's solicitation, wrote a favorable review in the *Christian Union*.[40] "I think no man in the country is more widely known or more cordially liked by the clergy than Professor Ely," Washington Gladden wrote to Gilman. "It is greatly to the honor of Johns Hopkins that she has given him the chance to do his work."[41] By December of 1886, Ely believed that, despite Gilman's "becoming shaky under pressure from the *Nation* crowd," his position was safe.[42] The next year, 1887, Ely was not only reappointed but promoted to an associate professorship.[43]

Gilman's reaction to the dispute which threatened to explode within the walls of the university apparently was less vacillating than Ely thought at the time. The support of Herbert B. Adams, who put away personal grievances, may have been crucial, for Adams had recommended Ely's advancement to associate professor a few months before the Newcomb review. In glowing terms he wrote Gilman that Ely "justly deserves the honor and, considering his present leading position among economists of the country I think it highly inexpedient to withhold it any longer."[44] The trustees

[39] Ely to Shaw, Oct. 3, 18, 1886, in Hawkins, *Pioneer*, p. 183.

[40] Albert Shaw, "Seven Books for Citizens," *Dial*, VII (1886), 149-152; John Bascom to Ely, Dec. 6, 1886, T. Edwin Brown to Ely, Oct. 11, 1886, H. W. Mabie to Ely, Oct. 21, 1886, Ely MSS.

[41] Gladden to Gilman, Dec. 25, 1886. Gilman MSS.

[42] Ely to Shaw, Oct. 18, 19, 1886, in Hawkins, *Pioneer*, p. 184.

[43] Lyman Abbott to Ely, July 5, 1887, Ely MSS; *Johns Hopkins University Studies*, III-IV (1891), p. 204. Several years later Herbert Adams reputedly told Ely that Newcomb was a candidate for Ely's position at Hopkins. See Ely to Frederic C. Howe, Oct. 10, 1903, Ely to Davis R. Dewey, Dec. 8, 1903, Ely MSS.

[44] Adams to Gilman, May 29, 1886, in W. Stull Holt, ed., "Historical Scholarship in the United States, 1876-1901: As Revealed in

and Gilman awarded the raise in rank. Also, E. L. Godkin, editor of the *Nation,* exercised unusual restraint by refraining from using his personal friendship with Gilman as a lever to force Ely out. Not until 1892, when Ely had left for Wisconsin, did Godkin allow his true feelings to be known to Gilman.[45] Whatever Ely's suspicions in 1886, he could write in 1938 that Gilman "held firm to his belief that academic freedom must prevail."[46]

After 1886 the Ely-Newcomb hostility subsided. During the 1886-1887 term Ely even included one of Newcomb's books as a reference for his basic course. And when Newcomb offered an undergraduate course on business and financial institutions in the 1887-1888 term, he found that Ely had firmly grounded his students in the fundamentals of classical economics. By 1893, although still believing the new economists had exaggerated the differences between the two schools, Newcomb was willing to agree with their proposal to nationalize the telegraph. In 1894 he reviewed the first and second edition of Ely's basic textbook with much milder criticisms. By 1906, when both men had lost some of the youthful evangelism which had driven them to battle in 1886, they could speak warmly of each other.[47]

---

the Correspondence of H. B. Adams," *Johns Hopkins University Studies in History and Political Science,* LVI (Baltimore: Johns Hopkins Press, 1938), p. 86.

[45] Godkin to Gilman, Feb. 17, 1892, Gilman MSS.

[46] Ely, *Ground Under Our Feet,* p. 102. In his autobiography Ely speaks of an "indiscreet" attack he made upon the president of the Baltimore and Ohio Railroad. Although the president reported he would not send one of his children to Hopkins as long as Ely was there, Gilman said nothing of the incident.

[47] Hawkins, *Pioneer,* p. 185; Newcomb, "The Problem of Economic Education," *Quarterly Journal of Economics,* VII (July, 1893), 375-399; Ely, *Socialism: An Examination of Its Nature, Its Strength and Its Weakness, with Suggestions for Social Reform* (New York: Crowell, 1894), pp. 271, 271n; Newcomb, review of Ely, *An Introduction of Political Economy* and *Outlines of Economics,* in *Journal of Political Economy,* III (1894-95), 106; Ely to Davis R. Dewey, Dec. 8, 1903, Ely MSS; Ely to Newcomb, Feb. 7, 1906, Newcomb MSS, Library of Congress.

The review by Simon Newcomb and the ensuing danger to Ely's position at Johns Hopkins helped to give the *Labor Movement* an immense audience. Reform sympathizers across the country wanted to join Ely and do battle with "the new Church of Mammon," as one reform minister put it. After reading the review, the Reverend T. Edwin Brown reported that "It took away my appetite. It turned my stomach." He accused the *Nation* of "contemptible insolence, the Pharisaic arrogance, the air of Papal infallibility, the sneaking cussedness,—I shall swear if I don't stop." He planned to use his pulpit, in "which the shades of Roger Williams yet linger," to combat the enemy which placed materialism above Christianity.[48] Labor leaders added their support with friendly editorials, excerpts, and recommendations to locals that it be read.[49] The work was important as a tract of the times and as a personalized response to the critical state of labor-capital relations in the mid-1880's. Three editions appeared before 1890; it remained the standard work on labor history and the contemporary labor movement for three decades. The spirit of this work set the tone for the monumental studies in the twentieth century by Ely's student, John R. Commons.

The theoretical basis for opposition to the labor organizations rested primarily on the classical commodity-labor thesis. Ely explained that the classicist regarded labor as merely another economic commodity, like other goods subject to the mechanism of the marketplace. Without any sort of market restrictions, the labor supply and wages responded to demand exactly as did other goods. Thus, if the demand increased for gloves and decreased for hats, the manufacturer would shift his production from hats to gloves. And

[48] Brown to Ely, Oct. 11, 1886, Ely MSS.
[49] E. T. C. to Ely, April 12, 1887, Adolf Donai to Ely, Sept. 18, 1886, H. S. Schulteis to [?], Jan. 14, 1889, William Volkmar to Ely, Oct. 26, 1888, Ely MSS. See Henry F. May, *Protestant Churches and Industrial America* (New York: Harper, 1949), pp. 141-142, 142n, for some of the impact of the book on the social gospel advocates.

so it would be with labor, for the worker would be laid off at the hat factory and hired at the glove factory. If population remained stable and the demand for labor increased, then wages would spiral upward. Built into this neat mechanism was the assumption of pure freedom for the laborer to seek the highest price for his commodity, labor. David Ricardo, basing his ideas on Thomas Malthus, added a crucial amendment to Adam Smith's unending pageant of progress for entrepreneur and laborer alike. The worker could never raise his wage above the subsistence level, Ricardo explained, for with every wage increase the laborer had more children. Thus the labor supply always tended to glut the labor market, driving wages back to the subsistence level.

Ely rejected the thesis that labor corresponded to any other commodity. Relying heavily on his economic training in Germany, in particular on the criticism of labor as a commodity by Ludwig J. Brentano in G. V. Schönberg's *Handbuch der Politischen Oekonomie,* Ely argued that labor should be distinguished from other commodities. The fundamental distinction for Ely was ethical; this "commodity" was, after all, a human personality, an end in itself. He also maintained that as a matter of historical fact labor was the victim of imperfect competition, thus falling outside the classical model. Manufacturers selling needles or farmers selling wheat offered inanimate objects in which they did not sacrifice their own person or actions. On the other hand, the laborer had only his own person to offer for sale. This did not deny that in a purely economic sense labor tended to respond like other commodities to the pull of supply and demand. But it did make a vital ethical distinction. Nonhuman commodities were means to an end, "while the laborer who parts with [his] labor . . . is an end in himself, for man is the beginning and the termination of all economic life."[50]

Ely rejected on factual grounds the belief of the class-

[50] Ely, *Labor Movement,* p. 99.

icists that labor maximized its position by being purely competitive, that is, by being able to accept the best market for its product. He denied that pure labor competition existed in the present order. Businessmen and the public generally recognized that they determined conditions of employment and wages, even though theorists ascribed these phenomena to natural law. But when labor attempted to control these conditions, it was called "dictation." The basic reason that man fell outside of the beautiful supply-and-demand marketplace mechanism was owing to the peculiar characteristics of labor.

The laborer, unlike other commodities, was unable to seek the best market. Moving required money, sufficient intelligence, and information. More important, labor could not be withdrawn from the market when the demand fell for its services. Instead, a decline in demand brought forth an increased supply of labor, for other members of the individual laborer's family would be forced to seek work. And since labor demand normally fell during periods of depression, members of the white-collar class would also be forced into competition with the laborer. The workers could not diminish supply unless they died, killed themselves, or as a long-range solution practiced sexual abstention, while the production of goods could be steadily cut back with the fall in prices. Conversely, Ely denied that wages rose immediately with the increase in demand, for the first laborers hired were the reserves. Wages only increased when the reserve was used up and competition ensued for the remaining workers.

In an unorganized state the employer also could determine the conditions of the labor contract by influencing the worker's expenditures "in such a manner as to render him nearly as dependent as a serf."[51] The employer frequently paid his workers at long intervals, the result being that the

51 *Ibid.*, p. 103.

employee became dependent on credit and debt. Company stores and housing were widely used in the United States. Ely even cited state labor bureau reports of numerous charges of cheating in weight, quality, and price by company stores.

Likewise, the employer determined working conditions. The laborer was at the mercy of ill-ventilated factories and improper safety equipment. Ely estimated that nearly 15,000 railroad accidents were needless. The laborer must work next to a scoundrel, if his employer chose, and he must work the number of hours required. Especially evil was the lack of consideration shown for pregnant women and children. In sum, the employer influenced the mental, moral, religious, and political life of his employees. Although Ely admitted that employers seldom interfered with religious beliefs, they frequently exerted pressures on political opinions. In one town Ely found that the inhabitants were "marched like sheep to the polls, and ordered to vote in a manner well pleasing to a great corporation."[52] Without organization or the intervention of government it was well-nigh impossible for the laborer to provide security for himself and his family.

According to Ely these peculiarities of commodity labor and the changes in the pattern of industrial growth made the analysis and hopes of Adam Smith and his friends irrelevant. Continually improving technology had led to the supremacy of the machine over man, and experienced journeymen lost their jobs to women and children. In what resembled a Marxian historical analysis, Ely maintained that "thousands of laborers became tramps, their daughters prostitutes, and their sons criminals. Reduction after reduction of wages followed." When the worker tried to withdraw a portion of his commodity from the marketplace, as the industrialists frequently did, "they were thrown into prison; for the old conspiracy and combination laws continued long

---

[52] *Ibid.*, pp. 107-108.

after the legal protection offered labor by a previous generation had been abolished."[53]

Although condemned by the better classes, refined techniques of "cruelty"—the blacklist and the yellow dog contract—made the worker no less than a slave. A laborer could
be placed on the blacklist for whim or for disfavor, but once
his name appeared on the list it remained, barring him from
employment across the country. The yellow dog contract,
upheld by the courts, was signed by an employee when he
began work and prevented him from joining a union. It
was the "beginning of a system of white slavery," Ely maintained.

These historical developments had driven a wedge between the workers and their employers, between their interests and their ideas. Although the class separation was
more characteristic of European society, it was reaching a
critical point in the United States. In England and Germany
reform through state action and labor organizations had
brought the two classes within each nation closer together.
In America the trend was in the opposite direction—an "omin-
ous separation of the American people into two nations."
Already the capitalist and the laborer did not understand
each other. They supported "two public opinions" and two
separate presses. "Already there begins a class struggle for
political supremacy; already religious lines are becoming,
have become to an alarming extent in our great cities, social
lines, and there is a widespread feeling among the working
classes that the church of their employers cannot be the
church for them, that the God of the rich is no God whom
they can worship."[54]

Typically Ely made his primary appeal directly to the
upper classes rather than to the worker. He asked the respectable middle class, the morally conscious industrialists,

[53] *Ibid.*, p. 109.
[54] *Ibid.*, p. 113.

and the Christian ministers to recognize their true ethical obligations in the new industrial world. Christ set the example with His humble life as a carpenter and His crucifixion on the Cross. He supplied the ethical bond between not only God and man, but man and man. In this light Ely urged the reader to consider labor organizations.[55] Did they fulfill valuable functions in restoring the brotherhood of men or morally elevating men?

Ely answered in the uncompromising affirmative. The labor union enabled the worker to overcome the imperfect competition of the present system. Labor organizations placed the worker more on a par with the capitalists, for he could hold his product off the market in order to gain fair demands. If the demand for labor fell, the union could prevent its workers from working below the usual rates, for one decrease led to another. Moreover, labor unions could make the labor commodity more competitive by finding jobs. Even the more enlightened companies hired their workers through the union. Labor organizations would assist the worker in overcoming the gloomy Ricardian thesis of subsistence wages, according to Ely, because men would be more prudent in marriage.[56]

Following consistently his emphasis on class harmony, Ely urged arbitration as a "conservative" first step to the solution of labor-capital problems. Logically, arbitration should be a natural result of the wage system. Unfortunately, because of "imperfect moral development" businessmen hesitated to meet the worker on equal grounds. Thus, arbitrating disputes could only come by legal compulsion or when labor organizations had reached an equal strength with employers. Experience showed that government compulsion

---

[55] Ely, "The Labor Movement: A Reply to the Editor of the Christian Register," *Christian Register*, LXVI (Oct. 27, 1887), 675; Ely, "Labor Organizations," p. 55; Ely, "Arbitration," pp. 318-319; Ely, "Conditions of Industrial Peace," p. 640.

[56] Ely, "Labor Organizations," pp. 55-58.

would not likely work in the United States, for legislative bodies "too often" passed labor laws without any intention of enforcing them. "One might almost at times suspect a secret conspiracy with the administrative authorities that labor-laws should remain a dead letter. Yet we talk about the moral depravity of the working classes!"[57]

In order to overcome the "pride and arrogance" of the captains of industry on the question of arbitration, Ely believed labor unions had to be strengthened. For the individual employee had no chance of winning a compromise or just settlement against the giant corporation. "To ask a single laborer, representing a ten thousandth part of the labor factor, to place himself against a man who represents all the combined capital, is as absurd as to place a boy before an express train and expect him to stop its progress." Through the joint compulsion of labor organization and a higher moral development, Ely was convinced that the Knights of Labor in the "not distant future" would introduce arbitration for all workingmen. Already, a surprising number of employers saw labor "as connected with a human personality . . . superior to capital . . . and [recognized] that labor ought to be given an even larger and larger measure of ruleship, as it shows a fitness for it, until it gains its goal,—complete sovereignty." Strong words indeed! But this was only the admonition of Christ, Ely argued. How difficult it was for some men "to learn of social inferiors, like a carpenter's son and fisherman," Ely wrote.[58]

Although Ely in his theoretical and descriptive analysis tended to credit labor unions with almost every conceivable good, he skirted the vital question of whether labor organizations could actually have a substantial effect on general wage rates. John Stuart Mill had popularized the thesis that

[57] Ely, "Arbitration," p. 324n. Also see Ely, "Suggestions for Social Topics: VIII, Labor Organizations," *Christian Advocate,* LXVI (Sept. 10, 1891), 602.
[58] Ely, *Labor Movement,* pp. 146, 149.

a natural and set allocation of capital went for wages. Individual wages thus depended upon the number of workers as a divisor of the available capital. If the "wages-fund" was sufficient to pay labor higher than subsistence wages, then population would increase and wages would fall back to the subsistence level. Mill stated the wage-fund theory as follows: "wages not only depend upon the relative amount of capital and population, but cannot, under the rule of competition, be affected by anything else. Wages (meaning, of course, the general rate) cannot rise, but by an increase of the aggregate funds employed in hiring labourers, or a diminution in the number of competitors for hire; nor fall, except either by a diminution of the funds devoted to paying labour, or by an increase in the numbers of labourers to be paid."[59] In a single reference to the wage-fund theory, Ely called it "antiquated." Although, on occasion, he implied that general wage levels might be affected through organization, he definitely believed a serious limitation existed. For example, he wrote that "laborers are forced at times to hold their commodity, labor, [via the strike] back from the market in order to receive for it *the price which the state of the labor market justifies*."[60] All that Ely asked for was perfect competition on an equal basis, that is, labor's bargaining on an equal power basis with capital. But wages were definitely limited to what the market justified. "Where the national product is small, and there is little to divide between the various productive agents, they [labor unions] cannot raise wages to a satisfactory standard."[61] They first had to raise the general productive level. Then the Ricardian doctrine might come to play again.

Not surprisingly, considering his concern with higher

59 John Stuart Mill, *Principles of Political Economy* (London: Longmans, Green, 1909), p. 344.
60 Ely, *Labor Movement*, p. 149 (emphasis added).
61 Ely, "Labor Organizations," p. 57. Also see Ely, *Problems of To-Day*, p. 83.

moral development, Ely devoted almost as much attention to the educational and moral advantages of labor organizations as to the economic. Next to churches and the public schools, labor unions exercised the largest "influence upon the culture of the masses." They elevated the masses mentally, morally, and spiritually. In the usual Ely manner, he listed a series of examples, often superficial and unconvincing, of the ways in which labor organizations served as a valuable educational agency. They sponsored libraries, supported public education, morally coerced their members, and encouraged temperance. Ely attributed to labor organizations the coming of the public school in the United States in the face of "men whose political wisdom and sense of social justice I prefer not to characterize in terms which would seem to me fitting."[62] He examined several union libraries and found that union officials selected books more wisely than the young ladies in the best society. He discovered many workers reading Henry George's *Progress and Poverty*. Although Ely "decidedly" disagreed with George's teachings, he rejoiced at the intellectual stimulation and growing interest of the laborers in economics.

Labor organizations trained their members in the arts of practical politics and social grace. They encouraged debate of current issues and improvement in the art of oratory. Although most of the labor leaders had risen from the ranks, Ely stated that the popular image of them as "idle" demagogues was entirely false. Ely's examples were trivial and reflected more of himself than the labor movement. For example, he told of attending a meeting of the Central Labor Union of New York in which one of the members shouted "damn." According to Ely's account cries sprang up from across the hall of "I object to the language!" And the chairman immediately reprimanded the offender by reminding him

---

[62] Ely, *Labor Movement*, p. 123.

that he had violated union rules. Fines were imposed by other unions, Ely claimed, for the use of profanity.

Labor unions were "perhaps the chief power" encouraging temperance, Ely wrote. Excessive drinking had always been a curse to the workingman, whose environment encouraged it. High-speed machinery, poor working conditions, idleness, and slums drove men to drink. If the drinking problem was to be solved, general reform would in part have to precede it. Considering the circumstances under which laborers toiled, Ely marveled at their temperance. The Knights of Labor especially played a large role in promoting sobriety. Under the leadership of Terrence V. Powderly, an acquaintance of Ely, they denied membership to anyone connected with the manufacture and sale of intoxicating liquors. And Ely cited with unabashed approval Powderly's comment that he would rather admit a serpent than a drunkard into the union. Furthermore, unions levied fines for drunkenness at work and at meetings of the lodges. "How many rich men's clubs exclude the use of intoxicants, and impose fines for profanity?" Ely rhetorically asked.[63]

Apart from the Christian church, which in many cases failed to exercise its function properly, the labor movement furnished the strongest impetus to the brotherhood of men. While the churches were discarding the use of "brother" and "sister," unions had adopted its usage. These were not empty words, for labor organizations extended thousands of little services to each other. Labor unions, as international organizations, reached an international brotherhood. The workers, "I am often inclined to think . . . are the only large class who really and truly desire peace between nations, the abandonment of armies, the conversion of spears into pruning-hooks, and swords into ploughshares." German laborers had protested against the slaughter of their French brothers in

[63] *Ibid.*, p. 135n.

the Franco-Prussian War of 1870. Veterans of both Union and Confederate armies joined the Knights of Labor in peaceful accord under the motto, "Capital divides, labor unites us." In the future, Ely predicted, organized labor would force the governments of the world to arbitrate their differences and war would end. A huge international parliament would be formed as a federated world state. "Strange is it not? that the despised trades-union and labor organizations should have been chosen to perform this high duty of conciliation! But hath not God ever called the lowly to the most exalted missions, and hath he not ever called the foolish to confound the wise?"[64]

To young economist Richard Ely class conflict overshadowed all other social problems of the 1880's. To avert a violent revolution and to restore the practice of brotherhood required dramatic and imaginative action by the better educated, the clergyman, and the responsible employer. Because of Ely's association with an esteemed university and his training in political economy, he commanded a higher aura of authority than the minister who was busily engaged in the daily details of his pastorate or the capitalist who was far removed from the life of the ordinary worker. Few laymen committed themselves so firmly to the social role of the church. While, indeed, Ely's social ideas and his description of the labor crisis were controversial, neither posed a direct threat to American interest groups. He seldom directly confronted the existing power structure of society. Neither did he promise the working class any utopia in terms of economic growth or a redistribution of income. He was inclined to feel that almost any arrangement of society could be infused with Christian brotherhood. Increasingly, however, he recognized the need of promoting a program of more specific reforms, reforms which would serve as a "golden mean" between socialism and a competitive order.

[64] *Ibid.*, p. 139.

Chapter Four

"THE GOLDEN MEAN"

When Ely wrote his *Labor Movement* in 1886, he firmly believed that the labor movement was preparing the way for a moral regeneration of the American industrial system and for the establishment of the "ideal" system, "the union of capital and labor in the same hands, in grand, wide-reaching, co-operative enterprises, which shall embrace the masses."[1] The cooperative movement, already well underway, would sweep everything before it, for each day autonomous trade locals joined the Knights of Labor in support of cooperative enterprises. While American cooperatives had often failed in the past, Ely admitted, eventual success was inevitable. Then class warfare would disappear and all rational wants would be satisfied. Eventually the corporations would become cooperatives. He likened the corporation to the limited monarchy form of constitutional government. As the limited monarchy had been the intermediate stage between despotism and democracy, the corporation was the stage between industrial despotism and industrial democracy in the evolution of the economic organism. Both corporations and cooperatives involved numerous investors. By simply changing the principle of one share, one vote to all shareholders having an equal voice in management, the corporation could become a cooperative.[2]

But the years 1886 and 1887 forced Ely to revaluate his position as to the best means of achieving reform. As he watched the grand dream of the Knights of Labor collapse, his fascination with cooperatives faded. By 1894, when he published *Socialism and Social Reform*, he seldom mentioned cooperatives. In eleven chapters devoted to social reform only two pages dealt with the cooperative management of production. He explained that the "tendencies toward centralization of business have raised up new difficulties which have impeded the extension of co-operation."[3] Ely's experience in the years following 1886 turned his attention to more concrete and conservative methods of achieving the practice of brotherhood, a "golden mean" between socialism and a competitive order.

Ely's appointments to the Baltimore (1885) and the Maryland (1886) tax commissions forced him to confront problems requiring specific suggestions for reform. He seized the opportunities to make a firsthand study of the problems of city franchises held by private corporations and of the problems of public administration and taxation at both the city and state level. Ely pioneered in examining the facts and figures of public finance. In preparation for the report to be submitted to the state legislature, he visited Charleston, South

[1] Ely, *The Labor Movement in America* (New York: Crowell, 1886), p. 136.

[2] *Ibid.*, chap. vii; Ely, "Social Studies: I—The Nature and Significance of Corporations," *Harper's New Monthly Magazine*, LXXIV (May, 1887), 970-972.

[3] Ely, *Socialism: An Examination of Its Nature, Its Strength and Its Weakness, with Suggestions for Social Reform* (New York: Crowell, 1894), p. 340.

Carolina; Savannah and Columbus, Georgia; Columbus, Ohio; Madison, Wisconsin; and three Canadian cities: Montreal, Toronto, and Quebec. Ely refused to sign the majority report which provided for more stringent enforcement of existing laws. Instead, he published a 108-page "Supplementary Report on Taxation in Maryland" (1888). The same year, assisted by one of his graduate students, John H. Finley, he published *Taxation in American States and Cities,* which was based on his investigations for the Maryland commission. Even the *Nation,* in reviewing Ely's work, admitted it was "almost invaluable to students of American politics," although it quickly added that the professor's suggestions for reforming the present system were "to speak temperately, worthless."[4] Over twenty-five years later the state of Maryland cited Ely's Maryland report in a tax suit against the Baltimore and Ohio Railroad.[5]

Ely's experience on the Baltimore tax commission and his tour of the country for the Maryland commission provoked another crusade. Everywhere he went, local citizens and assessors testified to an almost universal evasion of taxes. As a rule assessors, cowed by the fear of losing their jobs, invariably underevaluated property. In Baltimore Ely found glaring inequities in assessment. While houses under $5,000 were assessed at near market price, those above $30,000 were grossly undervalued. Assessment practices varied widely from county to county within states, though all paid a uniform rate of state taxes. Efforts to strengthen enforcement by detailed tax forms, strict oaths, and heavy penalties had led to even lower assessments and to violations in reporting property holdings. "The truth is," Ely concluded, "the existing system is so radically bad, that the more you improve it the worse it

[4] [C. B. Spahr], "Ely's Municipal Taxation," *Nation,* XLVII (Nov. 1, 1888), 359.
[5] See Oscar Leser to Ely, Oct. 27, 1915, May 27, 1916, J. G. Schonfarber to Ely, June 25, 1901, Ely MSS, State Historical Society of Wisconsin, Madison.

becomes."[6] Although satisfactory for an agrarian society, the existing system had outlived its usefulness. For the new urban society, wealth often took the form of stocks, mortgages, bonds, and various other forms of easily concealed property. The general property tax no longer reflected the classical "ability to pay" principle.

Because the existing system of taxation failed to meet the "requirement of practical morality," Ely proposed a system with a separate tax base for local and state governments. Local units, Ely wrote, should have sole claim on property as a source of taxes. But the property tax should include only real estate, for real estate could not be easily concealed and it would eliminate the temptation of one county to undervalue its property in order to pay less taxes than another. All tax rates would be set to meet the planned expenses of the government. For the state Ely proposed a graduated income tax, estimating that a $600 deduction with the beginning rate at 1 percent would be sufficient to meet expenses. Although the income tax had long been advocated by various reformers and even tried during the Civil War by the national government, the distinction between tax bases was a novel feature of Ely's proposed system.

Ely felt that taxes on "invisible" property such as stocks, mortgages, and bonds, as well as business taxes, should be eliminated. Such property could easily be concealed and taxes on it tended to affect business adversely. Taxes on mortgages, for example, merely resulted in shifting the real burden to the debtor by raising the interest rate. And a tax on bonds or bank deposits would drive capital to other states. The state income tax, on the other hand, was the most consistent tax proposal for meeting the "ability to pay," or "equality of sacrifice," principle. Admittedly, personal income was difficult to determine, but not as difficult as the evaluation

---

[6] Ely, "Supplementary Report on Taxation in Maryland," in *Report of the Maryland Tax Commission to the General Assembly* (Baltimore: King, 1888), p. 9.

of all property. The techniques proposed by Ely to determine income were hardly convincing, however. He wrote that
income could be calculated by the assessor, considering
property holdings and the manner of living by the individual
as reflections of personal income. If the individual felt he
was overassessed, he could appeal by demonstrating that his
income was lower. Ely's cumbersome proposal would hardly
have solved all the inequities of the existing tax system.

In a series of essays on railroads published by *Harper's
Magazine* in 1886, Ely anticipated his subsequent advocacy of
the governmental ownership of natural monopolies. Although
not prepared to suggest the immediate nationalization of railroads, Ely denounced their operations with a fervor which
equaled any of the aroused midwestern farmers. The railroads
had plunged the country into a morass of immorality. "They
drag their slimy length over our country, and every turn in
their progress is marked by a progeny of evils. Thus is our
land cursed!"[7] Railroads controlled state legislatures; the
United States Senate was their "stronghold"; and at least two
members of the Supreme Court were popularly spoken of as
"railway judges." Railroad directors watered stock, formed
dummy construction companies, siphoned off profits, gave
rebates to favored shippers, and gambled with other people's
investments. They discriminated against producers by charg-
ing more for short hauls where no competition existed than
they did for long hauls where they were forced to compete.
The railroad magnates "are kings in very truth, and we are
their subjects, to whom the right of free speech and of an
independent press is denied."[8] Worst of all, these practitioners
of dishonesty were often recognized as public heroes.

At the time, Ely suggested no fundamental changes in the
American railway system, though he hinted that the railroads
would eventually become cooperative enterprises. In order

[7] Ely, "Social Studies: I—The Nature of the Railway Problem,"
Harper's New Monthly Magazine, LXXIII (July, 1886), 257.
[8] *Ibid.*, p. 255.

to protect the public, he felt that all future charters should be limited to a given number of years so that they could be resold or purchased by the public at expiration. Railroads should be forced to disclose all assets to the public, and each individual, whether the owner of one or of a thousand shares of stock, should have only one vote. Finally, Ely wanted the establishment of state and federal commissions with complete rate-making power. He felt that the Reagen bill, which became the Interstate Commerce Act of 1887, was "chimerical" because it allowed recourse to the railroad-dominated courts and would involve endless litigation. But it was not until the following year, 1887, that he began to advocate federal ownership as an eventual solution.[9]

A significant turning point in Ely's advocacy of specific reforms came when he read an essay by Henry C. Adams, "Relation of the State to Industrial Action," published by the American Economic Association in January of 1887. Ely immediately hailed it as "the profoundest study in the English language on that subject."[10] The rigid distinction drawn by Adams between natural monopolies or utilities and competitive enterprises especially impressed Ely. The economic reasoning behind the distinction seemed to offer a clear argument for the socialization of natural monopolies.

While the essay by Adams reached a small audience, Ely popularized the distinction between competitive enterprises and natural monopolies. In the spring of 1887 he published

[9] Ely, "Social Studies: III—The Reform of Railway Abuses," *Harper's New Monthly Magazine,* LXXIII (Sept., 1886), 571-578; Ely, "Social Studies: III—The Future of Corporations," *Harper's New Monthly Magazine,* LXXV (July, 1887), 260-262.

[10] Ely, "Social Studies: II—The Growth of Corporations," *Harper's New Monthly Magazine,* LXXV (June, 1887), 76. For a similar statement see Ely, *An Introduction to Political Economy* (New York: Chautauqua, 1889), p. 93. In his autobiography Ely wrote: "I was especially influenced, as were many of my contemporaries . . . by my friend Henry C. Adams . . . 'The Relation of the State to Industrial Action.' " Ely, *Ground Under Our Feet: An Autobiography* (New York: Macmillan, 1938), p. 252.

for *Harper's* a series of three articles on corporations in which he developed the conclusions of Adams. In the winter of 1887-1888 he wrote a daily column for the Baltimore *Sun* entitled "Problems of To-day" in which he suggested special treatment for natural monopolies. The series "attracted widespread attention," the *Sun* reported, "and [was] . . . the subject of eulogistic remark and comment from hundreds of newspapers and practical men, as well as thinkers of recognized eminence in all parts of the country."[11] Thomas Y. Crowell immediately published the essays, and they became a textbook for the elementary course in economics at several schools. Ely also incorporated the conclusions of Adams in his report for the Maryland taxation commission (1888) and in his *Taxation in American States and Cities* (1888). In both his popular *Introduction to Political Economy* (1889) and *Socialism and Social Reform* (1894), he explained that the government ownership of natural monopolies was a practical "golden mean" between complete socialized ownership and a completely competitive order. By 1900 Charles J. Bullock justly claimed that Ely had "perhaps done more than any other single writer to familiarize us with this distinction."[12]

The rising Alliance and Populist movements saw in Ely a champion of their program for the federal ownership of natural monopolies, in particular railroads. William A. Peffer, Populist senator from Kansas, declared that Ely's "Political Economy was the best work to be had on natural monopolies."[13] The president of the National Farmer's Alliance, H. L. Loucks, solicited and obtained Ely's cooperation in furnishing ideas for a series of articles on transportation. Min-

11 Baltimore *Sun*, March 27, 1888.
12 Bullock, review of Ely, *Monopolies and Trusts*, in *American Journal of Sociology*, VI (July, 1900), 122. For a similar conclusion, see Albert Shaw to Charles K. Adams, Aug. 8, 1894, in Transcript of the Ely Trial, microfilm copy in State Historical Society of Wisconsin, Madison.
13 As quoted in Charles Lee Smith to Ely, Oct. 13, 1891, Ely MSS.

nesota Alliance leader W. W. Gamble published an Ely letter in *Farm, Stock and Home,* which reached 40,000 subscribers. On his numerous speaking tours and through Alliance papers Gamble recommended Ely's books and articles as the best available on natural monopolies. In 1893 the alarmed editor of the Omaha *Bee* reported to the *Forum* that such men as Ely and Edward Bellamy shared responsibility for the "Menacing Socialism in the Western States." In particular, the editor warned, Ely, by connecting "socialistic ideas with Christianity," appealed to the intelligent and well-educated, the churchman, and the prominent businessman, as well as the farmer.[14]

Through his writings Ely converted an inestimable number of municipal reformers to the idea that "gas and water socialism," or at least limited franchises, should be a cardinal tenet of city reforms. In almost every major American city and hundreds of smaller ones Ely corresponded with reform-minded citizens. He presented the arguments favoring municipal ownership and, perhaps more important, the facts and figures from the experience of other cities. Several of his students became prominent city reformers. As a young attorney in the nineties, Frederic C. Howe joined the movement for better municipal government in Cleveland and assisted the famous reform mayors of the early twentieth century, including Newton D. Baker, another former Ely student. Between 1895 and 1900 Albion Small, editor of the *American Journal of Sociology,* carried no less than thirteen articles on some urban problem. Perhaps most influential of all was Albert Shaw, who wrote a series of articles in his *Review of Reviews* on English city governments. Indeed, Ely through his direct connections, his writings, and his students

[14] Loucks to Ely, Aug. 12 [1894?], Gamble to Ely, March 11, 24, Aug. 3, 1891, Ely MSS; Ely, "Education for Farmers," *Farm, Stock and Home,* VII (March 1, 1891), 125; Frank Basil Tracy, "Menacing Socialism in the Western States," *Forum,* XV (May, 1893), 330-332. See C. Q. De France to Ely, March 13, 1903, Ely MSS.

helped pave the way for the great urban reform movement which reached a climax in the progressive era.[15]

Ely leaned heavily upon Adams for his thinking on the economic peculiarities of natural monopolies, but unlike Adams he favored their socialization. Ely noted with Adams that natural monopolies were unique enterprises in that they were subject to the law of increasing returns. That is, when an established firm such as a city gas company decided to add a customer, the capital and labor, or costs for the additional customer, would not be as high as for the original customers. Thus, the gas firm would have a larger profit for each additional customer than it had for the original customers. Sustained competition was impossible, for the established firm could always make additions more cheaply than a new firm. Besides the principle of increasing returns formulated by Adams, Ely, borrowing from T. H. Farrer's *The State in Its Relation to Trade,* listed four other prerequisites for a natural monopoly: one, what they supply must have high utility; two, they must occupy peculiarly favored geographic positions; three, the "article or convenience they supply is used at the place where, and in connection with, the plant or machinery by which it is supplied"; four, they require unity in management.[16]

Competition as a built-in self-regulator did not exist for

---

[15] The Ely MSS contain hundreds of letters testifying to the direct influence of Ely. See George E. Mowry, *The Era of Theodore Roosevelt and the Birth of Modern America, 1900-1912* (New York: Harper and Row, 1958), p. 61, for an indication of his indirect influence.

[16] See especially Henry C. Adams, "Relation of the State to Industrial Action," *Publications of the American Economic Association,* I (1887), 511-528; Ely, *Problems of To-day: A Discussion of Protective Tariffs, Taxation, and Monopolies* (New York: Crowell, 1888), pp. 118-119; Ely and John H. Finley, *Taxation in American States and Cities* (New York: Crowell, 1888), pp. 269-270; Ely, *Socialism . . . with Suggestions for Social Reform,* pp. 263-265; Ely, *An Introduction to Political Economy,* pp. 80-82, 251-258. Almost every idea which follows in this chapter is repeated by Ely in all of the above works as well as in numerous articles. Thus, citation will be discriminatory, based on the most explicit statement of his position.

natural monopolies, Ely believed. Attempted competition inevitably gave way to combination and consolidation. Of over a thousand examples in the gas business, Ely asserted, "no one can yet point to one single instance of permanently successful competition."[17] In both England and America the tendency of telegraph companies to merge was equally inescapable. In 1894 Ely proudly reminded his readers that he had predicted the merger of the Baltimore and Ohio Telegraph with Western Union as early as 1889.[18] Although railroads in America covered vast areas and construction was as yet incomplete, it was simply a matter of time, Ely predicted, before monopoly would be secured. The state could not force natural monopolies to compete; they might "as well legislate that the water of all rivers shall flow up instead of down!"[19] His arguments had a strong appeal because they bore out the experience of so many Americans.

The very existence of natural monopolies, Ely wrote, depended upon the conferral of some special concession by the public, usually a favored location. Street railways used city streets as a roadbed and gas companies laid their lines under the streets. The public bestowed the right of eminent domain upon railroads. Because the public had given up a valuable portion of its property to private enterprises, it had a right to exact its just share from the privileges granted. Since natural monopolies could charge all the market would bear, these tremendous profits should be benefiting the public, Ely argued. The cities in Europe and the few cities in the United States which owned their utilities provided equal or better services at much cheaper rates. Ely estimated rates for street railways and for gas could be cut in half. Telegraph

[17] Ely, *Socialism . . . with Suggestions for Social Reform*, p. 265.
[18] Ely, "The Telegraph Monopoly," *North American Review*, CXLIX (July, 1889), 44-46; Ely, *Natural Monopolies and Local Taxation: An Address before the Boston Merchants Association, Jan. 8, 1889* (Boston: Robinson and Stephenson, 1889), pp. 5-9.
[19] Ely, *Problems of To-day*, p. 143.

rates in Europe were much cheaper, and state-owned railroads provided better service and lower rates than in America. Fares reduced to three cents on Baltimore street railways, Ely estimated, would be worth fifty dollars a year for a family of five. Municipalization, Ely wrote, would give the city businessman a tremendous comparative advantage over other cities.[20]

The socialization of natural monopolies would also eliminate most of the "artificial" monopolies. Businesses otherwise competitive became monopolies when they attached themselves firmly to natural monopolies. Especially responsible for the growth of artificial monopolies was the railroad. Coal mining, oil refineries, and many other manufacturers received special benefits or concessions from railroads. The notorious Standard Oil trust secured its monopolistic position from railroad rebates, Ely claimed. Government ownership, as illustrated from the German experience, would provide equal treatment for all users.

The problems of the laborer employed by utilities and the farmer who depended so heavily upon them would be largely solved by socialization. Strikes, which could be so detrimental to the public interest in these areas, would cease. Under public ownership the wage earner would be like a soldier, guaranteed just treatment but punished if he deserted public service in an emergency. The history of the post office demonstrated that workers could protect their interests under public ownership better than under private. For the farmers, low freight and express charges would mean an extension of markets, and purchasing power for farm products would increase.

For society as a whole, public ownership of natural

20 See especially Ely, "Social Studies in Europe: II-III," *Christian Union*, XL (Dec. 5, 12, 1889), 711-712, 763; Ely "Social Observations in Germany: IV," *Congregationalist*, LXXVII (June 30, 1892), 206; Ely, *Problems of To-day*, pp. 173-175; Ely, *An Introduction to Political Economy*, p. 255.

monopolies would mean a more efficient utilization of productive forces. The enormous wastes of competition, such as digging up streets for competing gas lines, would be avoided in the future. The erratic nature of private construction of utilities would be replaced by long-range planning. Instead of feverish activity followed by stagnation and depression, an orderly construction of new projects to help level out the business cycle would ensue. Whenever depression struck private business, Ely observed, materials were cheap, labor abundant, and interest rates for governments low. Construction of new projects at that moment would increase employment, supplement private endeavors, and help to lift the country from depressions.[21] Moreover, a program of public ownership of natural monopolies would encourage a better distribution of private income. Ely estimated that three-fourths of the great fortunes of the country were connected with some sort of monopoly. Most of this wealth was "unearned"; that is, it came from an excessive return on capital. Public ownership of such monopolies would diffuse the unearned income to more people.

Ely believed the favoritism extended to natural monopolies by public officials was the "most potent cause" of the corruption so characteristic of American cities. The monopolies knifed through every level of government. In order to escape regulation, street railways in almost every American city gave free passes to city officials and filled job openings through the local political organizations. Often the municipal monopolies controlled both political parties, and railroads controlled state legislatures as well as wielding tremendous power in the United States Senate and the federal courts. When judges retired from the bench they received promises of lucrative legal fees. "Everywhere the facts are the same," Ely concluded, "and it must be so. When it is attempted to control private corporations, a divergence of interest between

[21] See Ely, "Hard Times," *Interior*, I (Dec. 13, 1894), 1624.

public and private parties arises, and this makes the temptation to corruption irresistible."[22] Extension of public ownership with an increased civil service class would reduce corruption. In the first place, it would eliminate the control which natural monopolies exercised over the instruments of government in order to escape regulation. Secondly, the "policy advocated would tend to purify politics, because it would give to the mass of men a greater interest in politics, showing the real significance of public affairs."[23] Men would take a new interest in public affairs and civil service would improve. Men who now turned to the greater inducements of private life would turn to public pursuits. It was the political boss, Ely insisted, who loved the motto, "laissez faire."

The socialization of natural monopolies, Ely reasoned, was an example of self-help rather than state paternalism. Since paternalism, Ely wrote, implied a father-son relationship, private management of natural monopolies was, in reality, paternalistic. For private management rested on the assumption that the people were not sufficiently intelligent to manage for themselves. Citizens, by banding together to purchase their own waterworks for example, continued the American tradition of self-help. They now helped themselves collectively rather than transferring to private enterprise a paternalistic function.[24]

As a practical matter Ely advised that most municipalities handle natural monopolies on a piecemeal basis. Public sentiment needed to be strongly in favor of socialization, for, he warned, private interests always attempted to discredit such experiments. While every city in the country should purchase

[22] Ely, *Taxation in American States and Cities*, p. 277.
[23] Ely, *Socialism . . . with Suggestions for Social Reform*, p. 284.
[24] See Ely, "Fraternalism vs. Paternalism in Government," *Century Magazine*, LV (March, 1898), 780-784. The article was originally prepared in 1889 and was not changed for the 1898 publication. See Ely to Daniel C. Gilman, March 20, 1898, Gilman MSS, Johns Hopkins University Library, Baltimore.

its waterworks and gas supplies as soon as possible, purchase of street railway lines, wharves, slaughterhouses, and electric works could wait. These enterprises, however, should always, as a minimum of public control, be granted limited charters. The charter should specify such items as maximum charges, taxes, and length of agreement. At the end of the prescribed time the charter should be placed up for public auction or retained by the city. If the city decided to keep the franchise, it should pay the private concern on the basis of an agreement reached when the original charter was issued.[25]

Ely also advanced a practical suggestion regarding land located in or near urban areas. He agreed with Henry George to the extent that land in urban areas acquired an "unearned" or "social" value by its mere location. City growth and improvements increased the value of surrounding land, although the owner may have done nothing to improve his property. Where possible, such as in western cities, Ely wanted the municipalities to purchase all unused land in advance. Orderly development could then proceed with much lower costs to the homeowner, or possibly renter, if the city wanted to retain ownership.

Ely repeated his plea for the socialization of natural monopolies in *Socialism: An Examination of Its Nature, Its Strength and Its Weakness with Suggestions for Social Reform*, commonly called *Socialism and Social Reform* (1894). The work had origins in a typical Ely effort to isolate and list the strengths and weaknesses of socialism as a proposed economic system. He received extensive cooperation from European socialists, notably H. W. Lee, secretary of the Social Democratic Federation, Sidney Webb, Fabian socialist, and Charles Gide, a French professorial socialist. They generously sent him pamphlets, literature, and their own views. Ely then

[25] Ely, "Supplementary Report on Taxation in Maryland," pp. 75-76; Ely, *Problems of To-day*, pp. 129, 174-176; Ely, "Land, Labor and Taxation," reprinted from *Independent*, XXXIX (1887), 15, in Ely MSS.

wrote a tentative appraisal of socialism in a series of twenty-one consecutive articles for the *Independent* in 1891. They received a large hearing and Ely found, as the country moved into a terrible depression, demands for speaking engagements on socialism more numerous than ever.

Because of his move to Wisconsin in the fall of 1892, he delayed publication of the book until 1894. Although it received mixed reviews—scholarly journals were more critical, popular ones more eulogistic—it soon became the most popular work in the "Crowell Library of Economics and Politics." In England Swan Sonnenschein and Company published an extensive extract for their "Social Science Series." Five years later the Chautauqua published an abridged version for their Literary and Scientific Circle.[26] After publication Sidney Webb wrote that "it cannot fail to be of great use . . . in clearing up misconceptions as to what Socialism means, and in compelling Socialists to think out more precisely the methods of application of the principle they uphold." Webb added that the Fabian Society had included Ely's work in a short list of books "sent to every Fabian, urging them to agitate local libraries to buy them."[27]

In contrast to his earlier studies, this work was neither a history nor an analysis of socialist writings. Instead, Ely constructed his own socialist model, drawing from such diverse sources as Karl Marx, the Fabians, Edward Bellamy, and the Bible. He purposely presented socialism in a form "which seemed to him to contain the greatest strength." Ely stripped from his model all unnecessary and weakening accessories. The essence of socialism was a proposed industrial system, not an all-embracing theory of social activity. The major reason that socialists did not find substantial support among the higher classes, Ely claimed, was their inclusion of

[26] Swan Sonnenschein & Co. to Ely, July 10, 1894, Ely MSS; Ely, *The Strength and Weakness of Socialism* (New York: Chautauqua, 1899).
[27] Webb to Ely, Sept. 9, 1894, Ely MSS.

a total theory. Karl Marx had fastened a "cast-iron" materialistic philosophy "full of revolting crudities" on socialism which needlessly antagonized Christians by making it appear in conflict with Christianity. By appealing only to the working class, Marx had encouraged class hatred and strife rather than promoting class harmony. His historical evolution had no proof. If a tendency did exist toward increased class polarization and giant monopolies, it had, in part, been reduced and could be further reduced by social reform.

In contrast to the Marxist appeal to the selfish interest of the workingmen, Ely felt the strongest argument could be made for socialism on the grounds that it would morally cement all classes. A major evil of the competive order was increased class antagonism. It might be conceded that socialism was not practical at the present time, "but to it the brotherhood of man is something very real." Socialism would remove the "sham and hypocrisy" between man's professed brotherly love and his practice of the principle. For modern science had demonstrated that the improvement of morality was dependent on the improvement of environment. Statistics showed that nine out of ten children became good citizens when taken from poor surroundings and placed in a favorable moral environment. Socialism, Ely wrote, "seeks to establish an environment favorable to the development of moral qualities in human beings; and unless this feature of socialism is carried so far as to make everything, or nearly everything depend upon environment, it is unquestionably a strong characteristic of socialism."[28]

The first essential in Ely's socialist model was the

---

[28] Ely, *Socialism . . . with Suggestions for Social Reform*, pp. 147, 151, 151n. Also see Ely, "Supplementary Report on Taxation in Maryland," pp. 55-56; Ely, "Pauperism in the United States," *North American Review*, CLII (April, 1891), 399-400; Ely, "Heredity and Circumstances," *Outlook*, XLVIII (Sept. 16, 1893), 505-506. Ely carefully distinguished between the role of environment on morality and intellectual ability, for most of man's mental ability was inherited, he said.

"common ownership of the material instruments of production." As a scheme of production, socialism promised the reduction of waste, thereby increasing total production for useful purposes. Hundreds of millions of dollars had been wasted in the construction and maintenance of parallel railroads alone, Ely declared, a sum probably sufficient to build comfortable homes for every American family presently without one.[29] Gasworks, the telegraph, milk distribution, and most advertising also exemplified the wastes of the present order. There was no doubt, Ely wrote, that collective ownership would eliminate waste in these areas. Planning of production would be on a scientific basis, always mindful of actual needs. The evil of purposely limiting production to raise prices in the competitive order would disappear. The business cycle, "an essential part of the order of competition," would be eliminated under socialism. Distribution costs would be substantially reduced.

Ely admitted, however, that most socialists were overoptimistic about the possibilities of increased production. Many of them expected the new era to bring affluence for all. Because of limitations on natural resources, Ely argued, this was doubtful. Further, the socialists had not, as yet, presented even a "plausible" plan for collectivizing agriculture. They talked of nationalizing "bonanza farms." But Ely maintained that large farms were located only in the staple-producing areas, and most American farms required intensive farming on a small scale. How could central operation and planning cope with the variables of soil, climate, and the designation of tasks for such a complex occupation as farming?

Another essential of socialism, to Ely, was a principle of "distributive justice," although socialists differed among themselves on what standard should be followed. Ely took issue

[29] See Ely, "Social Studies: II—The Economic Evils in American Railway Methods," *Harper's New Monthly Magazine,* LXXIII (Aug., 1886), 450-457; Ely, *Problems of To-day,* pp. 140-142.

with a distribution system based on equality. The preferred system rewarded those with superior intellectual and managerial skills. For until moral attitudes improved, incentives would be required to attract the highest qualified personnel. Admittedly, the socialist had a strong argument when he claimed that social esteem would be a sufficient motive for service. "There can be no doubt," Ely flatly declared, "that social esteem has been the most powerful motive which has animated men in all times."[30] Men in the present system attempted to purchase esteem by an ostentatious display of their wealth, Ely wrote, anticipating Thorstein Veblen's "conspicuous consumption" emphasis by four years. But this was not enough, unless a radical change in human nature took place. By whatever standards it resolved the issue of distribution, socialism, in its idea, "would be more productive of well-being than is the distribution which we now witness. Socialism seeks a distribution which avoids the extremes of pauperism and plutocracy." Ideally, socialism would provide public luxury and private frugality. The present order esteemed the reverse. The rich spent lavishly on themselves. "On the other hand, when it comes to school buildings or structures for state universities, library buildings, or art galleries, which minister to the needs of the people as a whole, a legislator who would cut down appropriations to a minimum amount . . . is praised and petted as a 'watch-dog of the treasury,' while a president who uses the veto power freely to defeat appropriations for useful purposes, which have something else in view than the promotion of material interest, is supposed to be animated by a stern sense of duty."[31] Historically, in periods of public luxury western civilization reached an apex, such as in the case of Greece and Rome. Rome collapsed, Ely wrote, when private luxury became ascendant.

[30] Ely, *Socialism . . . with Suggestions for Social Reform*, p. 228.
[31] *Ibid.*, pp. 140, 142-143. Also see Ely, *Problems of To-day*, pp. 93-97.

Even in his own strongly presented argument for socialism, Ely found certain inherent difficulties which centered on
human nature at its present stage of development. Men were
currently so enamored with the pursuit of their own interest
that it was doubtful they could make the transition to the
socialist state. Because of the many producers and distribu-
tors, dissatisfaction was widely diffused in the competitive
order. In the socialist order, dissatisfaction would concentrate
on the state. Evidence of disproportionate dissatisfaction with
socialistic enterprises could be found in the present order, Ely
claimed. Men tended to sneer at any malperformance of
collective enterprises such as municipal gasworks. But when
a private enterprise performed shoddily, little or no criticism
was heard, as though it were expected.

Ely felt that the freedom of the individual in a socialist
regime would be in no greater danger than in the competitive
system. The defenders of the present order claimed that men
had more freedom because of the opportunity to change jobs
at will. This was more correct in theory than in reality, Ely
wrote, for no such freedom prevailed. Whenever or wherever
a man chose to work, he became economically dependent on
his employer. He was forced to submit to rigid discipline.
His dependence made his theoretical liberties impotent. Under
socialism he would, at least, have the opportunity as a part
owner to make the rules for himself. Obviously, however,
authority must exist for socialism to work. The question is,
Ely wrote, where should authority be located? In the capital-
istic system the workingmen exercised no power, but under
socialism decisions would be made democratically. Moreover,
in the United States socialist enterprises could be spread out
between the various units of government: municipal, state, and
national. Thus if an individual felt oppressed in his public
job, he could move to a different governmental unit or to
another location.

Perhaps, Ely wrote, the major contribution of socialism

to the present society was educational. For socialism established an ethical goal from which to view present conditions. A thorough study of socialism awakened the conscience of the ordinary man to the gap between the ethics of the competitive order and the ethical ideal set by socialism. Already, "the study of socialism has provided the turning point in thousands of lives, and converted self-seeking men and women into self-sacrificing toilers for the masses."[32] It was doubtful, Ely wrote, whether even the Bible had produced such a marked change in the attitude of students who had studied both. Socialism "largely" accounted for the present concern for the poor and unfortunate. Socialism, too, had contributed to remedial measures in the most pressing areas of the industrial world. Sanitary legislation, safety provisions in factories, and protection of women and children exemplified the adoption of the immediate demands of socialists. Socialism made public questions larger than a mere matter of personal booty. Ely concluded his study of the "strengths" of socialism with these ringing words: "Socialism has undoubted strength, especially strength of a negative sort. It points out real defects in our present order; its indictment of existing institutions is a powerful one. The wastes of the competitive system are so enormous as to be awful; its operations are as cruel as laws of nature. In its onward march it crushes and grinds to powder human existences by the million; its rubbish consists of human beings with minds, hearts, and souls–men, good men often; women, and very frequently, most frequently indeed, innocent women–women with precious rights which ought to be developed for themselves and others, and little children with all their possibilities."[33]

Ely's attitude toward the importance of socialism was somewhat ambiguous. On the one hand he found the so-

[32] Ely, *Socialism . . . with Suggestions for Social Reform*, p. 145. Also see Ely, "Fundamental Beliefs in My Social Philosophy," *Forum*, XVIII (Oct., 1894), 181.
[33] Ely, *Socialism . . . with Suggestions for Social Reform*, p. 253.

cialist indictment of the competitive order largely valid and their proposals for building a new order important enough to warrant serious consideration. On the other hand he consistently maintained that he was not a socialist and remained aloof from socialist organizations, except for a peripheral association with a few Christian socialists. Ely's demurral as an active participant rested both on considerations of strategy and on personal views. He recognized the unreasoned, stereotyped response of the public to the mere term "socialism." To a certain extent Ely took advantage of the public attitude by picturing social reform as a means of avoiding either the extreme economic system of socialism or that of competition. On the personal level Ely had genuine doubts about the desirability of a socialist society. The real questions were who would control it and what would be its nature. A paramount danger, in the view of Ely, was that it would be directed by the anti-intellectual farmers and laborers. Ely repeated again and again the necessity of recognizing the superiority of intellect and the necessity of maintaining social differences based on intellect and achievement. Doubtless in personal terms Ely was quite conscious of endangering his own status by his advocacy of a socialist society which might be directed by the very people who sneered at intellect.

Almost a third of *Socialism and Social Reform* dealt with the "Golden Mean, or Practicable Social Reform." In these chapters Ely anticipated almost every reform of the Progressive and New Deal eras. By 1894 the direction of his program was essentially modern rather than traditional. He had little loyalty or nostalgia for the older individualistic America of the early nineteenth century. Though inclined to criticize the moral character of the business community, he took no real stock in conspiracy theories to explain its suppression of the masses. In the final analysis, unbridled competition, which was cruel, wasteful, and outmoded, accounted for the immoral and irresponsible actions of the captains of industry. Competition tended to drive the moral sentiment of participants to the level of the lowest member. For example, if one barber remained open on Sunday, he forced the others to do likewise; the same was true of the employers of children and women. Legislation closing barbershops on Sunday, prohibiting the adulteration of products, establishing boards of arbitration and the like, would go far in raising the level of competition. Ely gave nominal support to the initiative, referendum, and proportional representation, but he was dubious of the recall and described these political reforms as hardly adequate to cure the ills of a modern industrial society. Unlike the genteel reformers of the era, he saw no magic in civil service, for he believed industrial reform must accompany it.

Society, Ely wrote, should guarantee everyone work. "It is much better," he added, "that subsistence should be furnished in return for work rather than without work." Public work projects should not interfere with private industry, but they should be expanded in periods of depression. In addition he suggested the establishment of a federal employment bureau and public loans to private individuals in hard times. Writing during the depression of the nineties, Ely sympathized with the shortage of circulating media, but he rejected the free coinage of silver and doubted whether international bimetallism could be secured. The establishment of a truly centralized banking system could do much to relieve the currency shortage. He added a long list of other reforms, one of which was a state program of medical services.[34]

To Ely, business consolidation was an inevitable product of competition and of a technological revolution. When he wrote his *Monopolies and Trusts* in 1900, in the midst of the first great merger movement, he firmly rejected antitrust legislation. The longing for a nation of small shopkeepers, he said, rested on an ignorance of the advantages of modern industry and on pure nostalgia. He carefully distinguished between

[34] *Ibid.*, pp. 332-366; Ely, "Hard Times," p. 1624.

bigness and monopoly, defining monopoly as the exercise
of an unity of control, particularly with respect to price, by
those engaged in the same business, a definition which was
later used by the Supreme Court.[35] He again advocated the
public ownership of natural monopolies but in addition proposed a "federal bureau of private corporations," modeled after
the controller of the currency. The bureau should aim to
secure the same sort of control over all private corporations
engaged in interstate commerce. It should insure honesty and
individual responsibility through complete publicity and adequate provisions for punishment.[36]

[35] *National Cotton Oil Co., v. Texas,* 197 U.S. 129 (1904). See
Ely and Frank Bohn, *The Great Change* (New York: Nelson, 1935), p.
142.
[36] Ely, *Monopolies and Trusts* (New York: Macmillan, 1900), pp.
268-269.

Chapter Five

NEW VISTAS IN THE WEST

ELY RETURNED from a short European trip in the fall of 1891 a troubled and sick man. Still weak from a serious attack of malaria contracted while in Germany, he felt that his position at Johns Hopkins University was no longer tenable. Disgusted with university policy, especially of keeping political economy and history in one department, he had attempted to obtain an endowed chair in "advanced sociology" at Hopkins—only to meet with failure. He was tired of playing a subordinate role to Herbert Baxter Adams. Despite an established reputation among reformers and reform-minded economists, due recognition from the academic world still eluded him. His own university refused his requests for more appropriations for the library, at least one assistant, and a promotion to a full professorship. Without any help, except that for which he himself paid, he laboriously wrote all of his articles and books in longhand and financed his own research ventures.[1] Self-righteous indignation toward the university and Adams propelled him to search for a new post. During the decade of the 1890's Ely's desire to win acclaim in the academic world increasingly absorbed much of his energies.

Ely's position at Johns Hopkins had never been fully secure. He constantly worried about salary, tenure, and adequate recognition from the university. After the first year he made overtures for other positions,[2] and even while a bachelor he found it necessary to keep his "eyes open for a chance to turn an honest penny." In 1883 he became incensed upon receiving a note from President Gilman that his appointment would be extended for one year at the same salary. Claiming that he had been promised a $500 increase, Ely's fiery spirit exploded in a letter to Adams. "Now there has been double dealing here, I promise to make a *fight about it*—unless indeed it is a mistake which I could wish—and the question is the method of warfare."[3] Entreating Adams to represent his cause to Gilman, Ely claimed he had passed up better opportunities elsewhere and had stayed only because of the promised pay increase and his dedication to the university. The rumor which circulated among the students that Ely had "bull-dozed" Gilman into a raise appeared to have foundation, for he received the salary increase. Nonetheless his pay remained inadequate to cover his living expenses. Apart from normal costs, Ely, after 1887, had to pay for his new house and his first speculative venture

[1] See R. Heber Newton to Ely, Dec. 9, 1891, Lyman Abbott to Ely, Nov. 24, 1890, Ely MSS, State Historical Society of Wisconsin, Madison; Ely, "Statement, J. H. U.," Nov. 27, 1886, Adams MSS, Johns Hopkins University Library, Baltimore; James E. Barbour to Edward A. Ross, Nov. 9, 1890, Ross MSS, State Historical Society of Wisconsin, Madison; Washington Gladden to H. B. Adams, May 13, 1890, Adams MSS; Ely, *Ground Under Our Feet: An Autobiography* (New York: Macmillan, 1938), p. 175.

[2] Ely to H. B. Adams, June 10, 1882, Adams MSS; Charles K. Adams to Andrew D. White, Aug. 25, 1882, Ely MSS; copy of promissory note to H. B. Adams dated Oct. 15, 1891, Ely MSS.

[3] Ely to H. B. Adams, June 11, 1883, Adams MSS.

—a small lot in the Catskills purchased with Edmund J. James.[4]

From the very beginning of his career at Hopkins, Ely earned a reputation as something of an academic empire builder. Jameson recorded in his diary that the little professor "is certainly on the make" and "wants to bring everything he can under political economy, including all social and political science."[5] Adams, who was equally ambitious and jealous of his position, resented Ely's efforts to swallow up the social sciences. Adams was "trying to rope in Ely (the little doctor is a tough customer for him)," Jameson wrote.[6] And on occasion, Adams' recommendations to Gilman with respect to Ely were less than enthusiastic. A large part of the difficulty between Ely and Adams stemmed from the indecisiveness of the administration toward the department during the 1880's. Even though history and political science had the largest single enrollment in the university, Adams did not enjoy even the nominal title of head and did not win a full professorship for himself until he forced the administration's hand in 1892. In 1889 Adams did go so far as to allow Ely to set up an "Economic Conference" separate from the general Seminary.[7]

The uneasy situation between Ely, Adams, and Johns Hopkins officials reached a head in 1890 and 1891 when William Rainey Harper, president of the newly founded

[4] J. Franklin Jameson Diary, April 4, 1884, Jameson MSS, Library of Congress; Hugh Hawkins, *Pioneer: A History of the Johns Hopkins University, 1874-1889* (Ithaca, N. Y.: Cornell University Press, 1960), p. 178; Smith & Schwarz to Ely, Aug., 1887, Edmund J. James to Ely, Dec. 12, 1892, Ely MSS.

[5] Jameson Diary, Aug. 14, 1884, Jan. 2, 1883. For similar evaluations by Jameson at other dates, see entries for Dec. 20, 1884, Jan. 7, 1886.

[6] *Ibid.*, Sept. 22, 1883.

[7] See H. B. Adams to Gilman, July 7, 1885, Gilman MSS, Johns Hopkins University Library, Baltimore; Ely, "Statement, J. H. U.," Nov. 29, 1886, Adams MSS; Gilman to Adams, June 25, 1886, June [1886?], Adams MSS; *Johns Hopkins University Circulars*, VIII (July, 1889), 93.

University of Chicago, attempted to wean both men from
Baltimore. Harper offered Adams a post as head of history
and political science, while Ely would head the political economy department. From their intimate association with Harper
at the Chautauqua, both men feared he would be a "stern
master," and they attempted to use the offers to force Gilman
to make concessions. Perhaps Ely also hoped that Adams
might go to Chicago alone, leaving him as top man at Hopkins. Apparently as a forcing action, he resigned in January of 1891, but, when the trustees still refused to grant his
demands, Ely, left in the lurch, decided to remain—at least
temporarily. In July of 1891 Harper made Adams a separate
offer of $6,000 annually. Adams quickly went to Gilman,
explaining that he felt the "pull of manifest destiny" westward, and the trustees promptly responded by offering him
a professorship and a substantial salary increase.[8]

Ely was completely exasperated. According to his account, Adams had broken a solemn promise to the effect
that if Johns Hopkins refused to meet their demands, they
would resign as a team and go to Chicago. Ely's hostility
toward Adams over the incident, which only slowly declined
over the years, may have been based on pure jealousy. But
Ely also feared, as one of his students put it, that Adams
"would never consent, never, never, never," to anyone being
placed on an equal status with himself in the history and
political science department at Hopkins. By July, when
Adams received the separate offer but had decided to stay,
Ely had apparently lost any chance for the Chicago post. No
formal overtures had been extended to him since March,
and it appears that Harper's original offer was made pri-

[8] Ely to Harper, Aug. 17, 1895, Ely MSS; Ely, *Ground Under Our
Feet*, p. 175; Gilman to Ely, Jan. 7, 1891, Ely MSS; H. B. Adams to
Gilman, July 21, 1891, Gilman MSS. Harper's negotiations with Ely
came in two private meetings. Thus the salary figure offered to Ely
is not disclosed in their correspondence.

marily to attract Adams. However, Ely might have rejected a chair exclusively in political economy, for he had for some time been inclined to branch out into sociology. Whatever the reasons, in the fall of 1891 Ely found his continued subordination to Adams unendurable and began looking for a more suitable position.[9]

Through the academic grapevine Ely heard that the Board of Regents of the University of Wisconsin had established a chair of "Finance and Statistics." The new chair had been created in part to relieve the aging vice president and professor of political science and economics, John B. Parkinson, from overwork. Since most of the students entered business after graduation, the board also had in mind a chair that encouraged "commercial science," similar to the Wharton School of Finance at the University of Pennsylvania. They wanted something akin to the modern business professor. Whether Ely was aware of the intention of the regents or not, in November of 1891 he wrote to Frederick Jackson Turner, one of his former students and now a professor of history at Wisconsin, detailing a long list of stiff demands which the university would have to meet in order to obtain his services. Contrary to the accepted view, Ely's interest in the position caught Turner by complete surprise. Though Turner was unaware of Ely's difficulties at Johns Hopkins, he realized from his work under Ely "how great a privilege" and boon to the recognition of the university it would be to have him on the faculty. He immediately disclosed the contents of Ely's letter to President Thomas C. Chamberlin.[10]

The president, also "highly gratified at the prospect" of

[9] Frederick Jackson Turner to Ely, Feb. 1, 1892, Ely MSS; Ely, *Ground Under Our Feet*, p. 176; Lyman P. Powell to Edward A. Ross, March 27, 1892, Ross MSS; Harper to Ely, March 20, 1892, Aug. 20, 1895, Ely MSS.

[10] Merle Curti and Vernon Carstensen, *The University of Wisconsin: A History, 1848-1925* (Madison: University of Wisconsin Press, 1949), I, 630-631; Turner to Ely, Nov. 25, 1891, Ely MSS.

securing Ely, went to work persuading the regents to make an offer and to transform the chair to meet his demands. Ely is "one of the foremost economists in the country, and is connected with one of the highest institutions," Chamberlin informed the trustees. "Probably no one among the younger generation of economists is more widely or favorably known. His employment would direct attention . . . to the University . . . and would aid greatly in giving it recognition as a leading institution."[11] The practical advantages to the school stressed by Chamberlin undoubtedly attracted the business-minded regents, for they treated Ely generously. As director of the new School of Economics, Political Science and History, he received $3,500, more than any other professor or dean on the campus. The trustees agreed to appoint an assistant professor of political economy, to provide one graduate fellowship at the outset, and to allocate the huge sum of $5,000 for library books.[12]

Ely had high hopes of making the new school "rank second to none in the country." When he arrived on the Wisconsin campus in the fall of 1892, the university had already established the groundwork for its renowned program in the social sciences. Although ranking far behind Hopkins in reputation, Wisconsin had encouraged faculty research and a modest graduate program. The seminar method had already been introduced to the graduate and undergraduate curriculum, and Wisconsin was the first western school to establish graduate fellowships. Chamberlin had strengthened the faculty by bringing in three young and promising Johns Hopkins men: Joseph Jastrow in 1888 to establish the psychological laboratory, Turner in 1888, and Charles H. Haskins

[11] Chamberlin to Regents Clark, Fratt, Dale, and Keith, March 5, 1892, as quoted in Curti and Carstensen, *University of Wisconsin,* I, 619.

[12] Turner to Ely, Nov. 25, 1891, Chamberlin to Ely, Jan. 22, April 29, 1892, Ely MSS; Curti and Carstensen, *University of Wisconsin,* I, 593n-594n.

in 1889 in history. Turner encouraged Ely by writing that the West was ripe for economic investigations and noted that the debating societies on campus had already shown a keen interest in the "practical bearings of the subject."[13] Ely widely publicized his own aims. "The time has come," he wrote in the Milwaukee *Sentinel*, "when a few institutions in the country . . . will assume a leading position in the United States, while the others will be obligated to take a second rank."[14] The new school should aspire for first rank by doing for civic life what West Point did for military life. The school should aim to broaden mental and ethical culture. Students and clergymen testified, Ely wrote, that training in economics and politics had drawn their attention to ethical problems. Since the university was located at the state capital, it was in a good position to train men for pursuits in journalism, law, and civil service. It should maintain close relations with state bureaus of labor, railroad, and insurance commissioners and boards of charity, penal, and reformatory institutions. In order to achieve these broad goals, research must be encouraged and knowledge diffused through university extension programs, newspapers, magazines, and learned treatises. Ely also hoped to raise an endowment of $150,000 for two or three additional professors and fellows.[15]

In the spring of 1892, before Ely arrived on the campus that fall, his exaggerated hopes for the new school caused an almost irresolvable rift between himself and President

[13] Curti and Carstensen, *University of Wisconsin*, I, 448, 545; Turner to Ely, Jan. 25, 1892, Ely MSS.

[14] Ely, "The State University: It Should Rank Second to None in the Country," Milwaukee *Sentinel*, Oct. 26, 1892.

[15] Ely, "School of Economics, Political Science and History," in Ely, "Miscellaneous Writings, 1876-1930," State Historical Society of Wisconsin, Madison; Ely, "The Proper Aims of Schools of Economics and Politics," *Independent*, XLIV (May 19, 1892), 682-683; Ely, "The State University"; Ely, "The Higher Education of Women in the Schools of Economics, Political Science, and History of the University of Wisconsin," *Christian Union*, XLV (May 28, 1892), 1025,

Chamberlin. Ely had insisted from the beginning that William A. Scott, who had just taken his Ph.D. under him at Hopkins, be brought along as an assistant professor at a salary of $1,500 and that David Kinley, one of his "pacesetting" graduate students at Hopkins, be offered a fellowship at $750. The calling of Scott broached a serious case of faculty rivalry. For Vice President Parkinson resented Ely's having an assistant while he had none in political science. To complicate things further, Parkinson demanded that his son be appointed as his assistant. Although Chamberlin did not believe young Parkinson was qualified for a permanent position, the regents made him an assistant professor anyway. Ely then demanded a clarification of his powers as director of the new school, for he had assumed he would control appointments of junior staff members. Chamberlin attempted to quiet the furor by explaining to Ely that the Parkinson case was out of his hands. Ely's powers were the same as the director of the observatory, Chamberlin wrote, but he warned Ely not to antagonize other members of the faculty.[16]

The small response of the people of Wisconsin in contributions to the new school also disappointed Ely. When the announcement of his transfer was made, William Dodge, railroad tycoon from New York, contributed $500 to the school, and Ely could not understand why Wisconsin citizens did not likewise make generous private gifts. Both Turner and Chamberlin warned Ely that Wisconsin capitalists were a "hard-headed" crew with newly acquired wealth and thus were not accustomed to making contributions to education. Ely became completely disgusted and was annoyed at the lack of public spirit in Wisconsin. He also objected to teaching undergraduates. Turner pointed out that the seniors were capable of original research and that the state would

[16] Chamberlin to Ely, March 17, 1892, Turner to Ely, April 22, 1892, Ely MSS.

demand that the undergraduates at least get a "taste" of him.[17]

Ely's anxiety turned into alarm when President Chamberlin resigned in June to accept a post as head of the University of Chicago geology department. Ely feared that he had made an irretrievable mistake in taking the Wisconsin post and had been "left in the ditch." "As nearly as I can gather," he wrote to Chamberlin, "you leave me in the hands of Parkinson. . . . What a mortification for me! What am I to say to students who come to Madison with enthusiasm and high expectations? They will feel that they have been deceived."[18] Ely further reiterated all of his past grievances, including the Parkinson affair and the lack of philanthropy in Wisconsin. His bellicose manner gave Chamberlin "a great deal of pain." Chamberlin explained that his leaving had no effect on the new school and took Ely to task for abusing his friends. "Your methods of treating your friends and those of whom you seek aid are the worst I have ever encountered in similar correspondences."[19] Turner, however, took Ely's anger good-naturedly and begged him not to despair of the original plan.[20]

Despite Ely's strained relations with President Chamberlin, the new school began under favorable circumstances in the fall of 1892. The press gave its establishment and Ely's appointment unusually large coverage. The Baltimore *American* described Ely's departure to the West as a "clap of thunder from out of an untroubled sky . . . [which] came down yesterday upon academic circles."[21] The *Churchman*

[17] W. E. Dodge to Ely, Feb. 23, 1892, Chamberlin to Ely, June 27, 1892, Turner to Ely, Feb. 23, 1892, Ely MSS.

[18] Ely to Chamberlin, June 24, 1892, in Curti and Carstensen, *University of Wisconsin*, I, 635.

[19] Chamberlin to Ely, June 27, 1892, Ely MSS.

[20] Turner to Ely, June 24, 1892, Ely MSS.

[21] Baltimore *American*, Feb. 13, 1892. Former Ely student Robert Finley, probably at Ely's solicitation, took the initiative in feeding news of his departure to all six of New York City's major daily papers. See Finley to Ely, Feb. 16, 1892, Ely MSS.

wondered how Johns Hopkins and the East could "consent to part with one who has done more than any other man in the country to make the 'dismal science,' a Christian science."[22] Wisconsin papers greeted the news with predictions that the university would no longer be a "feeder" for advanced students to Chicago and schools in the East. They noted that Ely had turned out a host of "eminent men" at Hopkins and concluded that Wisconsin would now attract the attention of leading citizens throughout the United States.[23]

The new president of the university, Charles Kendall Adams, was just as enthusiastic as Chamberlin had been. Ely had met Adams as early as 1882 and they had formed an enduring, though at times rocky, friendship. In 1884 Adams had sent the *Nation* a long protest of its review of Ely's "The Past and the Present of Political Economy." In his presidential inaugural address, Adams singled out the new school for special mention and explained that it deserved support from wealthy patrons. Throughout the nineties Adams supported Ely's judgment in selecting staff members and gave him a wide leeway in handling departmental affairs. The president's wife, Mary, took a special interest in Ely's philanthropic projects at Madison and assisted him in raising funds for needy students.[24]

Ely solicited the support of the local townspeople and immediately assumed an active role in the respectable Madison reform circle. In the fall of 1892 he joined and became vice president of the influential Madison Civil Service Reform Association and in November organized the Historical and Political Science Association of Madison, with himself as president and Charles N. Gregory, prominent Madison

---

[22] *Churchman,* March 30, 1892.

[23] Madison *Democrat,* Feb. 15, 1892; Madison *Wisconsin State Journal,* Feb. 16, 1892.

[24] Ely to H. B. Adams, July 19, 1882, Adams MSS; Charles K. Adams to Ely, Aug. 4, 1884, Mary M. Adams to Ely, April 26, *ca.* 1896, June 19, 1895, Ely MSS.

attorney, as secretary. The association brought together leading townspeople, including Lucius Fairchild, former governor
and Civil War general, and university people to discuss current social problems and "to create a close relationship between the graduate departments of the university and the
practical outside world." At Ely's instigation they invited
several prominent speakers, including Jacob Riis and Jane
Addams. He joined and took an active role as a vestryman
in the Grace Episcopal Church. He even took the initiative
in organizing the Four Lakes Kindergarten Association in
Madison and served as its president for several years.[25]

Ely bent his full energies to bringing immediate and
flashy results for the new school. He arrived on the scene
in an optimistic mood and exuberantly wrote Ross that he
had more graduate students in the first year than he had ever
had at Baltimore. However, recruiting high quality graduate
students without adequate fellowships proved a critical problem. Several of his former students at Johns Hopkins faced
the unpleasant task of deciding whether to move westward
with Ely to a school of lesser reputation, stay at Hopkins, or
take a degree elsewhere. Although most of them chose not
to follow their mentor, Ely did manage to pull to Wisconsin
one prize student, Charles J. Bullock. Bullock, later to become a leading economic theorist at Harvard, joined Kinley
as a pace setter and helped to buoy the reputation of the
new school.[26]

Ely's dramatic leap to the West reflected a movement
of the academic reform spirit from the privately endowed
eastern schools to the western state universities. Several of his

[25] Charles N. Gregory to Ely, Sept. 16, 1892, Ely MSS; Announce-
ment, "The Historical and Political Science Association" [1892], in Ely
MSS; "Notes," *Annals of the American Academy of Political and Social
Science,* III (March, 1893), 139; Alice Putnam to Ely, Aug. 24, 1894,
S. O. Y. Gurner to Ely, June 26, 1896, Ely MSS.
[26] See Ely to Ross, Sept. 15, 1892, Ross MSS; Bullock to Ely, Feb.
29, March 5, 1892, April 2, 1899, Ely MSS. Ely, *Ground Under Our
Feet,* p. 184.

students, including Commons at Indiana, Bemis at Chicago, and Ross at Stanford, led the westward trek of young rebels. In common they rankled at the overbearing and patronizing attitude of eastern professors. They often felt more akin to the spirited western social gospeler George Herron or the Chicago-based reform journalist Henry Demarest Lloyd. The insensitive response of the eastern conservatives to the bitter labor and farm unrest and to the millions of unemployed was beginning to push many western academicians toward a more radical position. Bemis spoke openly for the Pullman strikers and Ross even took to the stump for the Silverites. Although academicians generally hesitated to take the full step and commit themselves to Popularism, they suffered, with the agrarian radicals, from a feeling of eastern scorn and abuse.

Although Ely was moved less by the radicalism of the decade than some of his students, his relationship with the American Economic Association clearly reflected his disdain for his former eastern colleagues. No sooner had the association been formed than the leadership, except Ely, grew concerned about the prominent economists who refused to join. Conservatives J. Laurence Laughlin, Arthur T. Hadley, and William Graham Sumner apparently felt excluded by the platform. Laughlin complained to Ely's student Edward H. Bemis that the platform was aimed specifically at Sumner. Without Ely's knowledge Edwin R. A. Seligman and John Bates Clark pushed for the removal of the platform and even for sending Sumner a personal invitation to join. When Ely discovered their efforts, he demanded an explanation. Seligman vigorously denied that he wanted to "back down," but he felt that the platform was "not essential, [and] might be misinterpreted." Finally, aware that the tide had turned, Ely consented to dropping the statement of principles at the December, 1887, meeting of the executive council of the association. When Hadley heard that the "confession of faith" had been revoked, he "gladly" joined the association, but

Sumner still refused.[27] By 1890 Ely ingratiatingly acknowledged that "the old issues, which divided the economists a few years ago in this country, are no longer so important as they were and now is the time for a love-feast!"[28]

But in 1892, the same year that he assumed the Wisconsin post, he resigned his position as secretary of the American Economic Association. Still suffering from illness and anxious about his future, Ely privately expressed a desire to escape the burdensome job as early as November of 1891. However, a disruptive dispute over the scheduling of the 1892 meeting triggered his resignation. Apparently on previous occasions he had independently selected the time and place of association meetings, but they had always been held in convenient cities: Boston, Philadelphia, and Washington. Without conferring with other members of the executive committee, Ely announced that the 1892 convention would be held at Chautauqua, New York, in August. This location was convenient for Ely personally, as he spent each summer at the Summer School and his proposed date fell at the conclusion of the session.[29]

Whatever the reasons for Ely's decision, several leading

[27] Bemis to Ely, Sept. 29, 1886, Ely MSS; Francis A. Walker to Seligman, Sept. 24 [1887?], Clark to Seligman, April 25, 1887, Ely to Seligman, April 25, 1887, in Joseph Dorfman, ed., "The Seligman Correspondence, I-II," *Political Science Quarterly*, LVI (March-June, 1941), 109-110, 281; Seligman to Ely, June 29, 1889, Ely MSS; "Minutes of the Council, Dec. 30, 1887," *Publications of the American Economic Association*, I (1887), 19-21; Seligman to Ely, Jan. 2, 1889, as quoted in A. W. Coats, "The First Two Decades of the American Economic Association," *American Economic Review*, L (Sept., 1960), 558n-559n.

[28] Ely to Seligman, Oct. 22, 1890, in Dorfman, ed., "Seligman Correspondence, II," 282.

[29] See Amos G. Warner to Ely, Nov. 24, 1891, George Vincent to Ely, Nov. 27, 1891, Frederick B. Hawley to Ely, Nov. 27, 1891, Ely MSS. Thomas Nixon Carver, a student of Ely at the time, believes Ely scheduled the meeting purely as a matter of personal convenience. Carver, "The First Two Decades of the American Economic Association: Comment," *American Economic Review*, L (Dec., 1960), 1014-1015.

economists objected strongly to the Chautauqua location. A few suspected that Ely had acted unconstitutionally; others objected to the unusual summer date. But the most serious complaint came from those who feared the association would be cast in an unscholarly light by being identified with Chautauqua.[30] Perhaps President Walker's view of Chautauqua as "the first intellectual camp meeting in the Country" was typical of their view.[31] Ely placed the critics of the Chautauqua meeting in an embarrassing position when he publicly announced the site and threatened his resignation if his action were not approved. President Walker wrote to Seligman: "To my request for a call of the Executive committee of the Council, he replies that this can only mean a purpose to humiliate and insult him. And that he will straightway resign. . . . Small loss you say; and I don't disagree with you. . . . But he promises to resign peacefully in August, whereas if he goes out now there will be a specious row. All the Socialist and semi-Socialist papers will join in attacking the Association and raising Ely to the rank of a martyr. The whole Chautauqua influence will be invoked against us. The newspapers will take the affair as 'another row among the political economists.' "[32] Although some of Ely's friends thought he took the opposition too personally and advised him to back down. Ely steadfastly refused.[33]

At the meeting in Chautauqua, Ely resigned and an

[30] Seligman to Ely, Dec. 29, 1891, June 24, 1892, F. W. Taussig to Ely, Dec. 31, 1891, Davis R. Dewey to Ely, Jan. 10, 1892, George Gunton to Ely, Dec. 29, 1891, Charles Dunbar to Ely, Dec. 29, 1891, Ely MSS. William R. Harper, educational director of Chautauqua and later president of the University of Chicago, wrote in 1887, "I appreciate the fact that there is a strong prejudice in the minds of many College Professors regarding this work." Harper to Ely, Jan. 11, 1887, Ely MSS.

[31] Walker to Ely, Dec. 18, 1891, Ely MSS.

[32] Walker to Seligman, Dec. 23, 1891, as quoted in Coats, "The First Two Decades," p. 565n. For a similar view see J. B. Clark to Seligman, Dec. 30, 1891, *ibid.*

[33] See Davis R. Dewey to Ely, Jan. 10, 1892, James H. Canfield to Ely, Dec. 28, 1891, George Gunton to Ely, Dec. 29, 1891, Ely MSS.

entirely new slate of officers was elected. Deciding to rotate the presidency, the convention elected Charles A. Dunbar, a classicist, to replace Walker. For secretary, Edward A. Ross was chosen with the understanding that he would receive an assistant at $600 per year.[34] Henry W. Farnam wrote to Sumner in jubilant terms of the victory over Ely at the convention: "Though Ely was consoled by the office of Vice-President, this means practically the end of his regime in the Association. In fact it was rather amusing to see on how many occasions he found himself in a minority of one."[35] However, the council, as moved by Seligman, praised Ely for his work: "*Resolved,* That the Council [is] deeply sensible of the obligations of the Association to the faithful and painstaking labors of the outgoing Secretary in behalf of the Association since its formation, and hereby tenders the earnest thanks for his continued and successful efforts."[36]

Although Ely attended the 1893 convention and advised Ross on the intricacies of the secretarial post, he completely withdrew from the association in the midnineties. From 1893 to 1899 he did not attend a single convention, his name was dropped from the vice-presidency, and he even allowed his membership to lapse.[37] His withdrawal from the activities of the association was due to both personal and professional grievances. He felt very sensitive over the hostile reaction of his fellow economists to his unilateral action on the Chautauqua matter. Further, Ely viewed the new conservative leadership of the association as antagonistic, in particular the new president, Charles Dunbar, and a later president, Arthur T. Hadley. In 1886 Dunbar had severely

[34] Ross to Ely, Sept., 1892, Ely MSS.

[35] Farnam to W. G. Sumner, Sept. 5, 1892, as quoted in Coats, "The First Two Decades," p. 566.

[36] Ross to Ely, Sept., 1892, Ely MSS. For Seligman's authorship of the resolution, see William W. Folwell to Ross, Sept. 6, 1892, Ross MSS.

[37] See David Kinley to Ely, Feb. 29, 1895, Ely MSS.

attacked the new economics, and indirectly the American Economic Association, in an essay, "The Reaction in Political Economy."[38] In 1894 Hadley reviewed Ely's *Socialism and Social Reform* for the *Forum,* calling it "emotional" rather than "rational" in approach, and he "strongly" disapproved of Ely's apparent effort to "popularize economics by giving too much weight to the conclusions of uninstructed public sentiment."[39] Typically, Ely did not consider the review to be an honest criticism of his work. Since the editor of the *Forum,* Walter Hines Page, had requested an article from Ely for the same issue, he even accused Page of using his article as "an excuse for malignant attacks upon me."[40]

For a time Ely and his followers turned to substitute organizations to fill the function that they had hoped the American Economic Association would perform. The first of these short-lived organizations, the American Institute of Christian Sociology, founded in 1893, indicated by its title that the western professors wanted more than a purely academic society. The principal officers were all western men: Ely from Wisconsin, president; John R. Commons from Indiana, secretary; and the Reverend George D. Herron, Iowa College, principal of instruction and organization.[41] When the institute seemed doomed to failure from inadequate financial support, Ely and Commons attempted to organize an association of western "Progressive economists" in 1894. The two professors agreed that the organization should be composed of "congenial men" and "should be carefully limited in numbers."[42] Again their plan failed.

Ely's inability to establish a successful society of western

[38] Ely, *Ground Under Our Feet,* p. 149.
[39] Hadley, "Ely's Socialism and Social Reform," *Forum,* XVIII (Oct., 1894), 191.
[40] Ely to Page, Oct. 12, 1894, Ely MSS.
[41] David Kinley to Ely, Feb. 27, 1895, Commons to Ely, Jan. 30, 1894, Josiah Strong to Ely, Jan. 24, 1895, Ely MSS. Strong replaced Ely as president of the institute in 1895.
[42] Commons to Ely, Jan. 30, 1894, Ely MSS.

social scientists led most of the western professors to remain in the American Economic Association. They also encouraged Ely to resume an active role. William W. Folwell of Minnesota urged him "to stay in the ship. I heard many regrets at your absence in New York [meeting of 1894] & hopes that you would not lose interest, no matter how discouraging the circumstances might be. You have a strong body of friends in the Association, whom let me say you cannot desert."[43] David Kinley, professor of political economy at Illinois and a former Ely student, wrote him: "I am aware of the shabby treatment you have received from some of the men now in power there. I am sure, however, that if you count out Hadley and his satellites, and Walker and his, you have none but friends and well wishers in the management of the Association, and still more in its membership."[44] Others wrote in a similar vein. Eastern economists, aware of the real danger of a revolt of the West, made conciliatory gestures. The executive committee chose Indianapolis for the 1895 convention and selected Cleveland for 1897; it even made a special point of inviting Ely to read a paper before the Cleveland convention. Yet he still refused to have anything to do with the association.[45]

Ely, his ties with the eastern seaboard severed, had plenty of opportunity for educational experimentation at Wisconsin. From the start he encouraged a practical economics which encompassed the experience of those actually engaged in business, labor, and reform. In 1892-1893, as he did in the years following, Ely invited a series of prominent lecturers to campus. Frederick H. Wines of the Illinois Charities Board gave a course of lectures on punishment and reformation which he later published. The work remained the authority

[43] Folwell to Ely, Jan. 12, 1895, Ely MSS.
[44] Kinley to Ely, Nov. 28, 1896, Ely MSS.
[45] Kinley to Ely, Feb. 27, 1895, Edward H. Bemis to Ely, Dec. 27, 1895, Franklin H. Giddings to Ely, Oct. 25, 1897, Ely MSS.

in the field well into the twentieth century. Ely asked his former student, Amos G. Warner, to give a series of lectures on charities, which were published as *American Charities* and also became a classic. Apart from these prominent speakers Ely invited a host of local men to give public addresses or talks to his seminary or classes. Superintendents of state institutions were favorites, though businessmen occasionally received invitations.[46]

The nature of the addresses by special speakers indicated Ely's increasing interest in charities and correction as a branch of sociology. While at Hopkins, he started several students in research projects in the field, and when he moved to Wisconsin, he offered a regular course on the subject, which attracted sixty-three students by 1895. Ely wrote for the catalogue that the course was not intended to train specialists but to prepare students for good citizenship. Some twenty special lecturers, mostly from state correctional institutions, assisted with the course. Most illustrious of the group was Alexander Graham Bell, who addressed the class on techniques of teaching the deaf. In 1895 Ely was appointed to the executive committee of the State Conference on Charities and Corrections and began to work closely with state agencies.[47]

Ely also set up fieldwork in charities for his students. His most valuable connection was with the Associated Charities of Cincinnati. A former student, Philip W. Ayres, headed the organization and invited Ely to send several graduate students down each summer for firsthand experience. Local citizens in Cincinnati financed small fellowships, and Ely obtained a few gifts in Madison to meet expenses. When

---

[46] See Ely to Charles K. Adams, June 7, 1895, Ely MSS.

[47] Ely and Edward D. Jones, "Instruction in Charities and Correction in the University of Wisconsin," *Lend-a-Hand*, XIV (June, 1895), 406-411; "Announcement for 1895-6, School of Economics, Political Science, and History," *Annual Catalogue of the University of Wisconsin, 1894-95*, p. 116; Lynn S. Pease to Ely, Jan. 3, 1895, Ely MSS.

Ayres moved to Chicago to head the Associated Charities
there and then later to New York, Ely continued to send him
students. At the close of the nineties Ely assisted in super-
vising the Milwaukee settlement house and throughout the
decade remained in close touch with Hull House in Chicago.
Several of his students took up charity work as a career.
Charles M. Hubbard replaced Ayres at Cincinnati; George
S. Wilson headed the Associated Charities in Toledo and
then Washington, D. C.; Helen P. Bates headed the Unity
House in Minneapolis; and Kate Everest, the first woman to
obtain a Ph.D. at the university, headed the Kingsley House
in Pittsburgh.[48]

Ely worked tirelessly to raise funds to pay for special
lectures and fellowships. Since Wisconsin citizens contributed meagerly, he relied primarily on the proceeds of special
lecture tours. Through the extension division of the university he normally gave a series of ten or so lectures. Socialism proved to be a popular, though an emotion-laden, topic.
His first big lecture series at Minneapolis in the fall of 1892
netted over $500. He equaled that amount from a series on
socialism sponsored by the People's Institute at Milwaukee.
And during his first two years he made other major engagements at Galesburg, Illinois, Cincinnati and Dayton, Ohio,
and the Auburn Seminary.[49]

Each of Ely's lectures on socialism created a local furor.
The Alliance advocates turned out in substantial numbers in
Minneapolis, and Ely's advocacy of the socialization of natural

[48] "Announcement for 1895-6," p. 116; Ely to Charles K. Adams,
June 7, 1895, George S. Wilson to Ely, Nov. 25, 1895, Philip W. Ayres
to Ely, May 5, 12, 1894, July 22, 1897, A. M. Simons to Ely, March
13, 1897, H. H. Jacobs to Ely, April 22, 1897, Jane Addams to Ely,
March 12, 1895, Ely MSS; Ruth Harmon and Charlotte Lekachman,
"The 'Jacobs' House,'" *Wisconsin Magazine of History*, XVI (March,
1933), 254.

[49] H. P. Nichols to Ely, Oct. 11, 1892, Fred W. Speirs to Ely,
Oct. 17, 1892, John H. Finley to Ely, Oct. 24, 1892, Ayres to Ely,
Jan. 19, 1894, Arthur S. Hoyt to Ely, Nov. 10, 1892, Ely MSS.

monopolies infuriated some of the local businessmen. One of them denounced Ely as a "calamity howler and sower of dangerous seed." Much to Ely's chagrin, the Milwaukee socialist newspaper, *Advance*, claimed him as a "fellow agitator" in the movement. Fred H. Speirs, head of the People's Institute, attempted to persuade local socialists that Ely advocated only the public ownership of natural monopolies. But the "good people" of the city continued to look upon the institute with "alarmed suspicion."[50]

Students commonly reported that "if you take only one course from Dr. Ely you are apt to be disgusted with Economics, but if you take more you will devote your life to the subject."[51] Having read several of Ely's pungent books, Oliver E. Baker expected a scintillating lecturer, a large man similar to Edward A. Ross. "Instead I found Dr. Ely with a low squeaky voice who often shuffled along the road as he walked."[52] With a shock of chalky-white hair and slightly overweight, he looked the role of a small-town clergyman. In his typical classroom performance Ely would pace slowly back and forth; occasionally he would stop to study his notes, using his glasses which hung from a narrow black ribbon over his vest. Then he would walk slowly toward the window, continuing to discuss a point. Suddenly stopping, he would peer out the window; seemingly oblivious to the class, he would begin a new line of thought, a new subject for possible research. Students would abandon notetaking. Surprised at student stares, he would turn and start back to the lectern. His glasses would fall quietly down the length of the black ribbon. Then he would readjust them and continue with the lecture, "monotonously almost, but as he went on a subdued excitement pervaded the class."[53]

[50] W. W. Gamble to Ely, Dec. 20, 1892, Fred H. Speirs to Ely, Jan. 2, 1893, Ely MSS.
[51] Algie M. Simons to [H. C. Taylor?], [1944?], Ely MSS.
[52] Baker to Henry C. Taylor, Feb. 19, 1944, Ely MSS.
[53] E. D. Tetreau to Henry C. Taylor, March 8, 1944, Ely MSS.

Ely stimulated considerable enthusiasm among the under-graduates outside the classroom. They turned out in large numbers to hear his sporadic public lectures, especially on social Christianity. He also proposed a debate on the government ownership of natural monopolies for the Athenaean Joint Debate Team. The subject created a lively interest among the students and Ely assisted those on the affirmative side. He even called on his journalist friend, Henry Demarest Lloyd, for "full information" on the state ownership of Australian rairoads. The debaters, at Ely's suggestions, sent out form letters to officials in every city in the country over 25,000 population and to the larger cities of Europe, Australia, and South America. The letter posed a series of questions concerning the value of municipal ownership as taken from their own experience. The debaters even visited Chicago, viewing power plants, street railways, and all aspects of municipal administration. Ely announced that it was the most extensive research ever made on the subject. He offered to aid the debaters by editing, writing an introduction, and publishing the results of their work. The debates had a "fairly wide" circulation and received favorable notices in the *Outlook, Review of Reviews,* and *Independent.*[54]

Ely patterned the graduate work of the new school along the same lines as Johns Hopkins. Graduate studies centered in the general "economic Seminary," or Round Table, which met in Ely's home at eight o'clock every Tuesday evening. Each student chose a special research topic within a general area for investigation. Ely was more intense and less detached in the Round Table meetings than in the classroom. He was sometimes overly enthusiastic for fledgling research topics, and on occasion students felt Ely

[54] Communication of Supt. Wells to Investigating Committee, Aug. 20, 1894, Ely MSS; form letter of Athenaean Joint Debate Team, Dec. 12, 1892, Ely MSS; Ely to H. D. Lloyd, Sept. 30, 1893, Lloyd MSS, State Historical Society of Wisconsin, Madison; Curti and Carstensen, *University of Wisconsin,* I, 435, 437.

gave insufficient training in the techniques of criticism. But they could not quarrel with the results. Ely's Round Table always had a high *esprit de corps,* and when he occasionally took a leave of absence, faculty and students alike complained of a loss of enthusiasm and interest. Ideally, he liked to guide a small group of dedicated men toward a common goal. Cooperative research still appealed to him. He always carried a black pocket notebook in which he scribbled ideas for new projects, lecture suggestions, essay topics, and a new course to be offered.[55]

Many of the graduate students made the Ely home their "social center." He built a beautiful house on University Heights overlooking Madison's two lakes, Mendota and Monona. As Charles J. Bullock later put it, they came as much to see Mrs. Ely as to see the professor. Bullock and Robert Finley described her as having a "lovable" and "radiant" personality. The Elys did more entertaining than they had in Baltimore. "Never in my life—North, South, East, or West, in Europe, or in America—have I been more charmingly entertained than I was by Mrs. Ely and you at your home in Madison," exclaimed R. H. Jesse, president of the University of Missouri.[56] Practically all of the prominent speakers—Amos G. Warner, Albert Shaw, Bernard Fernow, Jacob Riis, Jane Addams, Theodore Roosevelt, Woodrow Wilson, Alexander Graham Bell, and a host of others—stayed overnight or for an extended period at the Elys'.

With Ely's guidance the graduates of the new school made a notable record in the nineties. David Kinley, the first fellow, published the *History, Organization, and Influence of the Independent Treasury of the United States,* received an appointment at the University of Illinois, and moved up the ladder from dean to president of the institution.

[55] See Ely, *Ground Under Our Feet,* p. 193, and reminiscenses of former Ely students gathered in 1944 by Henry C. Taylor, in Ely MSS.
[56] Jesse to Ely, Oct. 3, 1906, Ely MSS; Ely, *Ground Under Our Feet,* p. 206.

Edward D. Jones published a widely read work, *Economic Crises*, and became an expert in statistics. Jones prepared a grand-prize-winning exhibit of statistical charts and maps for the Paris Exposition of 1900. Balthazar H. Meyer became the outstanding authority in the economics of transportation and later served on the Interstate Commerce Commission. Before the decade was out, Ely added two capable young Wisconsin men to the political science staff: Paul Reinsch and Samuel E. Sparling. Reinsch published a stinging criticism of nationalism and imperialism, *World Politics at the End of the Nineteenth Century*, and later served as American ambassador to China.[57]

Ely could be proud of the record of the School of Economics, Political Science and History during the nineties. By the end of the decade the school offered fifty-three courses, and the staff had a notable record for original investigations and publications. Ely was burdened with extensive administrative duties, but he did manage to write and publish three books and several articles during the decade. He also accepted the editorship of the "Crowell Library of Economics and Political Science" series in 1892. Ely's initiative brought to the series several works which remained standard authorities in the social sciences for years, including books by William Scott, Amos G. Warner, Frederick Wines, John R. Commons, Frederic C. Howe, Jane Addams, and Edward H. Bemis. Although the placement of graduate students by Ely did not quite equal his success at Hopkins, he did well considering the stringent budgets of most schools during these depression years. The school also approached Ely's hopes for reaching the people of the state. Most of the staff, including Ely, offered courses through the extension division. And he established closer relations with the major state agencies, preparing the way for the peculiar nature of the Progressive Movement in Wisconsin.

[57] See Curti and Carstensen, *University of Wisconsin*, I, 636-639.

Ely's increasing involvement in administrative duties corresponded with the changing character of his role as a reformer. He became more conservative and tended to cloister himself within the academic world. His trial for economic heresy in 1894 was significant as a precedent in support of academic freedom, but it also helped to induce Ely to withdraw from an activist role in reform.

Chapter Six

RETREAT FROM REFORM

ON THE MORNING of August 14, 1894, a packed crowd of Summer School students and staff assembled in the vast Chautauqua Amphitheatre. They listened expectantly as Bishop John H. Vincent rose to read a prepared statement by Professor Richard T. Ely. Ely, who had recently acquired a beard and pince-nez, sat on the platform staring straight ahead. The audience sensed that Ely would deny the charges that he had been guilty of teaching and practicing heretical economic doctrines. As Vincent read in Ely's behalf, his voice rolled out across the amphitheatre. "Taking up, first, the series of charges brought against my conduct and character, I deny each and every one in each and every particular. I defy the author of these base and cruel calumnies to prove one statement he has made, and until he does so, I shall hold him up to the public as an unmanly and shameless slanderer." Ely added that, if the charges were true, "they unquestionably, unfit me to occupy a responsible position as an instructor of youth in a great university."[1]

So wrote Richard Ely two weeks prior to his trial by a special committee of the University of Wisconsin Board of Regents for teaching and practicing subversive economic principles. The 1894 trial and exoneration of Ely profoundly influenced his career and established an important precedent in the history of academic freedom in the United States. It came at the very moment when he had reached the apex of his popularity among both radical and respectable reformers. "No professor of political economy in America," reported the *Review of Reviews* in 1893, "has reached so wide a circle of readers or set to thinking those he has reached so much as Professor Ely, of the University of Wisconsin."[2] Never before or afterward did he have so large an audience awaiting his ideas and leadership. His trial for economic heresy made him a truly national figure, and reformers of all varieties sought his guidance. Yet, at the very moment of his greatest opportunity, Ely began a noticeable withdrawal from his peculiar role in the reform movements of the late nineteenth century.

Before 1894 Ely had worried about his radical image, for after all, he had tangled with such conservative giants as the *Nation* magazine, Simon Newcomb, and William Graham Sumner. In almost every one of his controversial works he was careful to deny that he was a socialist or an anarchist and bitterly denounced those who tagged him with such terms. He felt that he had always been more a critic of traditional ideology than an activist in reform. Even when he suggested specific reforms, such as the socialization of natural monopolies, he advocated a gradual approach. While he had preached direct action and participation in reform movements, he always maintained a degree of personal detachment. "Only twice in my life," Ely explained in 1894, "have I even spoken

[1] Ely's statement is published in full in *Chautauqua Assembly Herald*, Aug. 15, 1894. See also Ely, *Ground Under Our Feet: An Autobiography* (New York: Macmillan, 1938), p. 244.

[2] Review of Ely, *Outlines of Economics*, in *Review of Reviews*, VIII (Nov., 1893), 606.

to audiences of working men, and I had always held myself aloof from agitations as something not in my province—something for which I am not adapted."[3] He carefully avoided a clear-cut stand on those controversial issues which he considered to be largely superfluous to the main economic problems of the day. He seldom wrote on the politically explosive tariff issue and, in 1888, bitingly advised the irrepressible Bemis to avoid it. He warned both Bemis and Commons to ignore political parties and to take a higher ground that would cut across partisan lines.[4] His publications, he wrote in 1894, were "designed for men of wealth and culture—for those called the upper classes and by them chiefly my books have been read."[5] From his days at Columbia College he counted several wealthy men as personal friends. When secretary of the American Economic Association, he gained the personal acquaintance of men like Andrew Carnegie, Jonathan Love, George W. Childs, and William E. Dodge. On several occasions they made generous contributions to the association and to Ely's own work. Reform, Ely had always insisted, must not come primarily from the working class or farmers but from the superior classes, those with talents and an understanding of their ethical obligations.

Ely's increasingly cautious response to the entreaties for cooperation from the controversial Reverend George D. Herron indicated his growing conservatism. Ely first heard of Herron in 1891 when the minister wrote him asking for information on social problems. At the time, Herron had

[3] Ely to Amos P. Wilder, July 27, 1894, Ely MSS, State Historical Society of Wisconsin, Madison.

[4] See, for example, Bemis to Ely, Nov. 19, 1888, Julie H. Ward to Ely, Dec. 26, 1887, Ely MSS; Ely to Joseph A. Labadie, Sept. 18, 1885, in Sidney Fine, ed., "The Ely-Labadie Letters," *Michigan History*, XXXVI (March, 1952), 18. For Ely's only expressions on the tariff, in which he took an ambiguous position nearer free trade than protectionism, see his *Problems of To-day: A Discussion of Protective Tariffs, Taxation, and Monopolies* (New York: Crowell, 1888).

[5] Ely to Amos P. Wilder, July 27, 1894, Ely MSS.

just begun to attract a large audience for his brand of Christian sociology and sent the manuscript for his essays, *The Call of the Cross,* to Ely for criticism. Events brought them closer together when, in 1892, Ely assumed the Wisconsin post and Herron moved from a small church in Minnesota to be pastor of the Congregational church in Burlington, Iowa. Herron immediately seized the opportunity to invite the professor to give a series of lectures to his church. Ely responded favorably and assisted Herron in obtaining an endowed chair of "applied" Christianity at Iowa College (later Grinnell) from Mrs. E. D. Rand, a member of Herron's congregation. Herron in turn began to send his advanced ministerial candidates to Ely at Wisconsin.[6]

In the summer of 1893 Ely welcomed the support of Herron in forming the American Institute of Christian Sociology at the regular meeting of the Chautauqua. Ely as president of the institute and Herron as principal of instruction worked closely together in drawing up a program of social action modeled after that of the Christian Social Union. They hoped to publish papers on Christian sociology, recommend and preach sermons, and provide scholarships and endowed professorships. The institute claimed the supremacy of Christian law in the area of social control and presented "Christ as the Living Master and King of men, and His kingdom as the complete ideal of human society to be realized on earth."[7] For the following summer they scheduled two general sessions, one at Grinnell under the auspices of Iowa College in late June and early July, 1894, and the other later at Chautauqua. The proposed Grinnell meeting received national attention. With an avowed purpose of bringing together clergymen and social scientists, addresses were promised from Ely, Herron,

[6] Herron to Ely, July 6, Oct. 3, 1891, Nov. 16, Dec. 27, 1892, Feb. 2, Nov. 7, 1893, Ely MSS.

[7] "Notes," *Annals of the American Academy of Political and Social Science,* IV (Nov., 1893), 155.

John R. Commons, Josiah Strong, Leighton Williams, and Graham Taylor. Ely proposed to give five lectures on "Private Property as a Sacred Trust" and one on the "Social Aspects of the Lord's Supper."[8]

But Ely did not make the promised appearance. The increasingly radical image of Herron in the eyes of Ely's friends undoubtedly influenced his decision. Lyman Abbott's *Outlook* reported in May, 1894, that Herron was "too passionate" and that his demogogic appeal "robbed" his work of significant merit. The *Review of Reviews*, edited by former Ely student Albert Shaw, claimed that Herron's message was that of Ely, Strong, and Commons "on fire" and strongly deprecated his "fervid appeals to the heart rather than the head."[9] Albion Small, a former Ely student who headed the sociology department at the University of Chicago, presented more compelling arguments against Herron and George Gates, president of Iowa College. In a series of personal letters to Ely before the scheduled summer meeting, Small roundly condemned Herron's sociology, claiming it was unsafe, unfactual, and dogmatic. When Ely demanded a further explanation, Small wrote that the headquarters of the Christian sociology movement was shifting in the eyes of the public from men like Ely to Herron and Gates. The new interpreters of the movement disgust "every man of my acquaintance," Small wrote. "It is essentially . . . a repudiation of your own method of first making sure of the facts before offering to preach programs." Small concluded the discussion with a comment that undoubtedly shook Ely's confidence in continuing his close identification with Herron. "In so far as you encourage and tacitly endorse that unscholarly and illiberal course," the

[8] "Conventions and Summer Gatherings of 1894," *Review of Reviews*, IX (May, 1894), 540-541; Herron to Ely, March 30, 1894, Ely MSS.

[9] Charles Young to Ely, June 25, 1894, Herron to Ely, March 30, 1894, Ely MSS; *Outlook*, L (May 12, 1894), 837; "The Church and Society," *Review of Reviews*, IX (June, 1894), 749.

Chicago professor declared, "you must necessarily forfeit a measure of confidence."[10] Whatever the reasons, Ely not only decided to avoid the Grinnell meeting but also to resign his position as president of the institute at the Chautauqua meeting.

The year 1894 dawned ominously for the Elys when personal tragedy struck that spring. During a visit by Mrs. Ely to relatives in Richmond, their nine-month-old infant daughter, Josephine, suddenly and mysteriously died. Shortly thereafter, Mrs. Ely had an attack of diphtheria and recovered only slowly during the spring and summer. The Ely finances remained critical. His salary of $3,500, plus book royalties, ordinarily would have supplied a decent living in 1894. But the family budget strained under special expenses. In addition to a new house, Ely had to pay for several lots that he had speculatively purchased in University Heights. Perhaps the largest extra drain on family finances arose from extensive payments to his aging and unemployed father in Fredonia.[11]

As trying as these personal hardships undoubtedly were, Ely's position was endangered that summer by the historic trial for economic heresy. During the depression years of the nineties, unorthodox professors, including former Ely students Edward H. Bemis and John R. Commons, had been dismissed from their posts. With widespread unemployment looming in the background, proposed solutions to the nation's economic ills ranged from socialism and Populism to Cleveland's retrenchment program and hard money. Organized labor awoke from almost a decade of slumber. Beginning with the violent outbursts between strikers and Pinkerton agents at the Homestead steelworks near Pittsburgh in 1892, labor disputes appeared to reach a crisis in the spring of 1894. When the Pullman workers walked out, George M. Pullman closed

[10] Small to Ely, May 24, June 5, 1894, Ely MSS.
[11] See Thomas Y. Crowell to Ely, July 31, 1894, Ezra S. Ely to R. T. Ely, Aug. 11, 1894, Ely MSS.

down his plant. Then Eugene Debs, head of the American
Railway Union, called for a boycott of Pullman cars by the
railway workers. Even such a prolabor figure as Lyman
Abbott, editor of the *Outlook,* condemned the strikers.[12] It
was little wonder that hypersensitive men of property became
alarmed at academic figures who sympathized with labor
unions and advocated reforms affecting the rights of property.
Even academic discussion of possible institutional changes
antagonized the conservatives who usually controlled the
regents of higher educational institutions.

Another basis of the onslaught on college professors during the nineties rested on their acceptance of the German
principle of *Lehrfreiheit und Lernfreiheit* which, as defined
by Ely, meant "freedom to think and freedom to express one's
thoughts to one's fellows."[13] Those who came into conflict
with higher educational authorities, almost to the man, had
been trained either in a German university or in graduate
schools under German-trained professors. They presumed
that the scholar should pursue truth untrammeled and then
present his findings to the world. Whether the conclusions
should be presented outside the ivory towers or only inside
was an open question. Even the German professors dared not
criticize the policies of the state outside the university walls,
though they enjoyed such freedom within. However the
individual defined the concept of academic freedom, the
American professors tended to overreach the limits tolerated
by the schools of higher learning during the nineties.[14]

The attack on Ely began with a letter, dated July 12, 1894,
to the *Nation* from Oliver E. Wells, state superintendent of
public instruction for Wisconsin and an ex-officio member of

[12] Abbott to Ely, July 19, 1894, Ely MSS. Ely himself later condemned the railroad workers. See Ely, "Fundamental Beliefs in My
Social Philosophy," *Forum,* XVIII (Oct., 1894), 174.

[13] Ely, *Ground Under Our Feet,* p. 124.

[14] See Richard Hofstadter and Walter P. Metzger, *The Development
of Academic Freedom in the United States* (New York: Columbia University Press, 1955).

the Board of Regents. Wells, a little-known high school teacher, had been elected by a fluke in a Democratic upset in 1890. The Democrats had won only one state election in Wisconsin since the Civil War and, with little hope of victory, nominated Wells for state superintendent. However, before the election the Republicans had passed the Bennett Act, placing all parochial schools under state supervision. Catholics and Lutherans, reacting against the act, joined in full support of regular Democrats to overthrow the traditional Republican hold on the state. The Democrats swept their entire slate of candidates into office.[15]

Wells, who according to one report was "as pugnacious as an Irishman at a fair," had previously quarreled with other members of the Board of Regents as well as with President Chamberlin. He had accused the board of secretly conducting public business and charged that it was controlled by the executive committee. He had also attacked one board member for speculating on land which the university would need in the future. While on a visit to the offices of the *Nation* in New York City, according to Ely's later account, Wells had been invited to write the scathing letter.[16] Certainly the style of the letter bore indications that a *Nation* editorial writer had helped in its preparation. Entitled "The College Anarchist," it began with a general attack upon the university and upon Ely. The teachings and practices of the University of Wisconsin, Wells wrote, were the basis for "a sort of moral justification for attacks upon life and property."[17]

[15] William A. Scott to Ely, July 21, 1894, Ely MSS; Merle Curti and Vernon Carstensen, *The University of Wisconsin: A History, 1848-1925* (Madison: University of Wisconsin Press, 1949), I, 508.

[16] Theron F. Schlabach, "An Aristocrat on Trial: The Case of Richard T. Ely," *Wisconsin Magazine of History*, XLVII (Winter, 1963-1964), 146; William A. Scott to Ely, July 21, 1894, Ely MSS; Curti and Carstensen, *University of Wisconsin*, I, 508; Ely, *Ground Under Our Feet*, p. 222.

[17] Oliver E. Wells, "The College Anarchist," *Nation*, LIX (July 12, 1894), 27. The letter is reprinted in Ely, *Ground Under Our Feet*, pp. 219-220.

Wells then took up a series of personal charges against Ely. He wrote that in an 1893 printing strike in Madison, Ely entertained and counseled a "walking delegate," a strike organizer, from Kansas City. At the same time Ely, as secretary of the Christian Social Union, threatened to take his business away from a printing firm unless it unionized its shop. According to Wells, when the firm refused, Ely then withdrew his printing and "asserted that where a skilled workman was needed, a dirty, dissipated, unmarried, unreliable, and unskilled tramp, if a union man, should be employed in preference to an industrious, skillful, trustworthy non-union man who is head of a family." Ely supposedly said further that any man was a "crank" who had "conscientious scruples against joining the Union." Wells closed with a scathing criticism of Ely's writings. "Prof. Ely . . . differs from Ely the socialist only in the adroit and covert method of his advocacy," Wells wrote. Ely "masked" his socialistic teachings "by glittering generalities and mystical and metaphysical statements susceptible to various interpretations." His works abounded in "sanctimonious and pious cant, pander to the prohibitionists, and ostentatiously sympathize with all who are in distress." He assured his books a large sale by appealing to all who are religious, moral, or unfortunate. "Only the careful student will discover their utopian, impracticable, or pernicious doctrines, but their general acceptance would furnish a seeming moral justification of attacks upon life and property such as the country has already become too familiar with."[18]

Two days later the letter was reprinted in the New York *Evening Post*, which owned the *Nation*. The following week the *Nation* theorized that Ely would soon be removed from his post because of the opposition of President Charles Kendall Adams. They pointed out that Adams, in his annual baccalaureate address of that spring, had publicly condemned

[18] Wells, "The College Anarchist," p. 27.

the economic doctrines of Ely. The address, entitled "The Limitations of Reforms," had been "made up entirely of assaults upon his [Ely's] 'ethical concepts,'" the *Nation* claimed. "The President seemed to consider it his duty to remove from the minds of the graduating class . . . the rubbishy ideas which the director had planted therein."[19] Obviously, the *Nation* hoped to isolate Ely from the president and the regents of the university. In reality, it appears that Adams did not intend to attack Ely at all, but to quiet fears expressed in the press that the university was spreading "alien" and "revolutionary" ideas.[20]

To Ely, visiting in Virginia at the time, the attacks seemed to imperil all that he had worked for at Wisconsin. "I realized," he later wrote, "that all my hopes and ambitions to play a significant role in the educational history of the country were in danger of frustration."[21] The attack received attention from the press across the country. In Wisconsin the Oshkosh *Northwestern* led the demand for Ely's dismissal. But the two Madison newspapers handled the entire affair in a gingerly fashion. The *Wisconsin State Journal* reprinted Wells' letter, but felt the superintendent could not prove his charges and noted that he was hardly knowledgeable on economic matters. It also carried a story on July 21 from the Chippewa *Herald,* which roundly condemned Wells. The other Madison paper, the *Democrat,* completely ignored the charges until after the regents ordered an investigation on July 31.[22] While most commentators doubted the validity of the charges, several believed that Ely should be dismissed if evidence proved Wells' charges correct. The Milwaukee *Wisconsin* called for a fair

[19] [J. B. Bishop], "An Ethical Professor Rebuked," *Nation,* LIX (July 19, 1894), 41.

[20] See Charles K. Adams to Ely, July 23, 1894, Ely MSS.

[21] Ely, *Ground Under Our Feet,* p. 222.

[22] Ely to Amos P. Wilder, July 27, 1894, Ely MSS; Madison *Wisconsin State Journal,* July 17, 21, 1894. The Oshkosh paper had also attacked Ely before the Wells letter. See Charles K. Adams to Ely, Jan. 17, 1894, Ely MSS.

trial, but argued that the state could not tolerate "propaganda directed against the political and social principles embodied in the constitution." The Milwaukee *Journal* added that "our free institutions are too valuable to be imperilled by such teachings as are attributed to Dr. Ely."[23]

Responding to the attack posed a serious and difficult problem. Ely immediately consulted his friends, who gave suggestions ranging from a libel suit against Wells, the New York *Evening Post,* and the *Nation* to asking for a hearing before the regents, or both. Albert Shaw, editor of the *Review of Reviews,* proposed that Ely attempt to force Wells to retract the charges. If he refused, then Ely should sue for libel.[24] President Adams hesitated to suggest such drastic action, but he did write that if the specific charges could be categorically denied, then Ely should welcome a hearing by the regents. "I believe you can well afford to have all your writings put to the test of searching scrutiny, as, of course, they would be in case of a trial."[25] However, C. W. Gregory, a Madison attorney, advised against a hearing by the regents after contacting Regent Breese J. Stevens. Ely's colleague, William A. Scott, opposed either move. A libel suit, he wrote Ely, would lead to misunderstanding by the public and a fair judgment would be impossible "when the public mind is agitated over the strike." If a regents' investigation were held, Scott warned, they would surely attack the teachings of Ely's books. Supposedly, two or three regents had already expressed disapproval of his works. If true, a hearing would at least result in an unfavorable minority report, Scott asserted.[26]

On July 31 the president of the Board of Regents, William P. Bartlett, submitted a statement asking the consent of the

[23] As quoted in Schlabach, "An Aristocrat on Trial," p. 157.

[24] See Ely to George Raymer, June 17, 1894, Frederic C. Howe to Ely, Aug. 20, 1894, Shaw to Ely, July 19, 26, 1894, Ely MSS.

[25] Adams to Ely, July 23, 1894, Ely MSS.

[26] Gregory to Ely, July 19, 1894, Scott to Ely, July 21, 1894, Ely MSS.

board to appoint a committee to "investigate the charges made, the effect of Dr. Ely's teachings upon the students, and the whole matter connected therewith and report at our next regular meeting." Regent Stevens opposed the recommendation, arguing that "the times were too much disturbed to permit of a careful investigation into the facts charged and a careful judgment upon the facts found."[27] A majority of the regents, however, approved Bartlett's plan. Bartlett appointed three regents to make the investigation: H. W. Chynoweth, a Madison attorney; John Johnston, a Milwaukee banker and dilettante in literature; and Dr. H. B. Dale, a physician from Oshkosh.

The reports to Ely, who was lecturing at Chautauqua, were depressing. "The Committee, as you doubtless know," Scott wrote, "is a bad one. Mr. Dale has expressed himself in the matter in an unfavorable way, and I have my suspicions of Mr. Chynoweth." Frederick Jackson Turner added that recent "events show that the Regents have settled the question of an investigation for themselves." David Kinley, who was visiting from Illinois at Madison and had taken charge of the Ely forces, was even more gloomy, advising that "Shaw, [Carroll] Wright & the others cannot understand the situation here. Your friends have a right to a public denial before you can rightfully expect them to assume your public defense; the public must have it, else your silence will be interpreted as a lack of ability to defend yourself. You cannot expect your friends to defend you unless you give them definite ground to stand on."[28]

Kinley's suggestion of a public denial no doubt proved embarrassing to Ely, for Wells' charges of Ely's participation in the Madison strike were not absolutely false. In a statement apparently prepared for submission to the *Nation* but

[27] Curti and Carstensen, *University of Wisconsin*, I, 512-513.
[28] Scott to Ely, Aug. 3, 1894, Turner to Ely, Aug. 4, 1894, Kinley to Ely, Aug. 7, 1894, Ely MSS.

never sent, Ely admitted that the "statements of Mr. Wells are untrue . . . with the single exception of his account of my position as Secy. of the C[hristian] S[ocial] U[nion], the matter of a union printing shop; and that account is so perverted as to be equivalent to a false statement of facts."[29] Later evidence indicated that Ely had quarreled with W. A. Tracy, manager of the struck printing firm, over unionizing the shop and over the payment of a bill. He had also stated that members of the Christian Social Union might require him to take his printing elsewhere, if they learned he was dealing with a nonunion shop.[30] Further, Ely was, of course, recognized as one of the strongest advocates of government ownership of natural monoplies in the country as well as a strong sympathizer with the labor movement. An investigation of the facts might lead to the same distortions and misunderstandings that Wells had made.

Nonetheless, his friends had earlier impressed upon him the need for a categorical denial of the entire list of charges. C. W. Gregory wrote: "You will kindly forgive me if I say that I think I have noticed that your denials were often so qualified as to fail of the necessary comprehensiveness to carry conviction."[31] President Adams, David Kinley, and others wrote in a similar vein. Ely apparently acceded to the expedient course advised by friends. When the *Wisconsin State Journal* reported that Ely had accused Wells of "gross" misstatements, Ely indignantly answered: "Mr. Wells' letter contains nothing but lies. He may have heard them from others and believe them but nevertheless they are lies and nothing but lies—not facts twisted and distorted."[32] On July 28 the *Outlook* reported

[29] Statement, Aug. 5, 1894, Ely MSS.

[30] Ely to Amos P. Wilder, July 27, 1894, Ely MSS; Transcript of the Ely Trial, pp. 47, 54-55, in Papers of the Board of Regents, University of Wisconsin, microfilm copy in the State Historical Society of Wisconsin, Madison.

[31] Gregory to Ely, July 19, 1894, Ely MSS.

[32] Ely to Amos P. Wilder, July 27, 1894, Ely MSS.

Ely's claims that Wells' letter was "absolutely false." Ely further wrote to the editor that "I do not hold the views of which I am accused, and I have never been guilty of the acts with which I am charged."[33] With the regents' announcement of the investigation, Ely decided to deny the charges publicly at the Chautauqua Amphitheatre. Ely's friends gave the denial nationwide publicity.

Thus the central issue of the controversy became the validity of the charges made by Wells, not the rights or limitations implied in the German conception of academic freedom. The questions of Ely's rights as a private person or as a professor to entertain or counsel a walking delegate, to participate in a strike, and to teach and publish the doctrines which Wells claimed he held, remained secondary and were seldom raised. In fact Ely destroyed the possibility of making his case a *cause célèbre* by declaring publicly that if the charges were true, then he was unfit to teach. Ironically, only Edward H. Bemis, himself under attack at Chicago, recognized that Ely had sacrificed a valuable principle. "That was a glorious victory for you," Bemis wrote after Ely's exoneration. "I was sorry only that you seemed to show a vigor of denial as to entertaining a walking delegate or counseling strikers as if either were wrong, instead of under certain circumstances a *duty*."[34] Ely was certainly aware that academic freedom was an issue and had suggested earlier that the press could possibly take that position.[35]

With Ely's denial of the charges, the tide quickly turned in his favor. Although David Kinley failed to persuade Wells to drop the charges, he found the printer, W. A. Tracy, willing to testify favorably about his relations with Ely. After conversation with Tracy, Kinley reported back to Ely: "We have

[33] "Wisconsin 'Incident,'" *Outlook*, L (July 28, 1894), 127.
[34] Bemis to Ely, Oct. 4, 1894, Ely MSS.
[35] Ely to Amos P. Wilder, July 27, 1894, Ely to Albert Shaw, Aug. 8, 1894, Ely MSS.

Mr. Wells in a nice little hole of his own digging. It remains for you to bury him—and you can. I think the Comm. feels the favorable drift and any hostility one or two of them may feel toward you will not dare show itself."[36] Kinley also traced down information on the walking delegate with whom Ely was supposed to have had conferences. Friend O'Connell, who at the time of the strike headed the Federated Trades' Council in Madison, reported that he had accompanied the walking delegate, Frank Klunk, "almost incessantly during his stay in Madison" and that they never met Ely. It was true, O'Connell stated, that Klunk met a Professor Powers in a classroom and may have confused the two.[37] A letter arrived on August 17, 1894, from Klunk himself. Klunk did recall being "introduced to Dr. Ely by an old member of No. 313, who was present until the interview ended." But "Dr. Ely did not entertain me at his house . . . nor anywhere else. . . . Dr. Ely did not give me any advice in regard to the strike."[38] Now the Ely forces had concrete evidence that the specifics in Wells' charges were highly distorted. Kinley turned over the evidence he had accumulated to a highly respected Madison attorney, a Democrat and member of the Law School staff, Burr M. Jones, and allowed the contents to leak out to the press.[39]

President Adams suggested that Ely take the initiative of inviting the "fullest investigation" by the regents' committee, for this move would make it appear that Ely had nothing to hide.[40] On August 9 Ely wrote to each member of the committee. As far as the opinions expressed in his books, Ely commented, men would naturally differ, but the attacks on his private character were slander of the meanest sort. Nonetheless, Ely asked that both Wells and himself have "the privilege

[36] Kinley to Ely, Aug. 10, 1894, Ely MSS.
[37] O'Connell to [Kinley?], Aug. 16, 1894, Ely MSS.
[38] Klunk to Kinley, Aug. 17, 1894, Ely MSS.
[39] See Madison *Wisconsin State Journal*, Aug. 16, 1894.
[40] Adams to Ely, Aug. 6, 1894, Ely MSS.

of introducing . . . such evidence . . . as will leave no possible doubt as to the real truth."[41] On the other hand Kinley warned that Ely must "*Keep the investigation to Mr. Well's* [sic] *statements,* by all means."[42] By the date of the first scheduled hearing of the committee, August 20, Wells too had become aware that Ely had the upper hand. He saw that the specifics of his charges had been denied and realized that he had no concrete proof for them. Then the committee made the crucial decision that they would hear only evidence on Ely's teachings since his arrival at Wisconsin. Wells wrote each regent on the committee demanding an explanation. When he failed to receive satisfactory replies, Wells refused to attend the first hearing, maintaining he had to attend a meeting of the Board of Normal School Regents at Milwaukee on the same evening. Instead, he sent a long letter to the investigating committee declaring it had "disregarded the instructions of the board and undertaken an investigation not authorized by it."[43]

While Wells absented himself from the August 20 meeting, Ely, Kinley, and Burr Jones conferred with the committee behind closed doors for over thirty minutes. This and subsequent events suggest even more strongly that the committee was favorably disposed toward Ely from the start. Ely himself wrote a year later that the regents' committee "was as much a committee to try Wells as myself." The next night, August 21, the committee held its second meeting. Since Wells had no excuse this time, he attended, represented by George W. Bird, well-known Madison attorney. The law auditorium was packed with over 200 people, including professors and prominent townspeople. The meeting had all the elements of a courtroom drama, except that it was not clear who was on

41 Ely to Regents Chynoweth, Johnston, and Dale [before Aug. 9, 1894], Ely MSS.
42 Kinley to Ely, Aug. 2, 1894, Ely MSS.
43 Communication of Supt. Wells to Investigating Committee, Aug. 20, 1894, copy in Ely MSS.

trial—Ely or Wells. Chynoweth, Dale, and Johnston sat at the judge's rostrum, with Ely and his attorney on one side and Wells and his lawyer on the other.[44]

The two attorneys spent the first part of the hearing wrangling over the scope and procedure of the investigation. Bird insisted that Ely's writings must be examined, as they were the basis of his teachings. This issue was left temporarily unresolved. It was finally agreed that Wells' charges in the *Nation* would serve as the indictment against Ely. Furthermore, the committee decided to follow the rules of strict legal evidence. Burr Jones then read Ely's blanket denial of the entire list of charges that Wells had made in the *Nation*. The audience burst into applause and stomped their feet. The trial had almost turned into an Ely demonstration before Bird objected, claiming it appeared to be the "proceedings of a mob" rather than a court. Chynoweth warned against any further outbreaks.[45]

The attorneys and the committee then began to argue again over the submission of Ely's writings as evidence to substantiate Wells' charges. Obviously Wells hoped to prejudice the committee by proving, on the basis of his writings, that Ely was a socialist. Burr Jones objected that a few sentences from his works could easily be taken out of proper context. Regents Chynoweth and Johnston quickly showed that their sympathies were with Ely. Chynoweth humorously asked Wells if he planned to "inflict upon this committee a reading of these entire works." Regent Johnston took the issue seriously. "It seems to me it would be asking a great deal of this committee to purge the University library of every book which

---

[44] Madison *Democrat*, Aug. 21, 1894; Ely to Henry D. Lloyd, Dec. 24, 1895, Ely MSS; Madison *Wisconsin State Journal*, Aug. 21, 1894. Ely had had friendly correspondence with Regent Johnston prior to the incident. See Johnston to Ely, Jan. 19, May 3, 1894, Ely MSS.

[45] Transcript of the Ely Trial, pp. 19-20; Madison *Wisconsin State Journal*, Aug. 21, 1894. All information not noted concerning the hearing is from the Transcript of the Ely Trial.

might be subject to criticism," Johnston declared. "Vaillant, the anarchist . . . said that he got his views as an anarchist from Darwin and Spencer. Now we cannot exclude their books from the library here because some fellow says he got his anarchist ideas from them."[46] Although the proceedings give no indication of a definite decision by the committee, it appears that they planned to consider Ely's works as evidence only when they related to Wells' charges.

The committee finally took up the charge that Ely had participated in the local printing strike and had boycotted a local firm. W. A. Tracy testified that Ely had only suggested that it might be necessary to take his printing elsewhere because of the feelings of the members of the Christian Social Union. Ely had never, so far as Tracy knew, counseled the striking printers. The last witness, Thomas Reynolds of the local typographical union, testified that he did not know whether walking delegate Klunk had ever conferred with Ely or whether it was with some other professor.[47] The failure of Reynolds, from whom Wells apparently had obtained his information of Ely's participation, to identify Ely specifically weakened the factual basis of Wells' charges. And after a rather tangled legal foray between Bird and Chynoweth over proper questions for witnesses, Chynoweth even threatened to kick Bird out of the hearings.[48] The committee then adjourned.

The hostile attitude of the investigating committee and the audience toward Wells led him to refuse to attend the next meeting. Wells explained to the committee: "The demonstrations [of the 21st] that occurred and the sentiments of approval

[46] Transcript of the Ely Trial, p. 27.

[47] Apparently Klunk actually talked in Ely's seminar for a short time with H. H. Powers, an Ely student. Klunk and others assumed they were talking with Ely, for Powers and Ely both wore short beards and were of a similar appearance. See Transcript of the Ely Trial, pp. 68-70; Madison *Wisconsin State Journal*, Aug. 16, 1894; J. F. Klunk to Kinley, Aug. 17, 1894, Ely MSS.

[48] Madison *Wisconsin State Journal*, Aug. 21, 1894; Transcript of the Ely Trial, p. 73.

and disaproval [*sic*] expressed during the sitting, as well as the limitation the committee was disposed to place upon the scope of the inquiry . . . constrain me to concur . . . that an investigation conducted under such circumstances . . . would not be likely to subserve any useful purpose or to reach any satisfactory conclusion."[49] Though refusing to meet with the committee, he submitted a series of "damaging" quotations from the works of Ely.

When the committee reconvened the hearing on August 23 without the presence of Wells, they immediately reversed themselves and allowed the Ely forces to submit any sort of testimony they wished. Burr Jones read extracts from Ely's works showing that he had warned workers against violence and that he had a high admiration for the state. Jones concluded for the committee that a reading of Ely's works indicated "a growing tendency toward conservatism." David Kinley and Frederick Jackson Turner took the stand in Ely's behalf. Each stated that Ely was essentially conservative and that he was of the German Historical School of economists rather than a socialist or an anarchist. In the classroom, Turner said, Ely always allowed both sides of an issue to be fully explored and practiced the "look and see" method of investigation. Ely testified in his own behalf, stating that he had never favored strikes, though he did favor state ownership of natural monopolies.

President Adams, United States Commissioner of Labor Statistics Carroll D. Wright, Albert Shaw, Albion Small, President E. Benjamin Andrews of Brown University, and several others submitted long testimonials.[50] They impressed upon the regents that Ely had a high reputation in both academic and reform circles and that he was a great asset to the university. Wright typically wrote that if Ely's beliefs "make a man

[49] Communication of Supt. Wells to Investigating Committee, Aug. 23, 1894, copy in Ely MSS.

[50] Madison *Wisconsin State Journal*, Aug. 16, 1894.

responsible for strikes and violence, you and I ought to be arraigned along with Prof. Ely."[51] But the most crucial support came from President Adams, for in almost every other such case in the nineties the professor under attack failed to gain the support of his president. Adams admitted that he and Ely came to "different conclusions" on economic questions but wrote: "In regard to that I am quite indifferent."[52] The *Wisconsin State Journal* reported that the hearing closed almost as "an Ely demonstration." As one wag caustically put it, "All's well that ends Wells!"[53]

No one doubted, not even Wells, that the committee would completely vindicate Ely. However, the academic freedom portion of the committee statement was apparently an afterthought. Two days after the hearing, John M. Olin, formerly of the university staff, suggested the idea to Regent George H. Noyes. Not only should the regents exonerate Ely, Olin wrote, but they should use this event to promote the university. "If the committee should bring in a report to the effect that the policy of this University was to give to the instructors or professors, great liberty in teaching what they believe to be the truth on the living questions of the day, such a report, would, I believe, be an excellent advertisement for the institution."[54] The suggestion was passed on to the committee, and President Adams prepared the statement.[55] After clearing Ely of a list of charges, the board declared that "in

[51] Wright to Charles K. Adams, Aug. 11, 1894, in Transcript of the Ely Trial.

[52] Adams to Ely, July 23, 1894, Ely MSS.

[53] Madison *Wisconsin State Journal*, Aug. 24, 1894.

[54] Olin to Noyes, Aug. 25, 1894, quoted in Curti and Carstensen, *University of Wisconsin*, I, 524.

[55] Some doubt surrounds the authorship of the statement. Both Chynoweth and Johnston have been credited as the authors. However, Ely and Balthasar H. Meyer claimed that Adams had told them that he wrote the statement. See Ely to Edwin S. Witte, June 5, 1942, Ely MSS; Ely to W. S. Kies, June 8, 1942, Balthasar H. Meyer to Merle Curti and Vernon Carstensen, April 7, 1949, Herfurth MSS, State Historical Society of Wisconsin, Madison.

all lines of academic investigation it is of the utmost importance that the investigator should be absolutely free to follow the indications of the truth wherever they may lead. Whatever may be the limitations which trammel inquiry elsewhere we believe the great University of Wisconsin should ever encourage that continual and fearless sifting and winnowing by which alone the truth can be found."[56]

The exoneration of Ely and the famous statement of academic freedom resulted, then, from factors not bearing on the principle at stake. From the beginning Wells had not been popular with his fellow regents, had proved a poor strategist, and had incurred the animosity of the Madison newspapers. Indicative of his weak position to carry on the battle with Ely was the refusal of the Democrats to renominate him for 1894. Even the *Nation* reluctantly withdrew its charges.[57] The very fact that the regents called a hearing differentiated the Ely case from similar controversies. At the same time Ely skirted the vital issue of academic freedom. Ely's own stature surely contributed to the outcome. His colleagues at Wisconsin, Turner and Scott, and his former students, Shaw, Small, Kinley, Frederic C. Howe, Charles Lee Smith, and others lent the full support of their own positions to Ely. In fact, almost all the leaders of the social sciences sprang to his defense, including economists E. R. A. Seligman, Frank Taussig, John Bates Clark, and even the conservative Charles Dunbar. Only Albert Bushnell Hart, Harvard historian, who was vacationing in Europe, remained out of touch with the overwhelming favor of academic opinion to Ely. Hart had precipitantly condemned Ely in a published letter, but upon his return to the country, he profusely apologized.[58] Ely also had the support

[56] Statement signed by H. W. Chynoweth, John Johnston, H. B. Dale to the Honorable, the Board of Regents of the University of Wisconsin, Sept. 18, 1894, copy in Ely MSS. The statement is reprinted in part in Ely, *Ground Under Our Feet*, p. 232.

[57] Jerome H. Raymond to Ely, Sept. 7, 1894, Ely MSS; *Nation*, LIX (Aug. 30, 1894), 151.

[58] See Seligman to Ely, Aug. 13, 1894, Taussig to Ely, Aug. 23, 1894,

of highly respected journals such as the *Review of Reviews,* *Congregationalist, Dial,* and *Outlook,* as well as the Madison and Milwaukee newspapers. During the ordeal both George Herron and George Gates sent Ely encouragement. Gates even promised him a position at Iowa College in the event that Ely were dismissed at Wisconsin. They also asked Ely to become a nominal editor of the *Kingdom,* a journal of Christian sociology which they had set up to replace the *Northwestern Congregationalist.* Gates explained that no work would be required on Ely's part and that they only wanted to add his name to lend prestige to the reform organ. Ely refused. He likewise turned down invitations by the Federated Trades Council to speak on Labor Day, September 3, at Madison, and to write an article for a labor journal.[59]

In an article prepared for the October *Forum* at the request of the editor, Walter Hines Page,[60] and composed during the crisis, Ely emphasized his conservatism. "As far as my general social philosophy is concerned," Ely wrote, ". . . I am a conservative rather than a radical, and in the strict sense of the term an aristocrat rather than a democrat; but when I use the word 'aristocrat,' I have in mind of course not a legal aristocracy, but a natural aristocracy . . . an aristocracy which lives for the fulfillment for special service."[61] He rejected all panaceas for social evils and noted that since he regarded the state as a divine institution, he obviously was not an anarchist. He admitted that the difficulties of public ownership were vast

Clark to Ely, Aug. 27, 1894, W. J. Ashley to Ely, Aug. 23, 1894, Ely MSS; Madison *Democrat,* Aug. 26, Sept. 14, 1894; Hart to Ely, Sept. 7, 1894, Ely MSS.
59 Gates to Ely, Aug. 14, Sept. 18, 29, 1894, John O'Connell to Ely, Aug. 6, 1894, A. J. Arkin to Ely, Aug. 11, 1894, Ely MSS.
60 Page to Ely, Aug. 20, 1894, Ely MSS.
61 Ely, "Fundamental Beliefs in My Social Philosophy," p. 183. That Ely was growing decidedly more conservative was a common student opinion. See James Barbour to E. A. Ross, Feb. 7, 1896, Ross MSS, State Historical Society of Wisconsin, Madison.

and needed more study. An improvement of public morality
and civil service reform would be necessary steps for the public
ownership of natural monopolies. And in all cases, the private
owners must be paid the full amount of their investment.

With respect to labor organizations his views differed
markedly from those of 1886, when the *Labor Movement* appeared. Strikes, Ely wrote, could not be tolerated against railroads, telegraphs, gasworks, or any concern in which the
public welfare was dependent. Although he had rather
severely castigated the Pullman experiment in 1885, the strike
of 1894, he wrote, "is barbarism and not civilization. We
should not . . . allow a discussion of abstract rights to interfere with determined action which will prevent the recurrence
of events like those referred to, which are nothing less than a
national disgrace and humiliation."[62] The use of the injunction
in the Pullman strike, Ely wrote, was a step in the right
direction. His ringing rhetoric, which sounded so much like
that in the *Labor Movement*, now applied the role of villain
to organized labor.

The years 1894 and 1895 were trying ones for Ely. They
initiated several years in which he put himself through an
agonizing reassessment of his prior achievements. The humil-
iating trial for economic heresy, and perhaps his reaching the
middle age of forty, touched off his self-reappraisal. Even
seven years after the trial he wrote Ross that "I have not, myself, entirely gotten over the effects of the unjust attacks upon
me six years ago."[63] Certainly the dismissal of two of his
favorite students—Commons and Bemis—from their posts added to his self-concern.

The crowning blow came in January, 1895, when the
Chautauqua unexpectedly dropped him from their Summer
School staff. Ely was stunned. Bishop John H. Vincent had
defended him the previous summer and Ely understood that

[62] Ely, "Fundamental Beliefs in My Social Philosophy," p. 174.
[63] Ely to Ross, March 19, 1901, Ross MSS.

his position was a permanent one. He had been with Chautauqua for seven years, had even purchased two lots near the site, and had written his popular textbook for the extension division. While William Rainey Harper admitted some social science might be offered by E. R. L. Gould of Johns Hopkins, he weakly insisted that Ely had been dropped because of the need of more variety in the curriculum. Ely had good reason to suspect that a radical image and his open sympathies with Bemis, who just been fired by Harper at Chicago, lurked behind the decision.[64]

In August of 1895 Ely explained in detail his personal concern with such a radical image to Hamilton W. Mabie, associate editor of the *Outlook*. "Suppose if you should become known as a radical you would lose your position on the 'Outlook,' and on account of alleged radicalism you could never secure any other position. Would you not under these circumstances feel a little sensitive about the epithet 'radical'? You see what it can do in the case of Professor Bemis." He closed with a thinly disguised effort to excuse himself of any personal hypocrisy. "With all my faults," he wrote Mabie, "I do not think that anyone has ever accused me of cowardice. If I were a radical or a socialist, I trust I should have grace enough to say so, and to take the consequences."[65] Nonetheless, the central message remained clear. One took serious risks when his ideas or behavior led to such name calling, even when completely undeserved.

From 1894 to 1899 Ely withdrew practically all connections with activist reform organizations. In 1895 he refused for a second time to address Herron's retreat at Iowa College and continued to ignore the entreaties of Gates to become an editor of the *Kingdom*. He turned down numerous invitations to give addresses, attend meetings, serve as an officer, and

[64] Ely to Bemis, Jan. 12, 1895, Harper to Ely, Jan. 25, Feb. 23, 1895, Vincent to Ely, Feb. 16, 27, 1895, Ely to Vincent, March 14, 1895, Ely to Harper, Aug. 17, 1895, Ely MSS.
[65] Ely to Mabie, Aug. 24, 1895, Ely MSS.

write articles for a host of reform organizations, including the National League for Promoting Public Ownership of Monopolies, to which several former students and many old friends belonged. In one reform meeting that he did attend, the Chicago Conference on Trusts (1899), he made it clear that he stood among the "conservative element."[66]

After having shown an early interest and support for the Alliance movement, by the 1896 presidential election he refused to become publicly involved in the controversial campaign. Albert Shaw, perhaps Ely's closest advisor, invited him to write an article analyzing the issues for the campaign because Shaw believed Ely could sway thousands of votes. But Ely refused. While he privately deplored the free silver plank of the Democrats as a "cowbird" of the reform movement, he was determined to take no public stand.[67] Edward H. Bemis remorsefully wrote to Ely in 1899 a common complaint of reformers: "I wish you might occasionally return to your practice of years ago of writing advanced articles of social reform in the most popular magazines like the Forum and Harpers. The liberal movement has gained such headway that I don't want you to lose your leadership in it.[68]

Unknown to Bemis and other reformers, Ely had already decided to concentrate on "scientific" investigations in the future rather than "popular" writing. Soon after his trial for heresy, Ely wrote President Adams explaining that he planned to discontinue his "habit of publication" for a few years. Adams agreed to the extent that the time had come for Ely "to go into something perhaps a little more of the nature of investiga-

[66] See W. D. P. Bliss to Ely, Sept. 15, Oct. 25, 1899, H. H. Swain to Ely, March 17, 1898, George H. Shibley to Ely, Dec. 31, 1897, Frank Parsons to Ely, March 18, 1898, Ely to H. B. Fay, Nov. 24, 1897, Ely MSS; Ely, *Monopolies and Trusts* (New York: Macmillan, 1900), p. 264.
[67] Shaw to Ely, Oct. 3, 23, 1896, Ely MSS. Ely also refused to write a work on the "money crisis," and at least one person interpreted Ely's silence to mean he favored free silver. See Callaghan & Co. to Ely, Jan. 8, 1895, K. P. Woods to Ely, Sept. 13, 1896, Ely MSS.
[68] Bemis to Ely, Aug. 11, 1899, Ely MSS.

tion."[69] The less than eulogistic implication by Adams concerning Ely's past work stung his pride. "I have been," Ely explained to David Kinley, ". . . plundered, and have not received credit for my original contributions to the science of economics, including public finance."[70] He even accused his former students, like Kinley, of failure to recognize his past achievements. He wrote numerous letters to others expressing a similar concern with a "popularistic" image in economics.

Nonetheless, the criticism served to confirm his resolve to write a magnum opus that would insure his due recognition among fellow economists. He planned a multivolume study on the "Distribution of Wealth," which he called "a system of economic philosophy." In the first volume, *Monopolies and Trusts,* published in 1900, he believed that he had made a significant contribution in defining monopoly and its causes. He frequently claimed he had formulated a "new and fundamental law of monopoly price."[71] Ely explained these continual references to the originality and scientific nature of his theories to David Kinley. "What I want to do is to put certain stakes around what I claim as my own. I feel that I have not sufficiently asserted my claims heretofore."[72] He continually repeated the same refrain to his friends in 1899-1900. Although the new work fell far short of establishing Ely as a major economic theorist, it clearly reflected a new Ely, one who was concerned more with his reputation as an academician than as an evangelist to the American public.

Ely had always walked a tightrope between a reputation resting on his ethical preachments to public opinion and one resulting from studies directed at his fellow economists. The very reason for Ely's popular appeal, the *Review of Reviews* theorized, resulted from his preaching the "truths

[69] Adams to Ely, Sept. 19, 1894, Ely MSS.
[70] Ely to Kinley, Sept. 4, 1899, Ely MSS.
[71]Ely, "A Decade of Economic Theory," *Annals of the American Academy of Political and Social Science,* XV (Jan., 1900), 107.
[72] Ely to Kinley, Sept. 4, 1899, Ely MSS.

which are instinctively believed by the mass of men whose instruction in political economy has come from witnessing present events rather than reading books." By voicing the "instinctive beliefs of our times" Ely's work had a "vitality" lacking in the "work of most of his professorial contemporaries."[73] Earlier, in 1888, Ely vigorously defended his effort to reach a popular audience. While his "learned friends" thought that a "university professor ought not to write anything . . . popular in form or style," Ely felt that this was a "mistaken view of the functions of our higher institutions of learning, for I believe that . . . they ought to . . . elevate the masses, and to guide and direct their thought."[74]

The shift in Ely's attitude concerning the role of the economist became almost complete by 1900. He now frowned on the efforts of economists to reach the general public. When he became editor of a new social science series for Macmillan, he opposed the idea of titling the series "The Citizens Library" because the term "citizen" implied that the books lacked a scientific approach.[75] In an address before the American Academy of Political and Social Science at Philadelphia in December, 1899, he praised the efforts of economists to discover large theories that could be employed deductively. At the end of the paper he said: "I think it may be said that the theoretical work of the decade has as a rule lacked sufficient boldness. We have been too timid, and have in some cases spent much time in petty refinements while essentials have been overlooked."[76] Strange words indeed for the economist who, only a few years before, vehemently decried the efforts of the classicists to formulate general theories.

Beginning in 1899 Ely also attempted to reestablish his professional ties. After six years of aloofness from the American Economic Association he welcomed the opportunity to read

[73] Review of Ely, *Outlines of Economics*, p. 606.
[74] Ely, *Problems of To-day*, p. vii.
[75] Ely to John H. Finley, Nov. 3, 1899, Ely MSS.
[76] Ely, "A Decade of Economic Theory," p. 111.

a paper on Senior's "Theory of Monopoly" and was even elected president for 1900-1901. In the fall of 1899 he made an extended tour of eastern colleges, renewing acquaintances with all the major figures in economics. It was no secret that Ely was seeking to return to the East. In the early nineties Ely had refused repeated invitations from J. Laurence Laughlin, University of Chicago classicist, to address the Political Economy Club. But in 1899 he ingratiatingly accepted a request to speak, while carefully explaining that the paper was "not at all a popular one, but strictly scientific." He also asked Laughlin to contribute a work to the Macmillan series and praised Laughlin's money theories at the Philadelphia meeting of the American Academy of Political and Social Science in 1899.[77]

The story of Ely's declining reform zeal disclosed a deeper problem of the intellectual as a reformer. That was the inability or unwillingness of the middle-class intellectual to forge an alliance with farmer-labor reformers. Almost instinctively he rebelled against close identification with lower classes. When he did attempt to bridge the gap, he found himself in the unenviable position of losing his stature and identity in the academic as well as the larger intellectual community of the late nineteenth century. The intellectuals of the era, still clustered in the Northeast, were largely genteel reformers. Ely shared their common suspicion of, if not violent hostility toward, the populistic democracy which had become ascendant in American political life since at least the age of Jackson. It was the same uncultured farmers, laborers, and *nouveau riche* who had corrupted the American politics of the Gilded Age. The populistic majority had little respect for and paid small

[77] Ely to Charles H. Hull, Oct. 2, 1899, David Kinley to Ely, Feb. 11, 1899, J. W. Jenks to Ely, Feb. 14, 1899, Albert Shaw to Ely, Feb. 17, 1900, Laughlin to Ely, Dec. 10, 1892, Ely to Hamilton W. Mabie, Aug. 24, 1895, Ely to Laughlin, Oct. 8, 1899, Laughlin to Ely, Jan. 1, 1900, Ely MSS. Ely remained hostile toward both Laughlin and Harper as late as December, 1897. See Harper to Ely, Nov. 29, Dec. 6, 1897, Ely MSS.

deference to the intellectual community. Consequently the overriding concern of most of the intellectuals was not social and economic problems, but civil service reform. They were virtually obsessed with the idea of restoring government to an elite corps of trained gentlemen.

Thus the Ely suggestions for deeper social and economic reform appeared to many of the intellectuals of the period as pandering to the very groups which threatened their security. Ely seemed to be selling out his class. From the beginning of his career he incurred the animosity of the champion of the genteel reformers, E. L. Godkin, editor of the *Nation*. The opposition of Godkin was symptomatic of the suspicion under which Ely was held. Although he frequently attempted to show that he advocated no fundamental changes in the competitive order and that he recognized the superiority of intellect, the emotion of his rhetoric and his specific reform suggestions seemed to betray an unpardonable bias for the anti-intellectual masses. Ely became increasingly aware during the nineties that his status as an academician was being jeopardized by his activism in reforms beneficial to farmers and laborers. To hold his place in the larger intellectual community, he felt forced to retire behind the ivy-covered walls of academia.

Chapter Seven

A BAROMETER OF
WISCONSIN PROGRESSIVISM

NIGHT AFTER NIGHT in August of 1903, Richard Ely suffered
from enervating insomnia, but Madison's exhausting heat and
humidity had little to do with his deep anxieties and sleep-
less nights. He was forty-nine years old, and yet recognition
as a top economic theorist still eluded him. Charles J. Bullock,
former student and close friend, had recently explained that
he had decided not to review Ely's latest work, *Studies in the
Evolution of an Industrial Society,* because he could not do
so favorably. Ely had pinned so many hopes on the book;
he sincerely felt that finally he had made an enduring contribution to the science of economics. "Faithful are the wounds
of friends." Most upsetting of all, Bullock "could not help
reaching his conclusions— . . . he wanted to think well of it
and could not—and I hoped for so much on account of the
book."[1]

Lack of success in gaining recognition as a theorist led
Ely to divert increasing attention to his personal affairs and

academic leadership. Except for textbook revision, he did not write another book until 1914. He continued his penchant for pioneering in new fields, especially by recognizing and exploiting the potentials of obtaining research funds from wealthy patrons. He gathered the money for the monumental labor history project of John R. Commons, secured the appointment of Edward A. Ross in sociology, and initiated massive studies in land economics and public utilities. He was indeed a captain of organized and cooperative research. "Dr. Ely never let any modern invention go unnoticed," Professor Carl Russell Fish said in 1925. "I think he was the first scholar in America to surround himself with staffs of secretaries, filin[g]-systems, desk telephones, statistical research, and so forth . . . the first scholar in America to be organized like a business man."[2] His younger disciples, of which there continued to be many in the twentieth century, felt the same urge to strike out to new frontiers of knowledge and put their special skills to practical use in benefiting mankind. The Wisconsin Progressive Movement embodied the Ely formulas of research and experimentation and owed much to his direct inspiration.

Ely could take some consolation in the growing popularity of his textbooks. His lucid style, graphic illustrations, and sympathies for the underprivileged helped them outdistance all rivals in both the high school and college fields. *An Introduction to Political Economy* (1889) sold over 30,000 copies by 1904, when it was revised for high school use by Ely protégé George Ray Wicker as *Elementary Principles of Economics.* Revised again in 1923 by Samuel J. Brandenburg, it probably outsold all competitors combined until well into the thirties. In 1893 Ely issued a college edition, *Outlines of Economics,* which was somewhat more technical

[1]Ely to George Ray Wicker, Aug. 25, 1903, Ely MSS, State Historical Society of Wisconsin, Madison.

[2] Fish, Address at Ely Farewell Dinner, Grace Church, Madison, Sept. 21, 1925, copy in Ely MSS.

than the previous edition because of an elaborate presentation of the marginal utility doctrine. Revised seven times by 1937, the *Outlines* became the most popular economics text in the country, with more than 350,000 copies sold between the world wars. It was also translated into several foreign languages. John Finley, editor of the New York *Times*, claimed that Ely had sold nearly a million copies of textbooks by 1937, next in the sales in economic works to Adam Smith's *Wealth of Nations*. Used in over 250 colleges and universities in the twenties, Ely enjoyed book royalties that averaged almost $7,000 per year.[3]

Ely's reputation probably remained the major attraction of the *Outlines*, though he added three important collaborators who were not "mere imitators" or "cloistered academicians." Each made valuable contributions to economic theory and practice. The three editions of 1908, 1916, and 1923, in which Thomas S. Adams, Allyn A. Young, and Max O. Lorenz participated, radically altered the original *Outlines* of 1893. In most of the revised editions Ely handled only the historical chapters and those on public expenditures. Adams wrote chapters on public finance and labor, and Young, who took his degree under Ely, handled the chapters on value, money and banking, and distribution. Lorenz, another Ely student, added an important contribution to technique with a curve designed to measure the inequality of the distribution of income or of wealth. Despite the growing conservatism of Ely and the carefully measured views of his collaborators, the *Outlines* continued to embody the most progressive views of any text in the field.[4]

[3] Joseph Dorfman, *The Economic Mind in American Civilization*, IV-V (New York: Viking, 1959), 211; [Finley], "Still Going Strong," New York *Times*, Oct. 7, 1937, p. 26; "Ely: Outlines of Economics," brochure of Macmillan Company, 1926, copy in Ely MSS; Ely to William S. Kies, Sept. 8, 1939, A. H. Nelson to Ely, Oct. 5, 1927, Ely MSS. See also John Maynard Keynes to Henry C. Taylor, Feb. 16, 1944, copy in Ely MSS.
[4] See chap. VIII of Dorfman, *The Economic Mind in American Civilization*, IV-V, for an evaluation of Adams, Young, and Lorenz.

The first few years of the new century were probably the most frustrating for Ely of his entire career. His earlier rapport with President Charles Kendall Adams had become strained, partly because Ely's ambitions for his School of Economics, Political Science and History exceeded the resources extended by the university. The two men broke completely in 1900 when Adams secured the reorganization of Ely's school by establishing new Schools of Commerce and History. Ely approved the new School of History with Frederick Jackson Turner as director, but he angrily opposed the Commerce School headed by William A. Scott. He mistrusted Scott and argued that commerce was an integral part of economics. But above all, personal resentment over the curtailment of his own power led him to fight a running battle with the administration for several years. Conditions failed to improve when, early in 1900, Edward A. Birge, due to the illness of Adams, became acting president. During the interim period from 1900 to 1903, when Charles R. Van Hise was selected for the presidency, the university operated without aggressive or effective leadership.[5]

Disgusted, Ely attempted to secure a position at Harvard or Johns Hopkins University. To promote his candidacy at Hopkins and to heal the deep wounds of 1892, he wrote the ailing Herbert Baxter Adams. Adams, on his deathbed, was willing to let "bygones be bygones." Ely hired Thomas S. Adams, a Hopkins Ph.D., as an assistant professor, the first appointment from outside the university since Ely and Scott came to Wisconsin. He encouraged friends to write President Ira Remsen and, in the fall of 1901, he received an invitation to address a memorial service for the deceased Herbert B. Adams. Ely immediately concluded that Hopkins officials wanted to look him over. In his address, which Albert Shaw's *Review of Reviews* conveniently published in

---

[5] See Ely to Balthasar Meyer, April 1, 1901, Ely to Birge, March 7, 1902, Ely MSS; Ely, "The School of Economics and Political Science, 1900-1902, for the Report of the President" [Oct., 1902], Ely MSS.

advance, Ely gave unstinted praise to the educational contributions of his former colleague. The alumni and old friends in Baltimore "cordially" received him, he reported, and several spoke to Remsen on the subject of his employment at Hopkins. But the call never came, possibly because both Edwin R. A. Seligman and John Bates Clark, though writing Remsen favorable letters, explained to Ely that they also "felt bound in justice" to support the candidacy of Jacob Hollander, an assistant at Hopkins. During the same period, Ely's efforts to obtain a post at Harvard failed. Apparently Harvard decided to hire two younger economists, one of them ironically Charles J. Bullock, an Ely Ph.D. at Wisconsin.[6]

Beginning in 1899 Ely had also attempted to obtain a position as a special investigator of public finances for the United States government. At Madison he had acquired the friendship of several of the prominent Stalwart Republicans, including Senator John C. Spooner. And for the first time in his career he began to take a minor role in local politics, being elected town supervisor in 1900. On several occasions he had explained to Spooner the desirability of an appointment as a special investigator, noting that government finances were handled unscientifically and that several other scholars had obtained similar posts. In the spring of 1902 Spooner and Ely visited President Theodore Roosevelt, who "cordially" endorsed a plan for a special investigation of public finances. Spooner then obtained an amendment to the Sundry Civil bill asking for an initial appropriation of $4,000, only to see it killed in a conference committee by "Uncle Joe" Cannon, speaker of the House of Representatives. Ely found it difficult to understand why the "most influential senator in

[6] Ely to Albert Shaw, Jan. 12, 1901, Ely to H. B. Adams, Feb. 7, 1901, Adams to Ely, Feb. 12, 1901, Ely to John H. Finley, Sept. 11, 1901, Ely to Bullock, May 30, 1901, David Kinley to Ely, Nov. 1, 1901, Ely MSS; Ely, "Herbert B. Adams: A Sketch," *Review of Reviews*, XXIV (Sept., 1901), 321-323; Ely to Kinley, March 3, 1902, Seligman to Ely, Jan. 26, 1902, Clark to Ely, Feb. 8, 1902, Ely to William F. Willoughby, Jan. 30, 1901, Ely to Bullock, May 15, 1903, Ely MSS.

the United States" had been unable to obtain approval of the amendment.[7]

In August, 1902, Albert Shaw, a personal adviser to Roosevelt, met with the President at Oyster Bay and suggested the possibility of appointing Ely as an assistant secretary of the Treasury. Roosevelt was "delighted" with the prospect, provided that political approval would be forthcoming from Wisconsin. The President further promised to write Spooner personally. After the conference between Shaw and Roosevelt, Ely, against the advice of Shaw, disclosed the contents of the meeting to Spooner, perhaps giving the senator the impression that Ely was working outside normal political channels. Rather than concentrating his efforts on winning the support of local politicians and allowing the possible appointment to appear to originate in Wisconsin, Ely asked Senator Jonathan P. Dolliver of Iowa, one of his admirers, along with several college professors, to write Spooner in his behalf. No doubt Ely's overaggressiveness offended Spooner, for he failed to obtain the appointment.[8]

In addition to his frustrated efforts to obtain a post at another university or an appointment with the federal government, Ely faced grievous personal problems. After the birth of Anna in 1897 Mrs. Ely fell seriously ill from "nervous prostration." Failing to recover at the Palmyra Sanitarium near Madison, she went to the Johns Hopkins University Hospital in February, 1902. Immediately operated upon for female disorders, she soon showed improvement, though she remained an invalid for more than three years. Also, from

[7] Ely to Leslie Burd, March 14, 1902, Ely MSS; Ely, *Ground Under Our Feet: An Autobiography* (New York: Macmillan, 1938), p. 214; Ely to Albert Shaw, July 9, 1902, Ely to Spooner, Jan. 19, 1901, Spooner to Ely, May 10, 1902, Ely to Spooner, June 28, 1902, Ely MSS.

[8] Shaw to Ely, Aug. 21, 1902, Ely to Spooner, Aug. 25, 1902, Shaw to Ely, Sept. 23, 1902, Ely to Spooner, Aug. 30, 1902, Ely to Shaw, Sept. 25, 1902, Ely to Thomas S. Adams, Dec. 16, 1908, Ely MSS.

1900 to her death in 1923, she had painful arthritis. Because of their mother's illnesses and their father's heavy pace of work, the Ely children suffered from inattention. Ely wanted them to have all the educational advantages available. He sent his eldest son, Richard, to Phillips Exeter Academy and later to Harvard. After graduation, Richard tried private business for a time, eventually obtained a law degree at Wisconsin, and worked for the Virginia Railroad Commission before taking a post with the Federal Trade Commission. His second son, John, rebelled against parental discipline and caused the family much grief. Ely sent him to the Culver Military Academy, where he was dismissed, and then to a German school, where he was similarly discharged. Later John attended Harvard for a short time, fought in World War I, and then entered private business. Anna went to two European schools before taking up economics at Wisconsin.[9]

Ely's financial plight was desperate. In 1903 while attending Phillips Exeter Academy, Richard burned his arm and extensive skin grafts were required. In addition to the huge medical bills accumulated in 1901 and 1902, Ely had neglected to pay the family's personal physician since 1893, owing over $1,000. Ely attempted to supplement his income by requesting an advance from Macmillan, making a western lecture tour for the University Association of Chicago, and selling his lots on University Heights and at Chautauqua. Still short of funds, he finally decided to sacrifice his magnificent collection of labor materials. Assembled over the twenty years at Johns Hopkins and Wisconsin, and at con-

[9] See especially Ely to George Ray Wicker, May 17, 1901, Louis R. Head to Ely, Jan. 4, 1902, Ely to L. H. Prince, Feb. 6, 1902, Benjamin A. Schenck to Ely, May 8, 1902, Ely to Frederic C. Howe, Oct. 10, 1903, Ely to Charles R. Van Hise, Feb. 12, 1906, L. R. Gignillat to Ely, Dec. 5, 1911, Ely to John T. A. Ely, Oct. 18, 1912, Leslie Bissel to Ely, Oct. 28, 1912, Ely to Bissell, Dec. 26, 1912, Ely to Mrs. H. K. W. Bent, July 27, 1914, Ely MSS.

siderable personal expense, it contained some 550 bound volumes, plus numerous periodicals. Trying first the Library of Congress, Ely eventually settled on the richly endowed John Crerar Library in Chicago, for a net price of $12,500. The sale temporarily alleviated his financial difficulties.[10]

The library sale allowed Ely to begin an active career in real estate. In the late nineteenth century he had speculated on a small scale in vacant lots at Chautauqua and in Madison. Between 1902 and 1914 he organized five different realty companies and was president of two. He founded the Marburg Company, which built a $50,000 business block on State Street in Madison. His largest venture, the Madison Park Corporation in Charlottesville, Virginia, purchased 450 acres, built roads, sold lots, and had a capitalization of $100,000. He also owned property in the state of Washington, in Canada, and in northern Wisconsin. Altogether, he estimated that he had bought and sold over one hundred pieces of property. Not surprisingly he was sometimes criticized for his extra-university activities and even occasionally found himself a target for large charity contributions. Despite the scope of his activity, his personal investments probably never totaled over $50,000. Most of the capital in his projects came from wealthy friends and small investors.[11]

Ironically, shortly after the sale of his labor library, Ely, in one of his most successful academic entrepreneurial ventures, secured large funds for the study of American labor history. Since the publication of the *Labor Movement* in

[10] Ely to Davis R. Dewey, June 17, 1902, Dewey to Ely, June 24, 1902, Louis R. Head to Ely, Feb. 12, 1902, Ely to George Brett, May 3, 1901, J. F. Hunt to Ely, May 1, 1901, Ely to E. A. Birge, Dec. 18, 1901, Ely to Herbert Putnam, May 17, 1902, Ely to Albion Small, May 29, 1902, Ely to David Kinley, Nov. 8, 1902, Ely to Peabody, Houghteling & Co., Dec. 16, 1902, Ely MSS.

[11] For a summary of Ely's business experience, see "Memo, Concerning the Activity of Richard T. Ely" [1920?], Ely MSS. Internal evidence indicates the memo was written probably not later than 1914.

1886, he often talked of doing a thorough and systematic labor history, but he was aware of the tremendous cost and time needed to secure source materials. At the same time he had always held a special fondness for his wayfaring former graduate student, John R. Commons. Commons, along with Edward H. Bemis, had lost academic posts during the turbulent nineties, but Ely had assisted them in obtaining work with various private and public agencies. He apparently persuaded Mayor Tom L. Johnson of Cleveland to hire Bemis as head of the city's waterworks and as a general adviser on municipal government. Commons had served on the famous Industrial Commission and had worked in the field of labor arbitration and conciliation for the National Civic Federation. In 1902 Commons met Carroll D. Wright, who was in charge of the Carnegie Foundation funds, and explained Ely's hope of doing a labor study. Ely immediately submitted a plan calling for a subsidy of $10,000 and the use of three investigators for three years.[12]

Although the plan received the verbal endorsement of Wright, Ely was impatient for a final decision and suspected that Wright favored granting the funds to Jacob Hollander of Johns Hopkins. He decided to raise the funds from private sources. Robert Hunter, wealthy New Yorker and friend of Commons, assisted in soliciting over $30,000; $10,000 came from V. Everit Macy and, after several conferences with Ely, also from Stanley McCormick of Chicago. Ely used his full weight to obtain the appointment of Commons at Wisconsin. Despite Commons' age of forty-three and his radical reputation, Ely succeeded by promising to raise two-thirds of Commons' $3,000 salary from private sources and by securing eloquent testimonials from prominent economists and businessmen. In 1904 Ely incorporated the American Bureau of Industrial Research with himself and Commons as co-

[12] Johnson to Ely, April 13, 1901, Commons to Ely, March 17 [1902], Ely to David Kinley, April 26, 1902, Ely MSS.

directors and with an advisory board of John Bates Clark, Albert Shaw, and Henry W. Farnam of Yale. Eventually the bureau obtained substantial funds from the Carnegie Foundation.[13]

Commons supervised the research and editing of labor documents, while Ely handled most of the administration of the bureau. Assisted by several graduate students, Commons scoured the country in search of labor manuscripts, eventually obtaining a collection second to none in the country. Through old friendships Ely helped to acquire several personal collections, including that of Henry Demarest Lloyd. In 1906 Ely organized the American Association for Labor Legislation, with himself as the first president. As part of an international body, the association gathered labor statistics and promoted uniform labor legislation. At the second annual meeting of the association, held at Madison in 1907 in conjunction with the American Economic Association, Ely presented as his presidential address, "Economic Theory and Labor Legislation." The paper was the first time since the early nineties that he had publicly addressed himself directly to labor problems.[14]

Although Ely was much less the propagandist in 1907, his theoretical position on labor had shifted little since the publication of the *Labor Movement* twenty-one years earlier. In part Ely was caught up in the spirit of the Progressive Era and had reverted to a prolabor position stronger than that which he had taken in the midnineties. In the late nineteenth

[13] Ely to Commons, June 16, 22, 1903, Ely to Hunter, Dec. 14, 1903, McCormick to Ely, Jan. 27, 1904, Ely to Commons, Dec. 16, 1903, Ely MSS.

[14] See Ely, "Additional Statement . . . in the Matter of Professor John R. Commons," April 1, 1909, Ely MSS; Program of First Annual Meeting of American Association for Labor Legislation, Dec. 30, 1907, in Ely MSS. The international organization was founded at the Paris Exposition in 1901 with a permanent bureau at Basel, Switzerland. See Ely, "Economic Theory and Labor Legislation," *Publications of the American Economic Association*, 3d ser., IX (1908), 149-151.

century, he said, economic popularizers had used the population theory of Malthus and the wage fund theory to oppose all labor laws. But since the founding of the American Economic Association in 1885 a "surprising change in public opinion" toward labor legislation had occurred. Practically all economists now recognized a considerable elasticity in the wage fund and were willing to sacrifice possible increases in capital for the future in order to improve the temporary lot of the working class. "No theory of wages now widely accepted by economists in this and other lands [exists] which in itself need produce opposition to labor legislation."[15] The state should regulate contracts when they promoted positive liberty. Ely attacked the Supreme Court for striking down a New York law regulating the hours of bakers. For the decision, he declared, represented the antiquated and negative conception of liberty. By 1908 the climate of public opinion had almost caught up with Ely's views. "I shall try to use part of it in my message this year," President Roosevelt wrote.[16] And Oliver Wendell Holmes, Jr., one of the four dissenting justices in the bakers' case, felt that he and Ely were in substantial agreement on defining liberty, in that the police power of the state could be used to promote the public health of the worker.[17]

Unfortunately Ely's academic empire building and zeal to get fast results for the bureau clashed with the slower, methodical methods of Commons. The conflict, which extended over three years, became incredibly complicated. Ely complained that Commons, who he felt had the business sense of a "new born babe," kept inadequate expense accounts and worked far too slowly. Bitter accusations of personal profiteering resulted because of a misunderstanding on the anticipated royalties of the eleven-volume *A Documentary*

15 Ely, "Economic Theory and Labor Legislation," p. 134.
16 Roosevelt to Ely, Oct. 26, 1908, Ely MSS.
17 Holmes to Ely, Oct. 20, 1908, Ely MSS.

History of Industrial Society (1910-1911). The personal hostility became so intense in 1908 that Ely refused to shake hands with his former protégé. He privately informed staff members and friends on other campuses that Commons should look elsewhere for work and even tried to find him another job. Despite their differences, however, Ely defended Commons from charges of labor partisanship before the university president and the regents. Apparently Ely never felt disposed to try to force Commons out, possibly because Commons had considerable support from within and outside the university. In 1909 President Van Hise adroitly intervened and was able to obtain a general agreement on the issues as well as to install himself as arbiter for all future disputes. By June of 1910 Ely and Commons resumed personal amenities and eventually restored much of their older friendship.[18]

Though Ely showed considerable tolerance in protecting Commons from dismissal, he was more courageous in hiring Edward A. Ross in sociology. Fired up by Ely's teachings at Hopkins, Ross went to Stanford in 1893 ready to do battle for his principles. He spoke out repeatedly on subjects calculated to attract the attention of Mrs. Leland Stanford, matriarch of the university. He publicly defended Eugene V. Debs. He advocated the government ownership of utilities and a ban on Japanese immigration while in a university founded by a railroad magnate who used cheap Oriental labor. While most economists were for gold in 1896, as a Silverite, Ross wrote a pamphlet entitled "Honest Dollar," which was widely distributed by the Democratic National Committee. At first President David Starr Jordan tried to

[18] For a basic outline of the Ely-Commons dispute, see Ely to Robert Hunter, March 3, 1906; Ely, "My Relations with Professor Commons," Jan. 25, 1909; Van Hise to Ely, Jan. 28, 1909; Commons, "Supplement to Report of John R. Commons, 1904-1909," March, 1909; Ely, "Additional Statement," April 1, 1909; Ely to Van Hise, Oct. 9, 1908; Ely to Thomas S. Adams, Oct. 10, 1908; "Memorandum of Agreement" [July 26, 1909]; "Personal and Private," July 3, 1909; "Joint Statement of Ely and Commons," June 21, 1910; all in Ely MSS.

mediate with Mrs. Stanford, but in 1900 Ross was forced to leave. Eight other professors followed in protest, including Arthur Lovejoy in philosophy and Frank Fetter in economics. In a historic decision, Ely, as president of the American Economic Association, appointed a special committee to investigate the dismissal. In order to assure public confidence in the committee, he carefully selected conservative gold advocates, Henry Farnam of Yale, E. R. A. Seligman of Columbia, and Henry Gardner of Brown. In their report, which was a direct precursor of later investigations by the American Association of University Professors, the committee concluded that Ross had been dismissed on inadequate grounds.[19]

Despite the favorable report and genuine sympathy for Ross, he was, in effect, professionally blacklisted. Whenever a charge is brought against a professor, Ely wrote to Frank Fetter, "it seems extremely difficult for him to justify himself in any effective way, however groundless may be the accusation. . . . Notwithstanding all that has been done I fear that it is going to be extremely difficult for Ross to get back into any desirable academic position."[20] As evidence, he cited the failure of Bemis and Commons to obtain positions after similar dismissals. Charles H. Hull, former colleague of Ross, expressed the typical reluctance of the academic guild to accept Ross back into full membership after the Stanford incident. All professors, he wrote Ely, must agree that irresponsibility was adequate grounds for dismissal. Ross, he said, "has a good deal of ability, and absolutely no judgment." Responding that Ross had become increasingly responsible, Ely posed a serious question of academic freedom. "Don't you feel after all," he asked, "that a true university ought to be large enough to contain men of

[19] See Richard Hofstadter and Walter P. Metzger, *The Development of Academic Freedom in the United States* (New York: Columbia University Press, 1955), pp. 436-445; Edward A. Ross, *Seventy Years of It: An Autobiography* (New York: Appleton-Century, 1936), chap. VII.

[20] Ely to Fetter, March 25, 1901, Ely MSS.

various types? Should it not be large enough to contain a
man of Ross's gifts, even if he hasn't that balance which
many men of far less capacity have?"[21]

Ely had always appreciated the genius of Ross. As early
as 1901 he had tried to get him a post at Wisconsin, but,
owing to the instability of the university administration, had
failed. In the meantime Ross had strengthened his reputation by publishing *Social Control* in Ely's "Citizen's Library"
series. The book established Ross as one of the top sociol-
ogists in the country. With his success in hiring Commons to
buoy him, Ely went to Van Hise with glowing letters of
recommendation from Oliver Wendell Holmes, Jr., Albion
Small, Seligman, and several conservative businessmen.
Though the regents hesitated because of the Stanford incident, Van Hise used his full weight to obtain the appointment of Ross in 1906.[22] The hiring of Ross and Commons,
both unacceptable to most college administrators, increased
Wisconsin's reputation for radicalism. But, more important,
it gave them two inspiring teachers who were at the forefront of their respective fields in the first half of the twentieth
century. To the credit of Ely and Van Hise, they had been
willing to withstand considerable criticism in order to acquire the two scholars.

The appointment of Commons and Ross was symptomatic
of the reform spirit which was sweeping across the Badger
State and which intimately involved the university with the
state government. The immediate basis for the Wisconsin
Idea came with the election of Robert M. La Follette to the
governorship in 1900 and Charles R. Van Hise to the presidency of the university in 1903. La Follette, a graduate of
the university and imbued with the moral responsibilities
taught to him by former President John Bascom, felt that the

[21] Hull to Ely, March 5, 1901, Ely to Hull, March 9, 1901, Ely
MSS.
[22] Ely to Seligman, Jan. 29, 1901, Ely to Small, July 11, 1905, Ely
to Ross, Sept. 30, 1905, Ely MSS.

primary purpose of the university should be direct public service. He was instrumental in the selection of Van Hise, a former classmate, and after 1903 turned to the university for guidance and expert advice. By 1903 Ely, sensing the shift in public opinion, elated by the choice of Van Hise, and disgruntled with Spooner's failure to secure him a federal position, abandoned the Stalwarts for the Progressives. And Commons, while still working with the National Civic Federation, assisted La Follette in preparing the governor's controversial state message for the 1903 session of the legislature. During that session, in which the legislature passed a general primary law and an ad valorem tax system for railroads, the governor called in Van Hise, Ely, Commons, and Paul Reinsch for frequent round-table discussions at the so-called Saturday lunch clubs. A considerable portion of La Follette's program originated at these luncheons.[23] Ely admitted that he was never a "close personal adviser" to La Follette, "but I saw him frequently; often he was a guest at my house as I was his."[24]

Beginning with the 1905 session of the legislature and continuing until the election of Stalwart Governor Emmanuel L. Philipp in 1914, Ely's department took an even more active role in the reform movement. Balthasar H. Meyer received an appointment to the new railroad commission which was given the duties of regulating the rates, services, and construction of railroads in the state. Meyer later became a member of the Interstate Commerce Commission, but only after Ely assured La Follette that Meyer was a genuine Progressive.[25] For La Follette, Commons drew up the most com-

[23] Robert La Follette, *La Follette's Autobiography* (Madison: University of Wisconsin Press, 1960), pp. 14-15; Belle C. La Follette and Fola La Follette, *Robert M. La Follette* (New York: Macmillan, 1953), I, 157; Robert S. Maxwell, *La Follette and the Rise of the Progressives in Wisconsin* (Madison: State Historical Society of Wisconsin, 1956), p. 130. In 1909 Ely supported State Senator William Hatton to replace Spooner. See Ely to Albert Shaw, March 7, 1907, Ely MSS.
[24] Ely, *Ground Under Our Feet*, p. 216.
[25] *Ibid.*

prehensive civil service law in the United States and Samuel
Sparling, a product of Ely's school, served on the first civil
service commission. Under Governor Francis McGovern,
Commons helped to draft a host of legislative proposals dealing with labor. Later Commons served on the industrial
commission, the agency designed to enforce the legislation
which he had drawn. Thomas S. Adams became chairman of
the state tax commission and designed the procedure for
determining the physical valuation of railroads. He helped
to draft the first progressive income tax in the nation, which
influenced the form of the federal income tax law of 1913.
Associated in the popular mind with the university was the
Legislative Reference Library, headed by Charles McCarthy,
an enthusiastic disciple of Ely's economics. Though the
library was ostensibly nonpartisan, McCarthy made it into
a virtual "bill factory" for the Progressives. McCarthy, perhaps more than any other individual, was responsible for
calling in expert advisers from the university. By 1911 some
forty-six faculty members were serving both the state and the
university.[26]

Progressives throughout the nation began to look to
Wisconsin as a model state. Almost every national magazine
devoted at least one article to the unique relationship between the university and the state. In 1912 two books appeared on the subject: one by Frederic C. Howe, a former
Ely student, called *Wisconsin: An Experiment in Democracy*,
and Charles McCarthy's *The Wisconsin Idea*, with a glowing
introduction by Theodore Roosevelt. The legislative reference department, McCarthy explained, had been beseiged by
newspaper reporters and by those who wanted to emulate
the Wisconsin experiment. Through the union of "soil and
seminar," of brawn and brains, Wisconsin reformers had
successfully redeemed their promises.

[26] For more lengthy accounts of faculty participation in the state
government, see Charles McCarthy, *The Wisconsin Idea* (New York;
Macmillan, 1912); Maxwell, *La Follette*, chap. IX.

In explaining the genesis of the Progressive Movement in Wisconsin, McCarthy saw two particularly important influences, the large German population and the almost messianic coming of Richard Ely in 1892: "Here was another singular coincidence. The pupil of Knies and Wagner, coming from Germany with his German political ideals, succeeded Bascom as a teacher of political economy in the German university of the German state of Wisconsin. A curious condition surely!"[27]

As McCarthy implied, it was the succeeding "long line of young men," impressed primarily with the early ideas of Ely, who became the vanguard of Wisconsin progressivism. By the early twentieth century Ely's reputation as a reformer rested largely on the image which he had earlier projected. His books and articles written in the prior century continued to be widely read and discussed. From the younger Ely, reformers gained much of their inspiration, but both students and reformers often found his contemporary views not advanced far beyond the general public. During the era of close cooperation between the state and the university, Ely rejoined the Christian Social Union but took a minor role in its activities. His personal research had been so widely distributed and his central message so much a personalized philosophy that he was seldom consulted as an expert on any technical problems. Apparently no governor considered Ely as a possible appointee to the several new commissions until, in 1910 and 1911, Governor McGovern asked him to serve on either the tax or the railroad commissions. After some criticism by conservatives and after conferral with Van Hise, Ely decided not to accept an appointment.[28]

While the state was under Progressive control the university prospered. The university's total income leaped from

[27] McCarthy, *The Wisconsin Idea*, p. 28.
[28] See A. J. Arkin to Ely, Dec. 2, 1907, Allyn A. Young to Ely, Jan. 17, 1911, Charles J. Bullock to Thomas K. Urdahl, Dec. 22, 1910, Ely MSS,

slightly more than $600,000 in 1902-1903 to more than three million in 1913-1914, while enrollment in the same period had slightly more than doubled. Ely, by exerting some pressure, shared in the largesse. In 1907 he informed Van Hise that he had been offered the presidency of a New York trust company with a salary of $10,000 annually. Simultaneously, he was a candidate for the directorship of the Cooper Union at the same salary. Van Hise, who recognized Ely's capacity as an academic leader, filled all of Ely's requests—two additions to the staff, a $4,000 salary, and one paid semester of each academic year for research. The last concession may have given Ely the best economic professorship in the country. And by 1911 the department had six full professors—more than any school in the country—plus eleven assistants.[29]

Inevitably the activities of the university staff led to criticism from special interests affected by the state's reforms. Exaggeration of the role of the professors in the state government by national magazines provided ammunition for the conservatives. In 1909 *Colliers*, a muckraking journal, carried an article which declared that the conservative university regents frequently interfered in academic affairs and, in particular, had tried to throttle the reform activities of the economics department. The decision of Frederick Jackson Turner to take a position at Harvard in the same year was widely interpreted as resulting from pressure by the regents. A joint meeting arranged by Van Hise between faculty representatives and the regents temporarily cooled the excitement. But the next year, 1910, the irrepressible Ross announced a public lecture to be given by anarchist Emma Goldman, and when she arrived, he escorted her around campus. Four days later Parker Sercombe of Chicago, considered a radical by some, lectured at the university at the invitation

[29] Maxwell, *La Follette*, pp. 136-137; Ely to Van Hise, May 9, 1907, Ely to John H. Finley, June 19, 1907, Van Hise to Ely, Aug. 26, Oct. 16, 1907, Ely MSS,

of Ross. Though Ross admitted an indiscretion in announcing Miss Goldman's lecture in his classroom and in inviting Sercombe without the approval of the committee on lectures, he insisted that they should have the right to be heard. The conservative press howled that the "spirit of anarchy and revolution" was running rampant on campus and Van Hise recommended that the regents censure Ross, a move apparently calculated to save Ross from dismissal.[30]

In the meantime Ely attempted to convince the regents and the public that the economics department was in reality conservative. He admitted that Ross had been guilty of a "gross indiscretion" but added that "his conduct did not involve any reflection upon honor."[31] In reviewing the texts used in the department, Ely noted that his *Outlines* was "probably the most widely used text book in the United States," and it was even used at the most conservative institutions, like Yale. "In general I might say," he wrote to the president, "that so far as my own views are concerned several intimations have come from economists that I am becoming too conservative." To the charge that the department gave more attention to socialism than the subject warranted, Ely answered that no course had been offered in socialism for the present year and doubted "if there is any American University of equal rank in which so little attention has been given to Socialism." In conclusion, Ely wrote, "I may say that I think on investigation it will be found that no one of the universities is more conservative than the University of Wisconsin in its Department of Political Economy, while other institutions have men far more radical than anyone here—men whom I would not think of recommending for a position."[32] Ely had considerably overstated his case for the

[30] See Merle Curti and Vernon Carstensen, *The University of Wisconsin: A History, 1848-1925* (Madison: University of Wisconsin Press, 1949), II, 57-67; Ross, *Seventy Years of It*, pp. 289-290.
[31] Ely to Lutie M. Pleasants, June 23, 1910, Ely MSS.
[32] Ely to Van Hise, Feb. 15, 1910, Ely MSS.

conservatism of the department, probably because he, along with other departmental members, was genuinely alarmed. The Progressives saw an opportunity to turn the attack upon the university to political advantage. Progressive newspapers came to the defense, while the conservative ones become more virulent in the tone of their criticism. At the suggestion of muckraker Lincoln Steffens, the senior class of 1910 presented the red-faced regents with a plaque bearing the famous "sifting and winnowing" statement that the 1894 regents had adopted at the conclusion of the Ely trial. Suspecting that the students had been duped by radicals, the regents rejected the gift. In 1910 the La Follette Progressives responded by writing the 1894 statement into the state Republican platform. In 1912, after the board had come under the clear domination of the Progressives, the plaque was finally accepted, and three years later it was bolted on Bascom Hall. The tactics of the Progressives further deepened the fears and suspicions of the conservatives. The last Progressive-controlled legislature, that of 1913, attempted to still criticism by passing a resolution authorizing the investigation of the university by the State Board of Public Affairs. The board hired William H. Allen of New York to study the efficiency of teaching and the methods at the university. After more than a year of work the board filed a report of almost a thousand pages. The report, though friendly to the university overall, gave ammunition to the conservatives. Emmanuel L. Philipp, Stalwart Republican, rode home to victory in 1914 on a campaign attacking the university for extravagance and inefficiency.[33]

Even before the election of Philipp the economics department, perhaps sensing a reaction to Progressivism, indicated an increasing hesitancy in cooperating with the state's Progressives. As early as 1909 Ely and Thomas S. Adams

[33] Curti and Carstensen, *The University of Wisconsin*, II, 68-71, 267-283; Maxwell, *La Follette*, pp. 148-151.

became concerned with the tendency of the national press to picture the university as an advanced agency of reform. "I intend before long," Ely wrote, ". . . to say some things which will put us right before the general public. . . . I want to bring out the idea very clearly that capital has rights as well as labor, and that we want to do our part to make this State a safe place for enterprise and industry . . . [as well as to improve] labor conditions and to help the weaker classes in the community."[34]

Before the national party conventions in 1912, Ely, in response to numerous inquiries concerning his position on the potential presidential candidates, freely expressed his reservations with regard to La Follette. In all of his letters he gave La Follette credit for lifting Wisconsin "on a higher plane politically and ethically. I do not think we can ever go back to the ways of the olden time when the Capitol was full of mere politicians. Our Capitol building now is filled up very largely with scholars and gentlemen."[35] But La Follette, Ely felt, attached far "too much importance to purely political measures, such as changes in the ballot." Too many people voted already, he argued, and no ballot changes would give American cities good mayors; only giving mayors adequate training would accomplish that objective. The behavior of Taft and Roosevelt during the campaign of 1912 disappointed Ely, and for the first time in his life he voted for a Democratic presidential candidate, his former student, Woodrow Wilson.[36]

The election of Philipp in 1914 encouraged the conservatives to further their attacks on Ely's department. No longer did the legislators consult the university, and the

[34] Ely to Adams, Feb. 4, 1909, Ely MSS.
[35] Ely to Mrs. H. K. W. Bent, April 27, 1912, Ely MSS.
[36] Ely to Lucy M. Washburn, June 12, 1912, Ely to Samuel P. Orth, July 3, 1912, Ely MSS. For a more detailed view of Ely with respect to electoral reforms, see his "Progressivism, True and False— An Outline," *Review of Reviews*, LI (Feb., 1915), 209-211.

removal of Van Hise, Ely, Ross, and Commons seemed a distinct possibility. Shortly after the election Regent Granville D. Jones, long a critic of radicalism at the university, challenged Ely to defend a proposed land study. Ely attempted to reassure Jones that the investigators believed in "individual property in land" and planned no "revolution in [the] Wisconsin land system." But Jones was persistent. Had not Ely advocated the "government ownership of all public utilities, payment therefrom to be made, if at all, from inheritance taxes?" Furthermore the regent had the impression that it was through Ely that the "somewhat strong socialistic element came into the University." Ely replied to Jones' repeated allegations by again noting the conservatism of the department. Although Ely's explanations, particularly with regard to the Ross-Goldman-Sercombe affair, did not completely satisfy him, Jones' charges became less bellicose.[37]

In response to the attacks of Jones and others, Ely also defended his department by writing an article for the *Wisconsin State Journal* in February of 1915 entitled "The University as a Commercial Asset to Wisconsin" and by sponsoring the First Wisconsin Commercial and Industrial Congress, February 14-18, 1916, at Madison. Leading businessmen in the state came to the congress and met the members of the economics department. The staff discussed sympathetically the problems of the businessman and how the university might offer more assistance in the future. Ely spoke at the closing banquet on "Government and Business." He implied that governmental intervention in the economy had gone too far. "There have been so-called reformers," he said, "who have thought that prosperity could be secured by unjust oppression of business." But economists opposed any reform which would reduce the services or destroy a business firm. Even Regent Jones approved of Ely's address and

[37] Ely to Jones, March 22, April 27, 1915, Jones to Ely, May 12, 1915, Ely MSS.

Governor Philipp reported in the fall of 1915 that since he had removed the professors from the state commissions, the university no longer had an active role in state politics.[38]

While such cooperation between the businessmen and the university pleased the worried Stalwarts, it embittered arch-Progressive Charles McCarthy. "The University is so hopelessly reactionary, and the professors as a whole have shown such a timid spirit," he wrote in one of a series of letters to Ely in 1916, "it seems hopeless to suggest anything." When the politicians began to attack the Wisconsin Idea, the "glorious ideal" of the past had been abandoned. "A few weak professors joined in with the politicians. We began to hear the same mouthings of the politicians among the college professors. Professors became timid, and then it became very unpopular to have anything to do with the state." Of all of the university students recently questioned by McCarthy, he had yet to find a single one "with the slightest enthusiasm for political economy or political science. Without exception, the students . . . speak disparagingly or sneeringly (I am not exaggerating it a bit) of all with the exception of one man and two or three courses."[39] Ely invited McCarthy to "get at the economists" by addressing the Political Economy Club. But neither McCarthy nor the Progressives could take much satisfaction in the remote possibility that the Wisconsin Idea would be resurrected.[40]

During the World War I era Ely's attitude toward La Follette turned from apprehension to open hostility. As early as the Spanish-American War, Ely had welcomed the responsibilities imposed by America's new position as a world power. Although forty-four years of age, he was so anxious

[38] Program of Banquet of First Wisconsin Commercial and Industrial Congress, Feb. 18, 1916, Ely, "Government and Business," [Feb. 18, 1916?], Ely to Jones, March 22, 1916, all in Ely MSS; Curti and Carstensen, *University of Wisconsin*, II, 104.

[39] McCarthy to Ely, March 8, 28, 1916, Ely MSS.

[40] Ely to McCarthy, April 5, 1916, McCarthy to Ely, Aug. 30, 1916, Ely MSS.

to get into the thick of the actual fighting that he joined a volunteer outfit of students. To his deep personal regret the war ended before he had an opportunity to see combat. Blending humanitarian impulses with a concern for security he had no qualms about supporting the United States in holding the Philippines. From German student days he had held a certain admiration for the discipline and sense of duty imposed and encouraged by military service. In World War I he approved of measures to round up the "loafers" and put them to work. Compulsion, when applied to the soldiers, he wrote to a friend, was "magnificent in its results."[41]

Convinced that a German victory in World War I would endanger American security, he immediately became a champion of preparedness and the English cause. He declined to continue his membership in the Wisconsin Peace Society. "I differ radically from many of the Pacificists in regard to the proper methods of attaining the desired end," he explained in January of 1915. "I am in favor of universal military service in the United States. . . . I think we should prepare to defend ourselves against attacks, and I do not wish to belong to any society which uses its influence against military preparations for defense."[42] After returning from a trip to New Zealand late in 1914, he reported that the loyalty of Australia and New Zealand to the mother country was "inspiring." On September 1, 1916, he joined the National Security League, an organization which represented the vanguard of preparedness. Apart from security he believed the war would release the German people from the stifling autocracy so that "we shall have a great revival of German learning."[43]

[41] Herbert S. S. to Theodore Herfurth, Dec. 15, 1946, Herfurth MSS, State Historical Society of Wisconsin, Madison, Wis.; Ely to F. B. Garner, July 25, 1917, Ely to Charles A. Ellwood, May 22, 1918, Ely MSS.

[42] Ely to Arnold B. Hall, Jan. 27, 1915, Ely MSS.

[43] Ely to George Crum, Oct. 30, 1914, Ely to R. Henry Rew, Nov.

Once America entered the European conflict, Ely was intolerant of the opponents of the war. Even as a member of the academic freedom committee of the American Association of University Professors, he felt that the defense of academic freedom should be entirely suspended in wartime. Any professor who uttered "opinions which hinder us in this awful struggle" deserves to be "fired," if not "shot," he wrote to Allyn A. Young.[44] La Follette's criticism of war profiteering seemed to him little less than treasonous. "To hear some of our Bolsheviki politicians, who do not know what the word sacrifice means," he wrote to Walter Gifford, "talk about profiteers and apply the term to some of our big business men makes my blood boil."[45] War had been thrust upon us by Germany, Ely felt, and all should join in the crusade to defeat the enemy. Before American entry his youngest son, John, had rushed from Harvard to join the French army; he later served in heavy fighting with the American army. Ely felt that the activities of the war opponents stabbed his son in the back. Swept up by the Wilsonian rhetoric of making the world safe for democracy, he, like so many old Progressives, tended to become a victim of an expedient course which allowed the ends to justify the means. Ironically, in 1938, when he composed his autobiography, he regretted his campaign against La Follette and was prepared to be the first to place a wreath at the senator's grave.[46]

When Senator La Follette and Representative John M. Nelson of Madison voted against the war resolution of April 16, 1917, Ely, for the first time in his life, toyed with the idea of running for a major political office. He received encourage-

10, 1914, Ely MSS. See Ely, *The World War and Leadership in a Democracy* (New York: Macmillan, 1918).

[44] Ely to Young, Nov. 1, 1917, Ely MSS.

[45] Ely to Gifford, June 11, 1918, Ely MSS.

[46] Ely, *Ground Under Our Feet*, pp. 217-218.

ment from several Stalwarts to challenge Nelson's congressional seat. On June 30, 1917, Richard Lloyd Jones, editor of the *Wisconsin State Journal,* a newspaper which had formerly supported La Follette, carried a favorable editorial on Ely's candidacy. But his candid friends advised caution, for sentiment with regard to American participation in the war was as yet untested and Nelson particularly appealed to a large Norwegian block in the district.[47] David Kinley wondered if Ely would be happy in Congress. "You are too sensitive to endure the rough and tumble of the day's work, such as falls to the lot of a Congressman," Kinley opined.[48] Van Hise clinched the decision by flatly informing Ely that in order to run, he would have to resign his university position. By September, 1917, Ely had decided to withdraw.[49]

Nonetheless, Ely took an active role in the movement to unseat La Follette. Although Fighting Bob had supported the first bond issue asked by the administration as well as higher income taxes, he led the fight against the Espionage Act of 1918, opposed conscription, and continued to levy a barrage of criticism at war profiteering. After an extemporaneous speech by La Follette before the Non Partisan League convention at St. Paul on September 20, 1917, in which he reputedly said that the United States "had no grievances against Germany," former Presidents Taft and Roosevelt joined the chorus in asking for a Senate investigation of the "Grand American neo-Copperhead." Petitions for dismissal poured into the Senate Committee on Privileges and Elections. At a huge rally in the university gymnasium in October of 1917 the Wisconsin state and county councils of defense

47 See Ely to Francis E. McGovern, June 28, 1917, Albert Shaw to Ely, June 30, 1917, Robert Campbell to Ely, June 29, 1917, Irvine Lenroot to Ely, April 22, 1918, Henry C. Taylor to Ely, May 16, 1918, Ely MSS.
48 Kinley to Ely, Aug. 20, 1917, Ely MSS.
49 Ely to Albert Shaw, Aug. 9, 1917, Ely to Kinley, Sept. 1, 1917, Ely MSS.

adopted resolutions asking for La Follette's seat. And at a dinner held by the Northern California Alumni Association, Ely joined Senator Irvine Lenroot and Representative John J. Esch of Wisconsin in condemning La Follette. On January 10, 1918, the War Committee of the university, of which Ely was a member, approved a plan for circulating a faculty memorial which stated that "in certain respects Senator La Follette has misrepresented them, his constituents."[50]

To Ely the memorial was far too mild, for he wanted nothing less than La Follette's removal from the Senate. Simultaneously with the presentation of the faculty memorial for signatures, Ely circulated an invitation to faculty members to join the Madison chapter of the Wisconsin Loyalty Legion. As organizer and president of the chapter, Ely wrote a superpatriotic pledge specifically aimed at La Follette, a pledge far stronger than the faculty memorial or the state pledge of the legion.[51] The Madison members promised "to stamp out disloyalty, and to stimulate those whose loyalty is weak and thin into a militant love for our country and the principles for which it stands." They expressed unqualified support of the Espionage Act and pledged themselves to "work against La Folletteism in all its anti-war forms, realizing that any encouragement to the supporters of La Follette is in fact support of La Follette himself."[52] Early in January, 1918, Theodore Roosevelt agreed to address the legion at a huge rally scheduled in Madison for February 15. "We have one great task before us in this state," Ely explained to Roosevelt, "and that is to crush La Folletteism. I think every-

[50] See La Follette and La Follette, *La Follette*, II, 731-737; Curti and Carstensen, *University of Wisconsin*, II, 112-115; "Memorandum and Resolution" [Feb. 1, 1918], Ely MSS; G. C. Sellery, *Some Ferments at Wisconsin, 1901-1947: Memories and Reflections* (Madison: University of Wisconsin Press, 1960), pp. 7-8.

[51] See "Memorandum and Resolution" [Feb. 1, 1918], Ely MSS.

[52] Platform of Madison Chapter of Wisconsin Loyalty Legion [Feb. ?, 1918], Ely MSS. Internal evidence indicates the platform was written *ca.* Jan. 10, 1918.

thing else has to be subordinated to that at the present juncture, and I know your ringing patriotic address will be of great help to us."[53]

Ely's Loyalty Legion was born amid controversy. Faculty leaders Winfred T. Root and Carl Russell Fish found an inconsistency in pledging support to the President and at the same time sponsoring Roosevelt in his "carping" attacks on Wilson. Owing to a confusion over dates for the appearance, Ely postponed Roosevelt's speech indefinitely, but not before the faculty had begun to question the extreme position of the Loyalty Legion toward La Follette. Several faculty members viewed the legion as a front organization for the Stalwart faction of the Republican party. Both President Van Hise and Dean Birge refused to join because Ely frankly admitted the political nature of the legion, while denying that it was designed to benefit the Stalwarts. Although the legion had a membership of 442, an indeterminable number regretted that they had joined. And on February 1 the War Committee adopted a memorandum expressing "deep regret" that the Loyalty Legion had been "intimately associated with the presentation of the La Follette memorial" so as to convey the impression that both were politically inspired. The committee resolved that the list of those who signed the memorial—about 93 percent of the faculty—would not be publicly released.[54] During the summer of 1918 the Loyalty Legion rapidly faded away.

Despite unfavorable responses to the legion, Ely continued his campaign against La Follette. When La Follette filed a series of libel suits against the *Wisconsin State Journal*

[53] Ely to Roosevelt, Jan. 17, 1918, Ely MSS.
[54] See Root to Ely, Jan. 23, 1918, Fish to Ely, Jan. 25, 1918, Ely to Albert Shaw, Jan. 21, 1918, Shaw to Ely, Jan. 29, 1918, Ely to Irvine Lenroot, Feb. 4, 1918, Paul G. Clark to Ely, Feb. 9, 1918, Ely to Clark, Feb. 11, 1918, Edward A. Birge to G. M. Hyde, Feb. 1, 1918, Charles R. Van Hise to Ely, Feb. 1, 1918, "Report of the Madison Chapter of the Wisconsin Loyalty Legion," Feb. 23, 1918, "Memorandum and Resolution" [Feb. 1, 1918], Ely MSS.

for distorting his war record, Ely assisted the defense attorneys in gathering information. He especially wanted to uncover evidence that La Follette's activities had been used in Germany and Russia for propaganda purposes. "I think there can be no doubt," he wrote to Albert Shaw, "that he [La Follette] has been of more help to the Kaiser than a quarter of a million troops."[55] Guy Stanton Ford, head of the educational division of the Committee on Public Information, coordinated efforts to find materials to substantiate Ely's charge. From the facts gathered, Ely hoped to publish a pamphlet entitled "La Follette's War Record and its Effects in our Own Country, Germany and Russia." Researchers, however, found little evidence to indicate that Germany or Russia made any use of La Follette's activities.[56]

In the summer of 1918 Ely turned his patriotic zeal from the Loyalty Legion to the Wisconsin branch of the League to Enforce the Peace. As a delegate of the university, he attended the second national convention of the league held in Philadelphia on May 16-17, 1918. Although the league supported a postwar organization of free nations, the national convention, chaired by William Howard Taft, was more interested in securing the unconditional surrender of Germany. Their motto was "Win the War for Permanent Peace," but speakers emphasized victory instead of settlement of the war.[57] Throughout the convention, Ely reported, "there was a lot of determination and the greatest appre-

[55] Ely to Shaw, Jan. 29, 1918, Ely MSS.

[56] Ely to Ford, Jan. 30, Feb. 6, March 1, 1918, James G. Randall to John S. P. Tatlock, Feb. 16, 1918, Victor S. Clark to Tatlock, Feb. 14, 1918, Shaw to Ely, Feb. 2, 1918, Ely MSS.

[57] For the convention platform and speeches, see *Win the War for Permanent Peace* (New York: League to Enforce Peace, 1918). For the only history of the league, see Ruhl J. Bartlett, *The League to Enforce Peace* (Chapel Hill: University of North Carolina Press, 1944). Research on the Wisconsin branch of the league indicates that Bartlett fails to consider sufficiently the supernationalistic quality and political mechanizations that appeared behind much of the league activity.

hension in regard to German peace propaganda."[58] They feared President Wilson might succumb to a negotiated peace. Exuberant over the Philadelphia meeting, Ely determined to organize a Wisconsin branch as a weapon against "La Folletteism," though ostensibly the organization had as a major function the support of the League of Nations movement.

Upon returning to Madison, Ely organized the Wisconsin branch with himself as chairman of the executive committee and State Senator John M. Whitehead as state chairman. Van Hise advised Ely to go ahead with plans for a state convention to be held under the auspices of the university. As program chairman and with his usual vigor, Ely secured Taft as the keynote speaker and invited delegates from the entire Midwest. The Wisconsin legislature passed a joint resolution endorsing the Wisconsin Win the War for Permanent Peace Convention. In most of his correspondence relating to the proposed convention Ely explained that Wisconsin had been misrepresented in Congress and implied that the state wanted to bear testimony to its loyalty.[59] Taft's speech fired the convention, held on November 8-10, 1918, to adopt as its motto: "patriotic, sanely progressive and anti-Bolshevik." The Wisconsin convention was judged as one of the most successful in the nation.[60]

In the fall and winter of 1918, Ely, Senator Whitehead, and A. B. Hall, political science professor, gave a few addresses around the state under the auspices of the league. With the signing of the armistice the Wisconsin branch stepped up its activity. In the spring and summer of 1919, while the Treaty of Versailles was before the Senate, they

[58] Ely to Charles A. Ellwood, May 22, 1918, Ely MSS.
[59] Ely to Taft, May 28, 1918, Van Hise to Ely, Aug. 6, 1918, Ely to Franklin H. Giddings, Aug. 8, 1918, Ely to William H. Short, Sept. 26, 1918, Ely to Congressmen of the State [Oct. ?, 1918], Ely MSS.
[60] Ely to Kinley, Nov. 22, 1918, William H. Short to Ely, Nov. 12, 1918, Ely MSS; Bartlett, *League to Enforce Peace*, p. 96.

hired a professional campaign manager, William W. Powell. He spoke before county fairs, teachers' institutes, and farmers' conventions, sponsored high school debates, and brought in prominent outside speakers. Henry Morgenthau, Taft, A. Lawrence Lowell, Henry Van Dyke, and William Allen White all made swings around the state. They initiated a letter-writing campaign to obtain the support of Senator Lenroot for the League of Nations Covenant but made no effort to obtain the support of La Follette. Officers of the national League to Enforce the Peace felt Wisconsin was the "best organized State in the Union."[61]

But the purpose of the Wisconsin league continued to lack clear focus, and it is doubtful whether it was very effective in securing support for the League of Nations Covenant. At the conclusion of the war it began to absorb the "patriotic work" of the State Council of Defense. Ely thought the league had assumed responsibility for work formerly done by the Loyalty Legion. But now with the defeat of Germany a new enemy threatened American institutions and world peace. The league takes "the position," Ely wrote, "that the menace to a League of Nations is no longer autocracy, but Bolshevism, and this is a more serious menace than Czars and Kaisers were in the last century."[62] Throughout the history of the Wisconsin league, charges came to Ely that speakers were using the league as a forum to attack the Wilson administration. And personally Ely wished that Theodore Roosevelt were President rather than Wilson. He frequently explained that the league had never supported a particular "kind of League of Nations" but had emphasized educational work along lines of encouraging patriotism and

[61] See especially Ely to W. H. Short, Dec. 10, 1918, Ely to W. R. Boyd, Jr., June 9, 1919, Tom Jones Meek to Ely, May 12, 1919, Ely MSS. The Ely MSS appear to contain almost all of the official correspondence of the Wisconsin league as well as numerous letters relevant to it.

[62] Ely to Edward C. March, Jan. 28, 1919, Ely MSS.

opposing Bolshevism. Even before the Senate took a final vote on the League of Nations Covenant, Ely wanted to change the name of the Wisconsin branch of the League to Enforce the Peace to the Wisconsin Society for Civic and Industrial Improvement. Ely organized such a society, but, owing to a lack of interest, shortage of funds, and the existence of so many similar societies after the war, it was shortly dissolved.[63]

Ely also contributed to the postwar Red Scare. In an article published in 1920 he warned that Bolshevism was a "most serious menace, and one that we cannot disregard with impunity. It is a product of social disease germs which are spreading a pestilence over the world." The Wall Street explosions and the lawlessness of radicals in Chicago convinced him that "we must fight Bolshevism with repressive measures." Absorbed with the Wilsonian crusade for world democracy, though increasingly opposed to the President personally, he maintained that modern American democracy meant in essence that "right can control might—that might must be back of right." Unlike the earlier "aspirations of pacificism," modern democracy was "a kind of religion."[64] It required a high degree of conformity, unity in purpose, and the power to achieve its objectives.

Ely was a barometer of the rise and decline of the Progressive Movement in Wisconsin. His almost reflex responses to the tides of public opinion indicated a certain opportunism. But it also reflected what he believed to be a realistic appraisal of the direction of Progressivism and later of the war. La Follette's Progressivism placed far too much reliance on the intelligence and knowledge of the ordinary citizen,

[63] See Powell to W. H. Short, Aug. 28, 1919, A. L. Haugen to Ely, Sept. 5, 1919, Ely to Lucy Washburn, Feb. 17, 1919, Ely to John M. Whitehead, Feb. 26, 1920, Ely to D. O. Kinsman, Dec. 3, 1920, Ely MSS.

[64] Ely, "What Is Bolshevism?" *Review of Reviews*, LXII (November, 1920), 505, 501,

whereas Ely increasingly felt that the country required leadership by an elite. Although Ely seemed to turn his back on Progressivism completely during the war, he viewed the objectives of the simple war slogans as a continuation of reform, a reform to make the world safe for democracy. For Ely, it became a struggle between Good and Evil.

Chapter Eight

"UNDER ALL, THE LAND"

ONE FINE spring day in 1897, Henry C. Taylor, fresh from Iowa State College, trudged up the hill to Madison's University Heights. Filled with anxiety about his future, he planned to discuss his problems with the renowned economist Richard Ely. Greeted warmly by Dr. and Mrs. Ely, he explained his predicament. His father felt that Henry should abandon graduate work in economics and specialize in a practical subject like animal husbandry or soil science. But Henry wanted to study agricultural economics, a discipline not yet taught in American colleges. Since coming from Johns Hopkins, Ely replied, he had been searching for students interested in the "economic problems" of agriculture. By all means young Henry should specialize in the new field. Ely then wrote Taylor's father explaining that Henry would assuredly "make a name for himself" in the new field and within two years sent Henry to England to write a thesis on landholding.[1]

Thirty-four years later, Ely, at the age of seventy-seven, spoke before the National Conference on Land Utilization held in Chicago. Slightly balding and a little thinner, his smooth face belied his age. "Now as I look at this program," he reminisced, ". . . I feel that I am in the promised land." Before him as he spoke sat his former students: Lewis C. Gray, John D. Black, Milburn L. Wilson, and George S. Wehrwein, who, joined by Henry Taylor and Benjamin Hibbard, accounted for almost every prominent land economist in the United States. "Many years ago, in the nineties of the last century and even earlier," he explained, "I began urging some young men to develop agricultural economics in this country."[2] But Ely had been a "voice crying in the wilderness." During the thirty-four years between his meeting with Taylor and his address to the Conference on Land Utilization, Ely had fathered a new discipline, land economics, and had stimulated the changed attitude toward agricultural economics.

During the nineties Ely had shown considerable interest in the general field of land economics, especially government conservation programs. In his first textbook (1889) he explained that public ownership of the forests allowed for long-range planning, conservation, and the use of skilled personnel. In 1893 he proposed the formation of a forestry association in Wisconsin. Although the initial attempt proved abortive, he invited Bernard E. Fernow, chief of the Division of Forestry in the Department of Agriculture, to give a special course in forest conservation in 1896-1897. Fernow's lectures influenced geologist Charles Van Hise, who became one of the nation's leading conservationists in the Progressive era. Although Ely did not list a course called "land economics" in the nineties, nor during the first two

[1] Taylor to Edward W. Morehouse, July 28, 1930, Ely MSS, State Historical Society of Wisconsin, Madison.
[2] Ely, "Adjusting the Tax Burden to the Tax-Paying Ability of the Tax Bearer," *Proceedings of the National Conference on Land Utilization, Chicago, November 19-21, 1931* (Washington, D.C.: Government Publishing Office, 1932), p. 126.

decades of the twentieth century, he treated the subject under
"Landed Property and Rent" and various similar titles. Henry
C. Taylor began the first modern agricultural economics
course at Wisconsin in 1902 within the economics department,
but in 1909 switched to the College of Agriculture. Nonetheless, Taylor required all of his students to take a major
portion of their work in general economics. Under Ely's
editorial guidance Taylor published the first textbook in
agricultural economics in 1905.[3]

In 1903 Ely considered specializing in irrigation economics. As editor of the "Citizens Library of Economics" for
the Macmillan Company, he obtained the first scientific works
on irrigation by F. H. Newell in 1902 and Elwood Mead in
1903. Early in 1903, Mead, chief of the irrigation investigations for the Department of Agriculture, invited Ely to
prepare an economic study of irrigation on the Platte River.
Enthusiastic about breaking new ground, Ely announced that
the subject was "even more important than the railway
question, and it is quite truly an economic question." That
summer he visited the headwaters of the Platte in Colorado and Wyoming and prepared a paper for the National
Irrigation Congress held in Ogden, Utah, in September. He
outlined a new academic discipline, irrigation economics.
While the engineer handled the physical side of irrigation,
Ely said, the economist should deal with the social problems
surrounding property in water and interstate disputes. When
fully explored, the economics of irrigation should assist the
legislatures and courts in formulating intelligent policy. For

[3] Ely, *An Introduction to Political Economy* (New York: Chautauqua, 1889), pp. 91-92; Fernow to Ely, March 28, 1893, April 1,
1896, Ely MSS; "Announcement for 1895-96, School of Economics,
Political Science, and History," *Annual Catalogue of the University of
Wisconsin, 1894-95*, p. 114; Ely, *Ground Under Our Feet: An Autobiography* (New York: Macmillan, 1938), pp. 190-192; Merle Curti
and Vernon Carstensen, *The University of Wisconsin: A History, 1848-
1925* (Madison: University of Wisconsin, 1949), I, 636, II, 421-422;
Taylor to author [May, 1966]; Henry C. Taylor, *Introduction to the
Study of Agricultural Economics* (New York: Macmillan, 1905).

inexplicable reasons, perhaps because Ely had partially ignored his directives to concentrate only upon the Platte, Secretary of Agriculture James Wilson refused to publish the report. Although Ely gave no more attention to irrigation economics, his epochal paper influenced the later work of Henry C. Taylor and R. P. Teale.[4] Ely's study of irrigation economics further stimulated his interest in the economics of landed property. In 1909 he attempted to obtain a grant from the Russell Sage Foundation for a study of land tenure and taxes. Feeling that Lloyd George's heavy taxes on estates in England was confiscatory and that the single-tax advocates would soon carry to the United States the battle for a tax on the "unearned increment," he appealed for funds for an ostensibly "scientific" study of land economics. Arousing little interest from potential benefactors, he continued to work on his book, *Property and Contract*. In 1910 he asked Gifford Pinchot, president of the National Conservation Association, for financial assistance. Despite Pinchot's apparent interest, Ely decided the association was too "militant" and politically involved. Also in 1910 he toyed with the idea of organizing a Suburban and Country Homes Company which was to construct planned, low-cost communities near New York City. Several wealthy New Yorkers expressed an interest, but the project collapsed. Later such a company was organized in New York and served as a model for New Deal community programs.[5]

[4] See Ely to Albert Shaw, March 11, 1903, Ely, "Economics of Irrigation," abstract of paper for Irrigation Congress, Sept. 15-18, 1903; Taylor to Ely, Oct. 30, 1905, Mead to Ely, Nov. 3, 1905, Ely MSS. Henry C. Taylor and Anne Dewees Taylor, *The Story of Agricultural Economics in the United States, 1840-1932* (Ames: Iowa State College Press, 1952), pp. 830-837, contains a large abstract of Ely's unpublished report.
    [5] E. R. L. Gould to John B. Clark, Nov. 24, 1909, Ely to Robert Erskine Ely, Aug. 9, 1910, Pinchot to Ely, Nov. 29, 1910, Ely to Theodore Marburg, Jan. 18, 1911, Ely to Walter Hines Page, Nov. 10, 1910, Ely MSS.

In preparation for his major study on property and contract and to examine specific land reforms Ely visited Europe in 1911, 1912, and 1913. Escorted in Ireland by Sir Horace Plunkett, land reformer and head of the Irish Agriculture Organization, he collected documents, conferred with important officials, and viewed at close hand the transfer of large estates to the government and then to the actual cultivators. During his trip of 1913 he attempted to found an international Society of Land Economics, with headquarters in London. He obtained endorsements from Ambassador Walter Hines Page and prominent English agriculturalists H. Trustram Eve and R. Henry Rew. As outlined by Ely, the society would focus attention on such subjects as leases and rents, land utilization, the cultivation of land on both large and small scales, and the advantages of tenancy as opposed to cultivation by proprietors. Under urban lands he felt that the society should take into account town planning, taxation, and the relation of public to private land. His proposal of 1913 accurately forecast the purposes of his later Institute for Research in Land Economics and Public Utilities. Obtaining funds for the venture proved difficult, and the political excitement aroused by the recent land reforms in England led Ely to postpone action indefinitely.[6]

His most comprehensive work, *Property and Contract in their Relation to the Distribution of Wealth*, which appeared in 1914, provided the foundation for his later work in land economics. The two volumes originated in lectures Ely had given as early as 1892 on the distribution of wealth. By 1899 his lectures had taken a form similar to the published work. Each year he had added illustrations, quotations, and comments to his lectures. Several of his students

6 Ely to H. C. Taylor, June 27, 1913, Ely to Eve, Oct. 6, 1913, [Ely], "Draft of the Society for the Study of Property in Land (or the Society of Land Economics)," *ca.* July, 1913, Ely to B. H. Meyer, Jan. 5, 1914, Ely MSS,

had already given courses using Ely's lecture notes. Before publication he sent the manuscript to several economists and lawyers for criticism. Justice Oliver Wendell Holmes, Jr., read the entire manuscript, made many notes, and gave Ely references to court cases bearing on property and contract.[7] Typically Ely worried that he would not receive proper recognition for the original contribution that he believed he had made. Allyn A. Young explained the difficulty Ely faced: "The book will not strike the reader with the sense of freshness that it would have had if it [had] been published fifteen years ago. The social point of view, for which you have done so much, has become widespread and pretty thoroughly accepted in this country today."[8]

The reviews of *Property and Contract* confirmed Young's skepticism. Though the subject of a two-page eulogy in the *Review of Reviews* and a front-page review in the *New York Times Book Review*, Judge Learned Hand accurately summarized the impact of the work when he wrote, "there are interesting suggestions in detail, always moderate, never pungent, seldom novel."[9] Ely moderated the distinctive features of his earlier works: the biting criticisms of some phase of the existing economic order, the simple line of argument, and the moral indignation so typical of his writings. He repeated in more diffuse fashion the social philosophy he had expounded since his return from Germany. Laws and customs changed and circumscribed competition. The right to hold property, he said, was a product of society, not antecedent to the society which protected it. Thus society has

---

[7] See Ely, *Property and Contract in Their Relations to the Distribution of Wealth* (New York: Macmillan, 1914), preface; Ely to David Kinley, Feb. 23, 1912, Ely MSS.

[8] Young to Ely, Jan. 9, 1913, Ely MSS.

[9] For leading reviews, see *Review of Reviews*, LI (Jan., 1915), 114-115; *New York Times Book Review*, VII (Dec. 6, 1914), 549; Learned Hand, *Harvard Law Review*, XXIX (Nov., 1915), 110-112; Charles A. Beard, *Political Science Quarterly*, XXX (Sept., 1915), 510-511.

the right to regulate and use the institution which it had brought into being, subject to current needs which could not be expressed in advance. The same could be said for the right of contract. Thus society could regulate or even ultimately abolish both property and contract.

The most suggestive idea in the work, one missed by all the reviewers but not by later economists, was Ely's theory of vested rights. "*Strictly speaking,*" he wrote, "*vested interests are economic interests which are legally recognised to be such that they cannot be impaired by public action, directly or indirectly, without indemnification.*"[10] Compensation could come from either the public treasury or from private corporations. Since legislation defined vested interests, they could be indefinitely expanded. The wage earner could claim a vested right in his skill and, if suddenly thrown out of work by advanced technology, could claim restitution, just as a holder of property was paid when his land was taken for the construction of a railroad. The theory potentially justified extensive state assistance to protect the vested interests of underprivileged groups in times of social change. If a wide definition of vested interests were accepted, a maximum of social change could be achieved with a minimum of pain and sacrifice. The burden of change would rest on the entire community rather than on a few.

Ely, however, warned that society should hesitate to move rapidly in changing its laws of vested rights, including property and contract. Although judges lagged somewhat behind public opinion in interpreting the extant laws, he was confident that with more training in economics they would soon come to understand the significance of social questions. In dealing with the effects of the American system of property and contract on the distribution of wealth, the book was hardly adequate. The right of property, he

[10] Ely, *Property and Contract*, II, 755.

said, could be pushed so far that it would deprive large numbers from the benefits of private property. But he produced no analysis or statistics to indicate whether such was the case and none to indicate the relationship between institutions and capital accumulation.

Nevertheless, *Property and Contract* had a considerable influence in converting "conscientious Bourbons" to a larger view of the functions of institutions. Also, to young men not so familiar with Ely's earlier writings, like John Maurice Clark, Ely had written a classical work in institutional economics which helped shape their views in the institutional tradition. John R. Commons, who read the work in manuscript, elaborated many of Ely's ideas in *The Legal Foundations of Capitalism* (1924). A few law schools used Ely's work as a text and as collateral reading. Roscoe Pound of the Harvard Law School required it for a number of years in his seminar in jurisprudence. "There is nothing else on the subject worth talking about," he said.[11]

On December 12, 1914, former students and friends gave Ely a surprise banquet in commemoration of his new publication and his sixtieth birthday. David Kinley, president of the University of Illinois, spoke of Ely's contributions to the science of economics. Edward Bemis, who at this time ran a consulting engineering firm in Chicago, reviewed the services which Ely had rendered to society at large. At the conclusion of the gala celebration Edward Ross presented Ely with a beautiful loving cup.[12] Despite this loyalty of his students and friends, and the mildly favorable reviews

[11] See Joseph Dorfman, *The Economic Mind in American Civilization*, IV-V (New York: Viking, 1959), pp. 213-214, 440n; Clark, *et al.*, "Institutional Economics," *American Economic Review Supplement*, XXII (March, 1932), 106; [Ely], "Personal Statement in Regard to Two Reviews of Ely's *Property and Contract*" [1914], Ely MSS. Internal evidence indicates the statement was written sometime after the review by Hand in November of 1915.

[12] Ely to Albert Shaw, Dec. 24, 1914, Ely MSS.

of his book, Ely continued to feel unfulfilled and abused. In a multipage letter sent to friends he angrily replied to reviews by Charles A. Beard and Learned Hand. Of Beard: "It is not a review. [He] simply uses the appearance of the book to discredit me." Beard's statement that Ely's ideas came directly from German teachers was "absolutely false." "My development has been entirely independent," Ely wrote. He accused both Beard and Hand of not actually reading his work and of deliberately trying to destroy his reputation.[13] Ely still spoke with the self-righteousness of an Old Testament prophet, discrediting the motives of his critics and proclaiming the purity of his own.

During the war Ely initiated a series of important land studies with Professors Henry C. Taylor and Benjamin Hibbard, both of the Department of Agricultural Economics at Wisconsin. The university contributed funds for a study of cutover lands in northern Wisconsin. Ely proposed that they classify all unused land in the state according to economic use. They would determine the methods of bringing land into cultivation, means of sale, financing, and the work done by land companies. Hopefully they could suggest ways to promote more rapid settlement of the cutover regions.[14] In 1918 Ely published "Private Colonization of the Land" based on the Wisconsin study. He advocated planned settlement but insisted that it should be handled largely by private businessmen, who should receive a reasonable profit for the sale and for financing the new farmer. The settler would have the opportunity to consult the "greater brain power of the relatively few superior men in the community." The land companies of northern Wisconsin, Ely found, "recog-

[13] [Ely], "Personal Statement in Regard to Two Reviews of Ely's *Property and Contract*," Ely MSS.

[14] See [Ely], "Memorandum," Aug., 1917, Ely MSS; Ely, B. H. Hibbard, and A. B. Cox, *Credit Needs of Settlers in Upper Wisconsin* ("University of Wisconsin Agricultural Experiment Station Bulletin," No. 318 [Oct., 1920]).

nized that service in conspicuous degree must be the watchword of conspicuous success in land settlement."[15] Although the study represented pioneering scholarship, research methods were still quite crude. For supporting evidence they relied largely on the statements of the land companies themselves and a few short visits to new farmers. And the results were probably distorted by the high wartime prices for farm products.

In December of 1917 Ely and Taylor helped to organize the American Association for Agricultural Legislation. Elwood Mead, long-time advocate of public reclamation projects, was elected president, George F. Warren of Cornell, vice president, Ely, secretary, and Taylor, treasurer. At the founding session, held jointly with the American Economic Association at Philadelphia, Ely gave an address, "Tenancy in an Ideal System of Landed Property." The paper's conclusions confirmed the earlier studies of Hibbard and Taylor, except that Ely attempted to establish an ideal or benchmark from which to approach tenancy. Influenced by his European observations, he maintained that tenancy must be regarded as a final goal for perhaps one-third of the farmers in the country, and it should be especially high for Negroes in the South. Tenancy was frequently a means of transferring landed property from one generation to the next; it represented a rung on the agricultural ladder, from hired man to tenant to landowner. The evils of tenancy in the United States, Ely concluded, had been "grossly exaggerated."[16]

With high hopes for making the Association for Agricultural Legislation a success, Ely took charge of expanding

[15] Ely, "Private Colonization of the Land," *American Economic Review*, VIII (Sept., 1918), 527.

[16] See Taylor and Taylor, *The Story of Agricultural Economics*, pp. 804-826; "Minutes, American Association for Agricultural Legislation," Dec. 28, 1917, typewritten copy in Ely MSS; Ely, "Tenancy in an Ideal System of Landownership," *American Economic Review Supplement*, IX (1919), 180-212. For publication purposes the title was changed.

membership, obtaining funds, and even handling the minute
details of conventions. "It seems to me unfortunate," Oliver
E. Baker, former Ely student, wrote him after the 1918 convention, "that a man who has so many things to attend to
and so many interruptions by people who wish to meet him,
should in addition have these minor details to attend to."[17]
During the war the association issued several resolutions
which may have had some influence on federal government
policy. At Ely's instigation they published several bulletins
including papers by himself on the private colonization
of land and on tenancy. Farm bloc Senator Arthur Capper
of Kansas, after reading Ely's papers, wrote that they were
the "best discussion of the subject I have read" and contain
"information that will be of great value to me."[18] The state
auditor of Minnesota ordered copies of Ely's paper on private colonization for all of the legislators and county agents
of the state. Through the association Ely made several valuable acquaintances, including Milburn L. Wilson of Montana who, inspired by the work of Taylor and Ely, came to
Wisconsin for graduate work and later became a leading
agricultural policymaker in the New Deal. Gradually, the
association declined, until by 1922 it was largely absorbed
by the Farm Economic Association.[19]

The association helped to establish Ely as a leader of
land economists in the United States. In 1917 the Department of Agriculture asked him to prepare a plan for investigating the settlement of returning soldiers and sailors,
although it later refused to support Ely's plan. He also
prepared the sections on land utilization and tenure for the

[17] Baker to Ely, Dec. 30, 1918, Ely MSS.
[18] Capper to Ely, June 14, 1919, Ely MSS.
[19] See "Resolutions" of the association, *ca.* May 10, 1918, in Ely
MSS; Ely, "American Association for Agricultural Legislation: A De-
scription of the Association and a Statement of Its Aims" [1918], in
Ely MSS; Ely to Theodore Marburg, Feb. 14, 1919, Ely to Taylor,
Nov. 10, 1920, Ely to Members of the Association, March 4, 1922,
Ely MSS.

Agricultural Atlas of the department. Taylor, called to Washington in 1919 to reorganize a Bureau of Farm Management and Farm Economics, appointed Ely to a committee to consider the formation of a division of land economics. In 1919 Lewis C. Gray, an Ely-Taylor student, came to Washington to head the new division. From time to time Gray and Taylor called on Ely to present special lectures to department personnel on such diverse topics as the Historical School of economics and land problems in Wisconsin. In 1918 Governor Emmanuel Philipp appointed him to a Committee of Fifteen which was to frame a postwar land policy for Wisconsin.[20]

Ely clearly identified himself with the more conservative position on land settlement, opposing a policy formulated by Elwood Mead of the Reclamation Service of the Interior Department. The cutover regions, arid lands, and swamps, Mead proposed, should be reclaimed for returning servicemen. With the federal government purchasing the land, selling it to bona fide settlers on long-term payments, planned community development could be insured.[21] In letters to Senators Capper and Lenroot as well as to influential lobbyists such as Leo Day Woodworth of the Advisory Council of Real Estate Interests in New York City, Ely explained his reasons for opposing the proposal. Mead, Ely said, was familiar only with arid lands and furthermore had been "unduly influenced by working associates with radical

20 Ely to Charles L. Smith, Oct. 30, 1917, O. E. Baker to Ely, Feb. 20, 1918, Ely MSS; Leonard A. Salter, Jr., *A Critical Review of Research in Land Economics* (Minneapolis: University of Minnesota Press, 1948), pp. 16-17; U.S. Dept. of Agriculture, *Report of a Committee . . . to Consider the Subject of Land Economics,* Circular 138 (Washington, D.C.: Government Printing Office, 1918); Ely to Irvine L. Lenroot, Jan. 24, 1919, Ely MSS.

21 For the proposal that was prepared largely under Mead's supervision, see U.S. Dept. of Interior, Reclamation Service, *Farms for Returned Soldiers: Outline of Plans for Development of Arid, Swamp, and Other Unused Lands* (Washington, D.C.: Government Printing Office, 1918).

proclivities," in particular the single-taxers. The Wisconsin Committee of Fifteen, under Ely's influence, unofficially opposed the Mead plan. Disappointed, as he frankly admitted, with his own failure to receive an appointment similar to Mead's, Ely was also attempting to gain the support of private interests for an institute for the study of land economics.[22]

Ely did not oppose the public sponsorship of land settlement for experimental purposes but doubted that "any more than a minor part of the programme" could be "solved by public ownership."[23] Admittedly there should be a land policy which would promote widespread ownership and eliminate abuses. He suggested the establishment of state and federal land commissions similar to the railroad commission which had worked so well in Wisconsin. With increased population, land had become a utility, much like a natural monopoly in its economic relations. The commissions should license realtors, regulate tenancy contracts and land settlement, check credit arrangements, and serve in an advisory capacity to potential and actual landholders. Forests, valuable sources of water, and mineral deposits should be publicly owned.[24]

In the meantime Ely promoted the establishment of an institute for the study of land economics, primarily by exploiting the fears of special interest groups. Large property holders appeared particularly vulnerable to a revived single-tax agitation, which arose from the acute housing shortages, high rents, and the need for additional public revenues during the war and reconversion period. Several modified single

[22] See Ely to Capper, March 15, 1919, Ely to Lenroot, Aug. 12, 1918, Jan. 24, 1919, Lenroot to Ely, Dec. 21, 1918, Feb. 7, 1919, Ely to Woodworth, Aug. 1, 22, 1918, Woodworth to Ely, Aug. 12, 1918, Ely MSS.

[23] Ely to James E. Boyle, Oct. 9, 1918, Ely MSS.

[24] See especially Ely, "An American Land Policy," in Elisha M. Friedman, ed., *America and the New Era* (New York: Dutton, 1920), pp. 127-129, and Ely, "A National Policy for Land Utilization," in *Report of the National Agricultural Conference, January 23-27, 1922*, 67th Cong., 2nd Sess., 1921-1922, H.R. Doc. 195.

tax measures had come before Congress, although most of the bills would have excluded small farmers. Supporters believed such legislation would check land speculation, decrease tenancy, and force idle land into use.[25] To F. C. Schwedtman of the National City Bank of New York City, Ely gave a typical explanation of why he should receive support. Financial institutions, he wrote, "are seriously menaced by attacks on landed property." The proposed sum for the research project, $60,000, Ely claimed, was one-fifth of the amount spent by the single-taxers in the past few years. Every great railroad could well afford $1,000 per year for ten years. "Of course, I would not want it all to come from railroad companies, because that would create a prejudice; but I see no reason why part of it should not come from them, provided it is understood that the investigation is to be free and untrammeled."[26] Similar appeals, which sometimes included the danger of Bolshevism, went out to railroads, realtors, and large land companies.

Initially, large landholding interests showed little response to Ely's appeals for aid in doing general research in land economics. Several could not see how an institute would be of direct assistance and preferred to channel contributions through their own "educational" agencies. Despite his lack of success in 1918 and 1919, Ely continued to reiterate his pleas for research funds. He spoke to real estate associations in Milwaukee, Chicago, and Minneapolis, and to bankers' groups in St. Paul and Houston. Warning repeatedly that single-taxers had gained adherents in Washington, he unofficially adopted as his research motto, "Progress without Confiscation." A proposal submitted to the Carnegie Corporation in 1919 failed to win approval, partly because several board members wondered if Ely's investigations might "be interpreted by many as an effort to propagate a par-

[25] Dorfman, *The Economic Mind in American Civilization*, IV-V, 96-97.
[26] Ely to Schwedtman, Feb. 24, 1917, Ely MSS.

ticular theory or economic belief."[27] The University of Wisconsin Research Council, however, allotted him $1,000 for the academic year 1920-1921, and the university approved a special division of land economics under Ely's direction.[28]

In 1920 Ely's preparatory work began to pay dividends. In April the recently organized Interchurch World Movement agreed to pay traveling and research expenses for Ely, an assistant researcher, and a secretary. They proposed a general study of land economics as it affected religious programs. Before the summer was out, the movement collapsed, but Ely later received $3,000 from individuals connected with it. In July, William S. Kies, a former student who was now a wealthy investment broker in New York City, contributed $1,000 and contacted other potential benefactors. On September 16, 1920, Ely addressed the Farm Mortgage Bankers Association on the single tax at their national convention in Kansas City. Impressed by Ely's proposal, the association endorsed the institute and went to work to obtain financial support.[29] President Kingman N. Robbins wrote every farm mortgage banker in the country and included a copy of Ely's Kansas City address. Such questions as land taxation and tenancy, Robbins wrote, "are now the football of radicals and political opportunists. Only by meeting this propaganda with the true facts can we successfully combat it and certainly none is more interested in doing so than the farm mortgage banker."[30] In October, 1920, Ely announced the founding of the Institute for Research in Land Economics.[31]

[27] Henry Pritchett to Ely, May 30, 1919, Ely MSS.
[28] Charles S. Slichter to Ely, March 29, 1920, Ely MSS; *Land Economics* ("University of Wisconsin Bulletin," No. 1054 [May, 1920]).
[29] H. Paul Douglass to Ely, April 19, 1920, F. H. Partridge to Ely, July 14, 1920, Raymond B. Fosdick to Ely, Feb. 18, 1921, Ely to Kies, July 3, 1920, Kies to Ely, July 12, 1920, Ely to Kies, Oct. 8, 1920, Ely MSS.
[30] Robbins to Gentlemen, Jan. 12, 1921, Ely MSS.
[31] See Mary L. Shine, "Research in Land Economics at the University of Wisconsin," *National Real Estate Journal*, Dec. 6, 1920, p. 16,

In 1921 and 1922 Ely struggled ceaselessly to keep the institute alive. He hoped that it could furnish research for the immediate use of interested parties as well as general research in land economics. In 1921 the Farm Mortgage Bankers paid the institute to furnish statistics for use in opposing the Ralston-Nolan bill, a bill before Congress which would have levied a 1 percent tax on all land valued in excess of $10,000. The National Association of Real Estate Boards gave nationwide circulation to Benjamin Hibbard's detailed criticism of the bill. Hibbard's attack, one single-taxer claimed, "more than any other led to the bill's defeat." By January 16, 1922, thirteen railroads had given $200 each to the institute without requiring specific results, though they were fully aware of the position of the institute on land taxes. Yet the major financial support in 1922 came from the Carnegie Corporation, which allocated $10,000. The University of Wisconsin agreed to provide space for the institute, Ely's salary of $5,500 for five years, a full-time secretary, and $1,000 a year from the university for research, and to allow Ely to continue conducting his graduate classes and seminars, though he reached sixty-eight in April of 1922.[32] By the end of 1922 the institute employed over ten people and at times during the twenties included more than forty.

The institute and the National Association of Real Estate Boards jointly sponsored efforts to improve real estate education. In April, 1923, they initiated courses in real estate and land economics in over 150 cities through the Young Men's Christian Association. Several members of the staff taught in the course and the institute prepared several books

[32] See E. D. Chassell to Ely, April 2, May 27, 1921, Ely to Tom Ingersoll, June 11, 1921, Ely MSS; Emil O. Jorgensen, *False Education in Our Colleges and Universities* (Chicago: Manufacturers and Merchants Federal Tax League, 1925), p. 31; "Railroads Subsidized to the Institute," Jan. 16, 1922, Kies to Ely, Feb. 6, 1922, Ely to F. M. Davenport, Feb. 10, 1922, Ely to G. C. Sellery, May 19, 1922, E. A. Birge to Henry Pritchett, May 20, 1922, Ely MSS.

on real estate. Ernest M. Fisher of the institute wrote the first text and in 1923 joined the N.A.R.E.B. as an assistant executive secretary. The realtors contributed over $5,000 annually for three years to the work of the institute.[33]

In 1922 Ely began to establish a lucrative connection with the utility companies who were in the throes of a battle with public power advocates and were concerned with taxation and regulation. In August he wrote Martin J. Insull, brother of utility magnate Samuel Insull, that utilities were "especially vulnerable" to heavy taxation. "We feel . . . that what is needed now in the public interest is fearless, impartial, scientific research by an independent organization like ours. It makes no difference how honest the work may be that is carried on by interested parties, the results do not carry conviction."[34] The utility executives were anxious to cooperate but concluded that contributions should be channeled through the Carnegie Corporation so that they could escape criticism from state regulatory commissions and deduct their contributions from income tax payments. The Carnegie Corporation refused to become a party to the arrangement. But allocations of over $20,000 from individual utilities came to the institute in 1923 and 1924. From 1925 to 1929 the National Electric Light Association contributed $25,000 annually. And Martin Glaeser of the institute went to work preparing a book on public utilities, which the National Electric Light Association agreed to underwrite.[35] In 1923 Ely retitled his organization the Institute for Research in Land Economics and Public Utilities.

[33] See Herbert U. Nelson to Ely, Feb. 7, 1923, Ely MSS; *Institute News*, May, June, Nov., 1923; Nelson to Ely, Sept. 10, 1923, Nelson to Ralph E. Heilman, May 5, 1925, Receipts of Institute, July 1, 1925–June 30, 1926, Ely MSS.
[34] Ely to Martin J. Insull, Aug. 25, 1922, Ely MSS.
[35] See Margaret Schaffner to Ely, March 30, 1923, John C. Parker to Ely, May 31, 1923, George H. Harries to Ely, July 9, 1923, Martin Insull to Ely, March 24, 1924, Ely to Nicholas Murray Butler, Jan. 2, 1924, Ely to Charles J. Bullock, April 7, 1924, Ely to Martin Glaeser, Oct. 23, 1925, Ely MSS; Testimony of Martin Glaeser, in U.S. Senate,

From the outset, single-tax advocates and a few old-line Progressives criticized the relations between Ely's institute and special interest groups. Henry C. Taylor, after talking to Carl Vrooman, former assistant secretary of agriculture, found that several had the impression that the institute was an instrument of the realtors.[36] Ely was sensitive to such suggestions and constantly repeated that the institute was independent of donors. Every contributor, he claimed, had given them an "absolutely free hand" and "absolutely no one has made any suggestions in regard to our opinions or the nature of the results we reach."[37] Frequently Ely, in correspondence ot potential contributors, would attack the single tax or high land taxes, but he would conclude his letter by stating that the institute must be left completely free of any commitments. In selecting the directors of the institute he initially chose men not directly connected with a special interest. "The Institute," he explained in one brochure, "is supported entirely by private funds supplied by public-spirited individuals and organizations. . . . It has no thesis to defend nor preconceived conclusions to uphold; it obligates itself simply to search for the truth regardless of any special interest."[38]

In July of 1924 Emil O. Jorgensen of the Manufacturers and Merchants Federal Tax League, a single-tax organization, began a series of bold attacks upon the institute. Seven consecutive articles appeared in the *Bulletin* of the league, each purporting to show how a "Gigantic, Nation-Wide Scheme . . . Engineered by Prof. Ely of Wisconsin, and

---

Federal Trade Commission Hearings, Utility Corporation—Report, 70th Cong., 1st Sess., 1929, S. Doc. 92, pt. 11, pp. 48-61; Ely to Paul S. Clapp, May 21, 1930, Ely MSS.

[36] See for example Ely to G. C. Sellery, Nov. 25, 1921, Taylor to Ely, March 7, 1922, Ely MSS.

[37] Ely to Vrooman, March 9, 1922, Ely MSS.

[38] [Ely], "Institute for Research in Land Economics and Public Utilities" [1920], Ely MSS. Internal evidence indicates that the brochure was issued in 1921 or 1922.

Masquerading under the Guise of 'Research'" had been hatched to rob the producers of wealth and to protect "land speculators and rent profiteers." One leaflet contained a large picture of Ely in academic robes with "accusing" fingers pointing at him from three directions. In most of the bombastic propaganda of the league Jorgensen argued that Ely had formerly been favorable to the single tax but had become a large personal land speculator and had received donations from the National Association of Real Estate Boards to write a "special inflammatory article" against the Ralston-Nolan bill. Ely and the N.A.R.E.B. planned, Jorgensen said, to flood the country with books, pamphlets, reports, lectures, articles, "a steady stream of half-truths, false suggestions and misleading ideas regarding the proposition to transfer taxes from the fruits of industry to land values." Finally, whereas the institute claimed to be gathering the facts and then arriving at conclusions, they had already stated their conclusions and were now searching for facts to support them.[39]

Ely and his associates became genuinely alarmed by the repercussions of the Jorgensen attacks, for the tax league distributed 20,000 reprints of Jorgensen's first article to 2,000 Wisconsin newspaper editors, state officials, members of the Board of Regents, the university faculty, and leading scholars across the country. Moreover, in 1922 Robert M. La Follette, by winning reelection to the Senate, had swept the Progressive Republicans back into power in Wisconsin. The Progressives, who had regained control of the regents by 1924, now looked upon the university with suspicion, particularly Ely, who had led the fight against La Follette during the

[39] Seven articles were published by Jorgensen in the *Bulletin* monthly from July, 1924, to February, 1925. The articles were reprinted as Jorgensen, *False Education in Our Colleges and Universities.* See also "Do You Want the Public to be Deceived?" leaflet attached to Samuel W. Mendum to Ely, Feb. 15, 1925; form letter of Education Protective Association of America, Dec. 13, 1926, Ely MSS.

war. In hopes of bringing a retraction from Jorgensen, Ely called on his colleague John R. Commons, who frankly leaned toward the single tax and had, in fact, assisted Jorgensen's organization in drawing up the Ralston-Nolan bill. In a letter to Jorgensen, which the *Bulletin* of the league published in garbled form, Commons claimed that since Ely had always been opposed to the single tax, his views had not been influenced by the contributions of realtors. Instead of meeting Ely's arguments, Commons said, Jorgensen had impugned the motives of Ely and the University of Wisconsin.[40] The responder failed to halt the irrepressible Jorgensen.

Worried by the continued attacks on the institute, Ely began to consider a move from Wisconsin. Within the state the Progressive concern about the contributions of corporations to university research mounted. In January, 1925, La Follette blasted the Rockefeller General Education Board and the Carnegie endowments, both from which Ely had obtained funds. "Our universities, colleges and other educational institutions," he wrote, "are cringing and fawning for the favors of predatory wealth." The next month he lashed out again, arguing that the University of Wisconsin must lead the way to restore that "fearless 'winnowing and sifting of truth' which is paralyzed by the subsidies, direct and indirect, of the Monopoly System."[41] Although La Follette did not mention the institute and his "winnowing and sifting" statement may have been merely fortuitous, Ely saw the "handwriting on the wall." During the same period Commons was offered a grant from the Rockefeller Memorial for finish-

[40] See form letter of Education Protective Association, Dec. 13, 1926, Ely to Thomas S. Adams, Oct. 29, 1923, Commons to Jorgensen, Sept. 23, 1924, Ely MSS; Commons to G. C. Sellery, Dec. 4, 1924, E. A. Birge to Theodore Kronshage, Dec. 23, 1924, Presidents' Papers, University of Wisconsin Archives, Madison. For Ely's only public response to the attacks, see Ely, "Open Letter," *Institute News*, Nov. 1924.

[41] Signed editorials, *La Follette's Magazine*, XVII (Jan.-Feb., 1925), 2-3, 19-20,

ing his labor history. President Edward A. Birge, who succeeded Van Hise in 1918, advised Commons to turn it down,
for hostility to private gifts was growing in the state capital.
Ely confronted Birge. "What about the money that I am
receiving?" he asked. "They do not know about it," Birge
responded. "I think further comments are unnecessary,"
Ely wrote Henry C. Taylor. The sooner the institute could
be moved "the better."[42]

After briefly considering Columbia University, Ely settled
on Northwestern University at Evanston, Illinois. Already
he had added General Nathan W. MacChesney, general
counsel of the N.A.R.E.B. and a trustee of Northwestern,
to the institute's board of trustees. Martin Insull and John
C. Parker of the utilities industry, who were also trustees
at Northwestern, urged Ely to transfer his institute. Since
the university was privately endowed, Ely reasoned that
outside attacks would be less bothersome. Chicago, he said,
would provide the institute with an urban laboratory. Ralph
E. Heilman, dean of the Commerce School, and Walter
Dill Scott, president of the university, promised to raise
enough funds for an endowed chair in land economics and
$100,000 annually for the operating expenses of the institute,
out of which Ely was to receive a salary of $10,000 annually.
On July 1, 1925, the institute officially moved from Madison
to Evanston.[43] Apparently they left none too soon, for the
University of Wisconsin Board of Regents adopted a resolution in August barring any future gifts from "educational
endowments or organizations of like character."[44]

Moving to Northwestern failed to halt attacks on the in-

[42] Ely to Taylor, March 18, 1925, Ely MSS. See also Ely to Taylor,
Jan. 17, March 4, 1925, Ely MSS; Chicago *Daily News,* June 1, 1925.
[43] Ely to John Finley, Oct. 24, 1924, Heilman to Ely, Aug. 18,
1924, E. M. Fisher, "Confidential Memorandum," Sept. 15, 1924, Heilman to Ely, Dec. 22, 1924, Feb. 27, 1925, Ely to Heilman, April 24,
1925, "Minutes of the Meeting of the Board of Trustees of the Institute," May 22, 1925, Ely MSS; New York *Times,* Aug. 21, 1925, p. 12.
[44] Curti and Carstensen, *The University of Wisconsin,* II, 227,

stitute. Jorgensen continued his efforts to discredit the scientific work of Ely's group by organizing the Education Protective Association in 1926. In April he induced the Chicago branch of the American Federation of Teachers to ask for a resolution by the American Federation of Labor condemning the institute. Though a resolution was killed at the 1926 A.F. of L. convention, the executive council was instructed to make further investigations. John R. Commons again intervened in Ely's behalf. Writing to his friend, President William Green of the A.F. of L., Commons noted the past friendship of Ely to organized labor and the strong endorsement by the A.F. of L. of Ely's textbooks. The council made a perfunctory investigation. But Jorgensen persuaded several school boards, including Chicago's, to investigate and discontinue the use of Ely's texts. And President Edwin W. Kemmerer agreed to propose an investigation of the institute to the council of the American Economic Association, but Ely's friends on the council made certain that nothing came of the move.[45]

Amid the breaking storm of controversy, Ely had severed his connections with the university which he had served for thirty-two years. It was personally painful. In 1923 the university had awarded him an honorary LL.D. and twice, by special action of the regents, his retirement had been extended beyond the mandatory sixty-five. In 1924 his friends, students, and colleagues celebrated his seventieth birthday by having his portrait painted. It was later hung in the economics department in Sterling Hall. He left behind old friends such as John R. Commons, Edward A. Ross, and Benjamin Hibbard. His wife, who had served so many

[45] See Education Protective Association of America to Bowker, Oct. 1, 1926, form letter of E.P.A., Dec. 13, 1926, Ely MSS; Chicago *Evening News,* Oct. 8, 1926; Commons to Green, Oct. 9, 1926, Green to Commons, Nov. 17, 1926, Edward Morehouse to Ely, Nov. 27, 1926, Ely MSS; Chicago *Daily Tribune,* April 19, 1929; Jorgensen to Kemmerer, Sept. 30, 1926, Allyn A. Young to Ely, Oct. 13, 1926, Ely MSS.

splendid dinners to visiting dignitaries in Madison and had watched over the Monday night Round Tables, had passed quietly away on March 13, 1923. His youngest daughter, Anna, who remained close to her father, married Edward W. Morehouse, a staff member of the institute, and they moved to Northwestern with Ely. During the twenties both of his sons resided in Washington, D.C. Richard was a counsel with the Federal Trade Commission; John struggled to make a success of the Washington School for Secretaries, which he had founded and in which his father had invested heavily. As a parting gesture to the University of Wisconsin, Ely set up a scholarship in land economics in memory of his wife.[46]

At seventy Ely's pace of work and self-demands had changed surprisingly little from his days at Johns Hopkins. Arising early each day, he handled all of the staggering administrative work of the institute. At Northwestern he struggled with some of the same administrative problems that had plagued him at Wisconsin. While he and Dean Ralph Heilman worked closely together, Ely resented the final authority that the trustees of Northwestern exercised over appointments. At the same time they failed to assume responsibility for financing the institute. Conflicts arose over potential sources of finances, as both the university and the institute often sought the same benefactors. Ely found, after briefly experimenting with a professional fundraiser, that he alone commanded the respect to obtain funds. He eventually raised a $100,000 annual budget for the institute.

Ely lent every effort to publicizing the research and practical results of the institute. Monthly the *Institute News*

[46] See Ely to E. A. Birge, June 6, 1925, Ely MSS. Family record contained in Ely family Bible, photostatic copy in Ely MSS; Henry C. Taylor and George S. Wehrwein, "Richard T. Ely," *Journal of Land & Public Utility Economics*, XIX (Nov., 1943), 390; Ely, "Response at Celebration of Unveiling of Ely Portrait, University of Wisconsin," May 9, 1924, Ely MSS.

appeared, carrying articles on the activities of the staff and summaries of research projects. In 1925 the institute established the *Journal of Land & Public Utility Economics,* a scientific quarterly edited by Ely and Edward Morehouse. In the twenties the typical edition included several technical articles on such subjects as valuation and depreciation of utilities property, written mostly by members of the institute, book reviews, and a summary of recent legislation and court decisions affecting land and public utility economics. Originally Ely hoped the *Journal* would be purchased by interested parties and show a return for the institute, but its audience remained rather limited.

"I am like a horse on the treadmill," Ely wrote a childhood friend, Mattie Bent, in 1924. "I have to keep going and there is no help for it. If I stop, it will imperil the work of years. The consequence of it is that I am scarcely able to lead a really civilized life."[47] He played no cards, chess, or checkers. He had no hobby, he explained to a newspaperman writing a biographical sketch, unless it was hard work. Henry C. Taylor introduced him to golf during the war, but much as he enjoyed the game, he rarely played. In 1922 he learned to drive a car, which afforded him some relief from overtaut nerves. Above all, he enjoyed a good dinner party and even after the death of his wife continued to give them.[48] Before prohibition he had on occasion served wine to dinner guests. He often remarked that the breaking of bread together was a semispiritual ritual that alleviated anxieties and encouraged free communication.

Though Ely had little time for personal research, he wrote the first general textbook in land economics. Assisted by George S. Wehrwein and Mary L. Shine, he published in 1922 a mimeographed four-volume general survey that

[47] Ely to Mrs. H. K. W. Bent, April 26, 1924, Ely MSS.
[48] Ely to Carl V. Getz, Dec. 11, 1922, Ely to Taylor, Aug. 8, 1922, Ely to Taylor, Jan. 17, 1925, Morton Bodfish to Taylor, Aug. 30, 1944, Ely MSS.

contained several earlier essays by Ely and some highly tentative material on urban land economics. In 1924 Ely nominally collaborated with Morehouse to write *Elements of Land Economics* and with Wehrwein in 1928 to publish *Land Economics,* which was revised in 1940 and reissued in 1964. The Wehrwein edition is something of a classic and is still considered authoritative. Like earlier Ely works, it was institutional and pragmatic in approach. "If the use of the land in certain ways leads to undesirable social consequences, it is an undesirable use and should be changed."[49] The major objectives of a land utilization policy should include a balanced production and distribution of goods, the conservation of natural resources, and the increase of the amenities of living. These could be partially accomplished by various means of social control such as price fixing and rate regulation by the state, the use of the police power, and the dissemination of useful information. In terms of immediate and practical policy, the book was cautious; it did suggest rather strongly that additional arable land should be turned into forest, grass, and park lands.

Ely continued to be a leading public advocate of planned land-use policy. In 1922 Taylor asked him to address President Harding's National Agricultural Conference, which was attended by more than 300 delegates representing every phase of agriculture. Amid a postwar farm recession, Harding opened the conference by denouncing the farm bloc; farm bloc supporters retaliated by claiming the leaders of the conference were attempting to dictate a "tailor-made" program which did not include price fixing. On the third day Ely strongly rejected price fixing but did call for a national policy of land utilization. Policy "means planning," Ely flatly declared. The national government must classify and continuously reclassify all land according to usage. Classi-

49 Ely and Morehouse, *Elements of Land Economics* (New York: Macmillan, 1924), p. 269.

fication could then guide tax rates and allow the farmer to avoid costly mistakes. The lack of balance between supply and demand could be adjusted more easily. And the federal or state governments should retire forest and grazing lands.[50]

Ely's speech established the basic position that he took in numerous articles throughout the twenties. In 1923, in an address to the National Association of Real Estate Boards, he again advocated the creation of a national land commission to guide land policy. In 1927, in order to obtain a "balanced production," he suggested the retirement of submarginal lands by government purchase. In the twenties, or long before, Ely anticipated almost every phase of New Deal agricultural programs.[51]

The depression years of the thirties provided an opportunity for Ely and his followers in the advocacy of land-use planning to put their ideas to work. In 1931 Secretary of Agriculture Arthur M. Hyde and the land-grant colleges called a national land utilization conference in Chicago to consider proposals. Ely and former students Lewis C. Gray, John D. Black, and Milburn L. Wilson presented papers on various phases of land planning. The conference recommended a program similar to the one Ely had asked for during World War I: a national classification of land, regulation of land development, a reduction of reclamation projects, and the public ownership of submarginal lands.

50 See New York *Times*, Jan. 24, 1922, p. 1, Jan. 27, 1922, p. 1; Ely, "A National Policy for Land Utilization," pp. 111-121; Russell Lord, *The Wallaces of Iowa* (Boston: Houghton Mifflin, 1947), pp. 235-237.

51 Madison *Wisconsin State Journal*, June 27, 1923; Ely, "Farm Relief and Flood Control," *Review of Reviews*, LXXVI (Nov., 1927), 485-487. Ely probably reached the largest audience through the *Country Gentleman*, in which he published the following articles: "City and Country," XC (Feb. 21, 1925), 3-4; "The Population Bugaboo," XC (May 16, 1925), 3-4; "Robber Taxes," LXXXIX (July 12, 1924), 1-2; "The Three G's: A Program of Prosperity," LXXXIX (Aug. 30, 1924), 1-2, 28; "Worthless Land: What Can We Do for Men on It?" LXXXIX (Oct. 25, 1924), 1-2, 16; "Country Playgrounds," XC (Aug. 15, 1925), 6, 28.

The National Land Use Planning Committee, created by the conference, made studies of land usage and merged with the National Resources Committee in the New Deal to become the "first truly national planning agency." Ely's former students took a leading role in New Deal agricultural programs. Wilson became the director of the Division of Subsistence Homesteads, the first land-use program put into practice, as well as a leading advocate of the domestic allotment program. And Gray directed the first nationwide program of land retirement in the Agricultural Adjustment Administration.[52]

From the standpoint of economic theory Ely broadened the Ricardian conception of land. Traditionally, economists felt that land income or rent arose from either the superiority of one piece of land over another or because of population changes, both factors for which the individual was not responsible. Thus when a growing population pressed upon the available land supply, a "social" or "unearned" increment of value appeared. Ely's theory of "ripening costs" justified the private receipt of the social increment of land value. Normally, Ely said, a period of time lapsed between a change from one type of land usage to another; the person who held the land during this nonincome period earned that percentage of increment needed to pay such carrying costs as taxes, special assessments, interest on the investment, and a normal return on his investment. Thus the private purchase of such land, according to Ely, benefited society by providing a means of transferring land usage. The theory became a standard answer to single-tax arguments and continues to be presented in land economics texts.[53]

[52] See *Proceedings of the National Conference on Land Utilization;* Paul K. Conkin, *Tomorrow a New World: The New Deal Community Program* (Ithaca, N.Y.: Cornell University Press, 1959), p. 80.

[53] For Ely's first formulation of the theory of ripening costs see Ely, Mary L. Shine, and George S. Wehrwein, *Outlines of Land Economics* (Ann Arbor, Mich.: Edwards Bros., 1922), II, 39-42. See also Ely, "Land Income," *Political Science Quarterly,* XLIII (Sept., 1928),

Ely took an interest in the development of planned communities as laboratories for the study of land problems. In 1924 he became a member of the board of the City Housing Corporation which financed the Sunnyside housing project on Long Island. Alexander M. Bing, chief organizer of the corporation, contributed $500 annually for several years to the institute for the study of planned communities. The only concrete result was an article by Ely on the Sunnyside project. Apart from attending board meetings, he also helped to secure a loan from John D. Rockefeller, Jr., for the undertaking. The apparent success of Sunnyside encouraged Ely to attempt a similar project near Chicago. Rather than planned housing for low-income groups, he hoped the Chicago project would attract the professional classes. He was unable to raise funds for the Chicago proposal, though he continued to work rather loosely with Bing on the establishment of the Radburn, New Jersey, project in 1927, serving as a board member, and from time to time advised the City Housing Corporation on policy matters. The depression brought the failure of Bing's projects, but they did serve as experiments for later New Deal community programs.[54]

Like the Sunnyside project, which Ely called the institute's urban laboratory, the Montana Fairways Farms was supposed to serve as a rural laboratory. Henry C. Taylor

408-427. For Ely's claim to originating the theory see William N. Loucks, "The Unearned Increment in Land Values and Its Social Implications," *Annals of the American Academy of Political and Social Science*, CXLVIII (March, 1930), 73.

[54] See Ely, "The City Housing Corporation and 'Sunnyside,'" *Journal of Land & Public Utility Economics*, II (April, 1926), 172-185; Ely to Beardsley Ruml, Sept. 29, 1924, Ely MSS; Ely, "The Child's Paradise: The Story of Radburn," *Child's Welfare Magazine*, XXIV (June, 1930), 527-529; Ely, "Taxing Land Values and Taxing Building Values," *Annals of the American Academy of Political and Social Science*, CXLVIII (March, 1930), 167-168; Conkin, *Tomorrow a New World*, pp. 70, 76; Ely, "Economic Factors Underlying Housing and the Experience of Limited Dividend Companies," in *Report of the President's Conference on Home Building and Home Ownership* (Washington, D.C.: Government Printing Office, 1932).

suggested to M. L. Wilson and Ely a plan to establish a
company to buy farms and to promote farm ownership. Organized in 1924, the corporation borrowed $100,000 from
John D. Rockefeller, Jr., at 5 percent interest and with no
required payment. Wilson, of Montana State College, directed the purchase and operation of the farms. From the Laura
Spelman Rockefeller Memorial the institute obtained $10,000
for two years of research in Montana in hopes of securing
results that would be useful for similar projects in other
areas. Except for a short trip to Montana by Ely, Wehrwein,
and Hibbard, the institute did little in connection with the
Fairways Farms. The money from the Rockefeller Memorial
did allow Wehrwein and Hibbard to continue research in
land tenure and ownership in Wisconsin, Illinois, and Iowa.[55]

When the institute was moved to Northwestern in 1925,
Hibbard remained behind at Wisconsin, leaving the institute temporarily without any prominent figure in rural
land economics. In 1925 Taylor left the Agriculture Department and joined the institute staff. Ely had selected Taylor,
a former trustee of the institute, for his successor as director.
But because of a personality clash with Ely, Taylor was
forced to resign in 1928.[56] While at Northwestern, Taylor
and Jacob Perlman published an important paper on agriculture's share of the national income. They used the years
1909-1914 as base years for determining the ratio between
the purchasing power of the farmer and the nonagricultural
sector of the economy. Agriculture's share of the national
income, Taylor and Perlman concluded, showed a decrease
from about 20 percent from 1909 to 1919 to slightly over

[55] See M. L. Wilson, "The Fairways Farms Project," *Journal of
Land & Public Utility Economics,* II (April, 1926), 156-171; Ely to
Wilson, June 17, 1924, Taylor to Ely, June 21, 1924, Wehrwein to
Ely, June 9, 1924, Ely MSS; Conkin, *Tomorrow a New World,* pp.
76-77.

[56] See especially F. S. Deibler to E. R. A. Seligman, Dec. 19,
1928, attached to Deibler to Ely, March 1, 1929, Ely to Seligman, Dec.
6, 1928, Ely MSS.

10 percent from 1920 to 1925. The study had some influence in stimulating a demand for farm price supports.[57] The work of the institute was more prominent in urban land economics. In 1928 Albert S. Hinman and Herbert B. Dorau published the first general text in urban land economics. Under the auspices of the institute six books on various phases of real estate appeared.[58] The institute sponsored studies of urban land values in New York, Chicago, and Philadelphia.[59] They all concluded that the social increment on land values was much less than commonly supposed, owing to better land utilization and "ripening costs." In Chicago Herbert D. Simpson conducted the most controversial urban land research project for the institute. Working under the auspices of the Cook County Joint Commission of Real Estate Valuation and financed by the Chicago Association of Commerce, he formulated a technique for measuring real estate tax inequities. His Chicago survey showed that office and bank property carried the highest assessment in proportion to sale value, and industrial properties the next highest. In 1928, as a result of the Simpson survey, the Illinois state tax commission ordered a complete reassessment of all the real estate in Cook County.[60]

As in the case of Wisconsin, Ely did much to put the

[57] Taylor and Perlman, "The Share of Agriculture in the National Income," *Journal of Land & Public Utility Economics*, III (May, 1927), 149-156; Taylor and Taylor, *The Story of Agricultural Economics*, p. 509.

[58] For the bibliography of the books published under the auspices of the institute, see Ely, *Ground Under Our Feet*, pp. 318-323.

[59] See G. B. L. Arner, "Land Values in New York City," *Quarterly Journal of Economics*, XXXVI (Aug., 1922), 545-548; H. L. Shannon and H. Morton Bodfish, "Increments in Subdivided Land Values in Twenty Chicago Properties," *Journal of Land & Public Utility Economics*, V (Feb., 1929), 29-36; William N. Loucks, "Increments in Land Values in Philadelphia," *ibid.*, I (Oct., 1925), 469-477.

[60] See Chicago *Daily News*, July 5, 1927; G. C. Leiniger, "Suggestions for an Article to be Written for 'Review of Reviews' " [April, 1928], in Ely MSS; Simpson, *The Tax Situation in Illinois* (Chicago: Institute for Economic Research, 1930); Paul H. Douglas, "Chicago's Financial Muddle," *New Republic*, LXI (Feb. 12, 1930), 324-325.

graduate work of Northwestern University "on the map." Former Ely students Alton Jones, dean of the Graduate School, and Frederick S. Deibler, head of the economics department, cooperated closely with the institute. Ely personally offered only his weekly Round Table; over forty staff members and graduate students generally attended. Graduate fellowships in land economics came from the Henry Strong Foundation and the university. By 1929 Northwestern rivaled any school in the country in the quality and quantity of students in utility and real estate economics.

At Northwestern Ely met Margaret Hale Hahn. A member of the debating team and president of the hockey team, as well as a superb student, she became a member of Ely's Round Table, later a member of Ely's staff, and published in the institute's *Journal.* She became an immediate admirer of "Uncle Dick," as he was affectionately called by his colleagues and students behind his back. Her admiration drew Ely's affectionate response and, after eight years of a lonely widower's life, Ely decided to win the thirty-two-year-old Miss Hahn's hand. Little is known of their courtship, which was a surprise to most of his friends, except that he promised her a leisurely life and travel abroad. On a sentimental visit to the Ely burial ground in Old Lyme, Connecticut, Miss Hahn accepted Ely's proposal and in 1931 they were married. Their optimistic plans fell victim of the Great Depression. The birth of William Brewster in 1932 and Mary in 1934 delighted Ely, and he was frequently seen pushing a baby carriage through the tree-shrouded streets.[61] Through the trying thirties the vitality and youthfulness of his wife greatly enriched his waning years. "You have the memory," William S. Kies wrote her shortly after Ely's death in 1943, "of having made a very great man happy in his last years."[62]

[61] See Ely, *Ground Under Our Feet,* pp. 250; James Washington Bell, "My Memories of Richard T. Ely," April 5, 1944, in Ely MSS; New York *Times,* March 30, 1934, p. 3.
[62] Kies to Margaret Ely, Oct. 25, 1943, Ely MSS.

Chapter Nine

HIS FINAL YEARS

LIKE SO MANY old Progressives in the twenties some of Ely's earlier optimism soured. "I think our civilization has slipped," he wrote in 1922, "and that we have gone backward as compared with 1914. It is going to take us a long time to get back where we were before the World War." Although still believing that problems would not "solve themselves," he had less confidence in the efficacy of government as a tool of reform. Impressed by the findings of the eugenicists of the decade, he increasingly felt that the Progressives had gone too far toward a direct democracy. The Constitution, he said, recognized inequalities in abilities and was "entirely in accord with the modern science of heredity. I think, in general, so far as we have departed from the principles of our Federal Constitution we have made things worse rather than better."[1] He uneasily combined subservience to the business cult with increasing disillusionment about the potentialities of reform. No longer did the easy theology of the social gospel seem to square with the reality of human nature. "It is pretty hard to keep one's faith in these days," he wrote Mattie Bent in 1929. "The Catholics have a logical position whether we agree with them or not; but what about the rest of us?"[2] At the Grace Episcopal Church in Madison he had served as senior warden and contributed $5,000 to a building fund, but after he moved to Evanston, he rarely attended services.

In the twenties Ely changed his views concerning public ownership of natural monopolies, particularly electric power. Though years had passed since he had been an active propagandist for public power, as late as 1917 he had spoken favorably of public ownership to a small group at Wisconsin. In an autobiographical note composed in 1929 he explained that the evolution of the American economic system had produced new conditions unfavorable to public ownership. But more important, the public had not responded to public enterprises.[3] Private utility groups had no doubt where Ely stood. "We are working continuously on public and private ownership," he wrote to M. H. Aylesworth, managing director of the National Electric Light Association on April 26, 1926, "and I am delighted with the results we are getting. I am sure also that you are going to be pleased."[4] On the same day he directed Samuel J. Brandenburg, who was revising the Ely-Wicker high school text, to change the section on public utilities because "complaint was made of it by one public utility man and I think justifiably so."[5] In 1926 Ely also became a

---

[1] Ely to Carl V. Getz, Dec. 11, 1922, Ely MSS, State Historical Society of Wisconsin, Madison.

[2] Ely to Mrs. H. K. W. Bent, April 27, 1929, Ely MSS.

[3] [Ely], "Notes for a Discussion of Public Ownership of Public Utilities," March 24, 1917, [Ely], "Autobiographical Note" [August, 1929], copies in Ely MSS.

[4] Ely to Aylesworth, April 26, 1926, Ely MSS.

[5] Ely to Brandenburg, April 26, 1926, Ely MSS. The complaint was made in a study prepared by John B. Sheridan, director of the Missouri committee on public utility information. The *Elementary Principles of Economics* "is an argument for public ownership," wrote Sheridan. [Sheridan], "Textbooks on Civics, Economics, Etc., Used in Public

member of the Committee on Cooperation with Educational Institutions of the N.E.L.A., which directed a campaign for writing favorable utility textbooks and the teaching of utility economics in colleges. The N.E.L.A. sponsored a textbook by Martin Glaeser which it intended primarily as a weapon against public power propaganda.[6]

Martin Glaeser furnished the most important research on public utilities for the institute. Glaeser took courses in engineering as an undergraduate, graduate courses in economics under Ely and Commons, and law under Roscoe Pound at Harvard. In 1921-1922 he undertook a general survey of the public utility situation in Milwaukee for a joint aldermanic and citizens' committee appointed by the common council of the city. His massive report dealt largely with the Milwaukee Electric Railway and Light Company and included a survey and evaluation of the principles and practices of regulation. As a result of Glaeser's work the city adopted an operating agreement with the company that transferred regulatory powers from the state to the city government. The company apparently viewed the results favorably, for they contributed substantially to Ely's institute. In 1923 Glaeser began work on a comprehensive monograph on public utility economics which was published in 1927.[7] When the institute moved to Northwestern, Glaeser stayed at Wisconsin, though he continued as a research associate and received some funds from the institute.

In reality the utility magnates found the institute rather ineffective in presenting the kind of information they wanted.

Schools which Give Incomplete Information on State Regulation . . . of Public Utilities," in U. S. Senate, *Federal Trade Commission Hearings, Utility Corporations—Exhibits*, 70th Cong., 1st Sess., 1929, S. Doc. 92, pt. 2, p. 461.

[6] See Ely, "Preliminary Report of the Institute," July 1, 1925 to June 30, 1926, in *Utility Corporations—Exhibits*, pt. 3, pp. 642-644.

[7] Glaeser, *Outlines of Public Utility Economics* (New York: Macmillan, 1927), pp. 702-704; Testimony of Martin Glaeser, in U. S. Senate, *Federal Trade Commission Hearings, Utility Corporations—Report*, 70th Cong., 1st Sess., 1929, S. Doc. 92, pt. 11, pp. 48-61.

The articles in the *Journal of Land & Public Utility Economics* usually avoided controversial issues and Glaeser took four years to complete his textbook. When Carl D. Jackson, chairman of the Committee on Cooperation of the N.E.L.A., read the proofs of Glaeser's book in 1927, he was surprised and chagrined. He felt the book was "distinctly antagonistic to the . . . utilities viewpoint" and refused to give it the endorsement of the N.E.L.A.[8] Glaeser, after reviewing Jackson's criticism, refused to make any changes. The next year, 1928, the subsidization of the Glaeser book came to the attention of the Federal Trade Commission. When the commission began hearings on utility propaganda, they called Glaeser to Washington to testify. His testimony and the revelation of payments by the N.E.L.A. to the institute received nationwide coverage by the Hearst newspapers and drew angry denunciations by public power advocates, including perpetual gadfly Gifford Pinchot, governor of Pennsylvania.[9]

Ely answered the charges with self-righteous indignation. The institute had not received "any money whatever" for supporting propaganda against public ownership, he wrote Robert E. Healy, chief counsel of the Federal Trade Commission. Typically, he turned on his accusers. Relieving the F.T.C. of any blame, he attacked the "sensational writers" who "have twisted and distorted information" in an effort to discredit scientific research.[10]

Yet the charges of unethical practices against both the institute and the Harvard Graduate School of Business Ad-

[8] R. R. Smith to Ely, Aug. 12, 1927, Ely MSS.
[9] Testimony of Martin Glaeser, in *Utility Corporations—Report*, pt. 11, pp. 48-61; "National Electric Light Association Statement" in *Utility Corporations—Exhibits,* pt. 3, p. 98. See Ely to William Thum, Oct. 25, 1928, Ely MSS; *Daily Northwestern,* Oct. 29, 1929; Ely to Pinchot, Oct. 29, 1929, Pinchot to Ely, Nov. 8, 1929; Ely MSS. For a summary study of the Federal Trade Commission hearings by a public power advocate, see Ernest Gruening, *The Public Pays: A Study of Power Propaganda* (New York: Vanguard, 1931).
[10] Ely to Healy, Oct. 29, 1929, Ely MSS. See also Ely to Editor, *Daily Northwestern,* May 30, 1928.

ministration became so serious that the American Association of University Professors instructed their standing committee on ethics to investigate. Edwin R. A. Seligman, who prepared the committee report, noted that the A.A.U.P. had been founded to protect the rights and tenure of faculty members. "At present the shoe pinches on the other foot—it is a question not of academic rights but of academic duties."[11] The central issue was not the professor's receiving funds for technical advice, Seligman said, but his providing opinions or facts bearing on public policy to private concerns. If the professor were to maintain confidence, he must be as impartial as a judge. No funds should be solicited, he concluded, for studies involving such political questions as public ownership and taxation policy. Realizing that the statement of ethics ran "counter to a widely recognized practice," the committee felt that as a minimum standard, solicitors should always insist on lump sums not subject to renewal.

Exposure of the extensive contributions of the N.E.L.A. to the institute coincided with the Great Crash of 1929. The N.E.L.A. abruptly discontinued its $25,000 annual contribution, and other benefactors quickly followed suit. The receipts for the institute fell almost 90 percent in 1930-1931 and the personnel had to be cut to five full-time members. The depression shattered all of Ely's grand hopes for the future. He desperately sought funds from contacts on the East Coast. Although the Equitable Tax Association agreed to sponsor a study of New York City's assessment practices, they were unable to finance it. In the summer of 1930 Ely weakened physically from the strain. Former students and long-time friends, John Finley, Albert Shaw, and William S. Kies, decided that the time had "come" for Ely to retire as director of the institute.

[11] Seligman, "Propaganda by Public Utility Corporations," *Bulletin of the American Association of University Professors*, XVI (May, 1930), 351. The report was approved by committee members C. P. Costigan, G. W. Cunningham, John Dewey, E. A. Ross, C. F. Taeusch, C. J. Tilden, J. H. Tufts, and U. G. Weatherly.

They asked Northwestern to continue his salary and take over the institute's management.[12]

In 1932 Ely transferred a small staff to New York City, where he organized the Institute for Economic Research. Northwestern continued to sponsor the *Journal of Land & Public Utility Economics* but, owing to financial plight, discontinued Ely's salary in 1933. Up to 1935 Ely's small staff offered regular courses in land economics and real estate; the classes attracted bank, utility, and real estate men. The primary source of income for the institute came from student fees, which apparently were always inadequate. The institute also sponsored small research projects, including a study of foreclosure conveyances in Manhattan between 1924 and 1928. By the summer of 1935 the institute was running desperately short of funds. From the outset Ely had contributed some of his own income to the institute and in the thirties dipped into his modest reserves. Between 1935 and 1937 family illnesses drained away the remainder of his personal savings. While Ely proudly tried to hide his poverty, old friends advanced him some money, and in 1937 they organized the Ely Economic Foundation. The foundation ostensibly was to provide money for Ely to finish his autobiography, a history of American economic thought, and several other books.[13]

Nonetheless, in the thirties Ely continued to contribute popular articles on current problems. He saw in the extreme fluctuations of land values an underlying cause of the depression. During World War I, Ely said, the federal government had encouraged the overexpansion of agriculture. After the war the demand for farm products fell sharply because of a

[12] See Dora E. Wallendorf to Fred J. Wright, Jan. 13, 1931, Ely to Herbert D. Simpson, May 12, 1930, Fred J. Wright to William A. Dyche, Nov. 25, 1930, Ely MSS.
[13] See New York *Times*, Sept. 4, 1932, sec. x & xi, p. 1; Ely to W. S. Kies, May 18, 1933, Ralph E. Heilman to Ely, April 4, 1933, Ely MSS; New York *Times*, Sept. 1, 1934, p. 24, Sept. 9, 1934, sec. x, p. 1; Ely to W. S. Kies, Feb. 15, 1934, July 3, 1935, Nov. 11, 1937, Robert H. Armstrong to Kies, July 28, 1937, Carl C. Kickey to Kies, June 7, 1937, Ely MSS; editorial, New York *Times*, Oct. 7, 1937, p. 26,

decline in the birth rate and in foreign markets. Land values collapsed, causing the failure of many rural banks and a loss in purchasing power by farmers, a loss which weakened the entire economy. In urban areas a similar overexpansion occurred. Increasingly, Ely said, cities, owing to the construction of skyscrapers and apartment houses, concentrated into smaller areas. If land had been put to proper use by a state policy, at least the severity of the depression could have been avoided. In 1931 he praised New York Governor Franklin D. Roosevelt's policy of purchasing submarginal lands and putting them into forests.[14]

Ely also popularized a program for general economic recovery. In 1931 he advocated the massive consolidation of American industry along the lines of European cartels. The Sherman Act and other efforts by the federal government to encourage competition had outlived their "usefulness." Unbridled competition seriously hampered the planning and direction needed to prevent the depression and promote recovery. Businessmen, if allowed freedom to consolidate and direct the operations of the economy, could avoid disastrous overproduction. Instead, he said, business leaders were continuously "harassed by administrative agencies of government." He completely rejected any state competition with private enterprise and opposed federal government planning. He also felt that property taxes should be reduced by basing them on use value. Increases in the state income taxes, selected sales taxes, and the sale of bonds would be adequate to meet the expenses of government.[15]

Long before the Great Depression, Ely preached an eco-

[14] Ely, "Real Estate in the Business Cycle," *American Economic Review Supplement*, XXII (March, 1932), 137-143; Ely, "Heavy Tax Burden Depreciates Value," New York *Times*, July 31, 1932, sec. x & xi, p. 1; Ely to Roosevelt, Nov. 11, 1931, in Edgar B. Nixon, ed., *Franklin D. Roosevelt and Conservation, 1911-1945* (Hyde Park, Franklin D. Roosevelt Library, 1957), I, 100-101.

[15] Ely, "Government in Business and the General Welfare," *Review of Reviews*, LXXXIV (Oct., 1931), 44-47; Ely, "Taxation in Hard Times," *Review of Reviews*, LXXXIV (Aug., 1931), 67-68.

nomic heresy which anticipated the major position of many New Deal economists; that is, depressions resulted to a large extent from underconsumption which in turn was affected by the distribution of income. Except for the socialist-oriented, economists generally approached the business cycle from the standpoint of production. In the depression of the nineties Ely suggested that greater purchasing power in the hands of the consuming masses could be provided by the increased construction of public buildings. Bonds for financing additional projects could be sold cheaply, and the money would be in effect transferred from the individual with a high propensity for savings to one with a high propensity for consumption. He proposed a method of leveling the business cycle without interfering directly with private enterprise or directly affecting the distribution of income. In the early part of the century he also encouraged the unconventional English economist, John Hobson, to work along underconsumption lines. He edited Hobson's *The Economics of Distribution* (1900), used it as a text for several years, and invited Hobson to Madison as a visiting lecturer in 1902. Perhaps because of the socialist tint attached to an undersconsumption approach, Ely himself failed to develop his ideas beyond his rather crude position in the nineties.[16]

In 1931 Ely proposed a novel program for dealing with unemployment in his little book *Hard Times—The Way In and the Way Out*. Doubtless in the long run the country would recover from the depression, he said, but for the short run, hard times meant "throwing on the competitive scrapheap hundreds of thousands . . . who somehow or other must live out purposeless lives, too often degenerating physically, mentally and spiritually." To meet this crisis, he advocated the

[16] See Ely, "Hard Times," *Interior*, I (Dec. 13, 1894), 1624; Joseph Dorfman, *The Economic Mind in American Civilization*, IV-V (New York: Viking, 1959), pp. 174-175, 175n; Ely, *Hard Times—The Way In and the Way Out, with Special Consideration of the "Seen and the Unseen"* (New York: Macmillan, 1931), pp. 48-49.

establishment of a "peace time army" to improve the "common wealth" of the nation. The common wealth included public parks, playgrounds, forests, roadsides, and grade crossings; the work that could be done to improve the common wealth had "no assignable limits." In the future, an increasing proportion of the nation's resources should be channeled into the common wealth. The proposal would not interfere with private industry, he said, and was not socialistic. "The common wealth and the peace-time army afford a way out of Hard Times. In my opinion they are the only proposals adequate to meet the situation."[17]

Ely had long held the notion that young men could be inculcated with discipline and morality by serving in the army. He quoted William James' *The Moral Equivalent of War* to show that "militarism is the great preserver of our ideal, of hardihood, and human life with no use for hardihood would be contemptible."[18] Previously the farm had furnished the discipline which had produced our great industrial leaders, but a peacetime army was needed as a substitute for the boy reared in the city. In times of prosperity the country could support an army of 25,000 men headed by a general staff. The staff would prepare plans for an indefinite expansion. The soldiers would receive regular salaries below that of private industry, and the army could serve as a pool of skilled manpower from which industry could draw. The country should have no difficulty financing the measure by the sale of government bonds, Ely said. For it was easier to sell bonds in times of depression. The long-term bonds could gradually be paid by taxation. Favorably reviewed on the front page of the New York *Times,* Ely's book attracted considerable attention. He popularized his proposal in an article for the *Review of Reviews* and in a speech before the American Association for Labor Legislation. Both President Hoover and Governor

[17] Ely, *Hard Times*, pp. 5, 93.
[18] *Ibid.*, p. 98.

Roosevelt were familiar with Ely's peacetime army proposal. And since it squared exactly with Roosevelt's views, Ely saw its embodiment in the Civilian Conservation Corps of the New Deal. However, Ely wanted the C.C.C. to draft all young men and women for at least one year.[19]

Ely had mixed feelings about the early New Deal. In 1935, when he cooperated with Frank Bohn, son-in-law of Secretary of Commerce Daniel C. Roper, on *The Great Change,* he fully approved of the Civilian Conservation Corps and the establishment of the Securities and Exchange Commission. But he condemned the National Industrial Recovery Act and the Agricultural Adjustment Act because they both attempted to limit production in a time of scarcity. He disapproved Roosevelt's tinkering with the gold content of the dollar but fully approved of the Federal Reserve System's expanding the use of its powers over credit. He praised Milburn L. Wilson's efforts to establish subsistence homesteads and felt that the program should be enlarged. But, like orthodox economists, he believed all levels of government should operate within balanced budgets.[20] In general, Ely said, the states should take a larger role in recovery programs. In 1935 a special legislative committee invited him to Wisconsin to testify. He again proposed a tax on land-use value, higher state income taxes, and the state purchase of submarginal land, and suggested a state-financed housing program.[21]

[19] Nathan W. MacChesney to Henry C. Taylor, Feb. 26, 1944, Ely MSS; Roosevelt to Ely, Nov. 30, 1931, in Nixon, ed., *Franklin D. Roosevelt,* p. 103; Ely, "Hard Times—And a Way Out," *Review of Reviews,* LXXXIII (March, 1931), 90-92; New York *Times,* Dec. 30, 31, 1931, p. 1; Ely and Frank Bohn, *The Great Change* (New York: Nelson, 1935), pp. 211, 256-259; Dorfman, *The Economic Mind in American Civilization,* IV-V, 671.

[20] See especially Ely and Bohn, *The Great Change,* pp. 138, 206, 210-212. The authors of each chapter are noted in the text. See also Ely to W. S. Kies, Nov. 19, 1935, Ely MSS.

[21] Ely and Bohn, *The Great Change,* p. 198; Ely, "Recovery Program for a State," *Review of Reviews,* XC (Aug., 1934), 39, 62; Ely to W. S. Kies, May 29, 1934, Ely MSS.

In the thirties Ely attempted to live according to his own advice: "THE FORWARD LOOK KEEPS ONE YOUNG IN SPIRIT."[22] A neighbor in Radburn, New Jersey, Louis Brownlow, reported that Ely was as vigorous in mind and spirit as any youth. He finished his autobiography in 1938, and after that date worked on a history of American economic thought. He was enormously pleased when, in 1937, Columbia University made him an honorary associate in economics with a small stipend and an office in which he occasionally conferred with graduate students.[23] In 1939 he developed pneumonia and was hospitalized for about three weeks. "Though he was convalescent two weeks of that time," Robert H. Armstrong wrote William S. Kies, "they nevertheless, had to keep a day and night nurse with him—just because he is 'cussed' and 'damn' contrary."[24]

Late in 1939 Ely decided to return to the city of his forefathers, Old Lyme, Connecticut. He bought a home there, moved his family, and each week came into New York City to take care of a few appointments at Columbia. When World War II broke out, Mrs. Ely took a job with the Gould Aeronautical Division, commuting thirty-five miles to work.[25] Ely continued to toil over the revision of several of his old manuscripts to his last day. On October 4, 1943, he quietly passed away at the age of eighty-nine. He would have been justly proud of the New York *Times* obituary. "Prof. Richard T. Ely," the editorial said, ". . . did as much as any man of his generation to make economics a less dismal science. . . .

[22] Ely, *Ground Under Our Feet: An Autobiography* (New York: Macmillan, 1938), p. 286.

[23] Louis Brownlow, *A Passion for Politics: The Autobiography of Louis Brownlow* (Chicago: University of Chicago Press, 1955), I, 68; Lindsay Rogers to Ely, Oct. 3, 1937, Ely MSS; editorial, "Still Going Strong," New York *Times*, Oct. 7, 1937, p. 26, *ibid.*, May 15, 1938, sec. II, p. 5.

[24] Armstrong to Kies, March 20, 1939, Ely MSS.

[25] See Ely to W. S. Kies, Sept. 8, 1939, Margaret Ely to Kies, Feb. 22, 1943, Ely MSS.

The modern economists whom he influenced, and many of whom he taught, have had a tremendous effect on national economic policies."[26]

To the very end Ely thought of himself as something of a reformer. In 1938, at the age of eighty-four, he wrote, "as I look about me, I am still fired by an ambition to 'set the world right,' just as my father before me."[27] But if he still had some faith in progress in 1938, he had changed his views on both the means of achieving it and on the nature of man and society. Benefiting and contributing to a common climate of opinion, his ideas and actions often mirrored the baffling anxieties, the frustrations, and the successes of the reformers. And his passion for public esteem sometimes blunted his reform zeal. It often posed a dilemma for the professor as a reformer. If he pursued a reform agenda which seemed to benefit only the lower classes, he endangered his status with his fellow professors and intellectuals. Yet, to achieve the practice of brotherly love, the lower classes would have to benefit more from the fruits of industrialism.

Ely's views shifted about the basic nature of man. He had always had some misgivings about the essential goodness of man. When writing in the nineties about a hypothetical socialist society he emphasized that at least rewards in public esteem would be necessary to obtain men's services, that restructuring society would not automatically produce moral men. Neither did he see men as equal in capacity. Whereas in his earlier years he had considerable faith that by the mere presentation of the facts, men would respond rationally, he increasingly doubted that they would do so. As he grew older, he became more convinced that rationality was a product of breeding and training.

[26] Editorial, "Professor Ely," New York *Times*, Oct. 6, 1943, p. 22.
[27] Ely, *Ground Under Our Feet*, p. 250.

In viewing society as a whole Ely tended to see it as a single unity in which all individuals were part of an organism. But he was quick to note that industrialism and urbanism had produced social fragmentation, in short, class warfare. For the social organism to work properly, both laborer and employer had to recognize their status and obligations; recognition required social reform. The principle of brotherly love bonded men into one humanity, which included all races and nationalities. However, this did not mean that men were endowed with equal capacities. Ely assumed a rather noblesse oblige attitude toward both the Negro and the laboring class. With age and under the influence of the eugenicists of the early part of the twentieth century, he agreed with Edward Ross that certain "races"—a term they used interchangeably with nationality—were inherently inferior.

Ely's age also affected his feelings toward the speed with which reforms could be accomplished. In his early years he was confident that man controlled his own destiny. Through the use of the state he believed change could be quite rapid. With his growing pessimism about the essential nature of man, he grew less confident that government was a useful tool. In the twenties and thirties he was willing to concede essential direction of the nation's economy to the private sector. Even in enterprises clothed in the public interest, such as utilities, he opposed public ownership. Earlier he had presented a host of legislative programs, his "golden mean," which read very much like the achievements of the New Deal. And Ely, even as an old man, approved of much of the economic experimentation of the New Deal.

The evangelical message which he had delivered remains part of the American heritage. To modern, supposedly hardheaded academic reformers, Ely spoke too much out of the clouds. They dismiss his early faith in progress and his belief that institutional reform can affect human nature. Nonetheless, it was the "visionaries" like Ely who humanized the middle class. They reinfected the class with a spirit of community welfare that, try as it may, it has never been able to rid itself of. Although Ely's specific suggestions for resolving the problems of his times were sometimes untenable, his criticisms of the competitive system have a modern ring. His indictment of an America in which amoral boosters set the criteria for success, in which the machine has become ascendant over man, still stands. What has perhaps been lost, what Ely himself partially lost over the years, has been the well-informed prophet-preacher. He has been replaced by the more inarticulate, cautious, and fearful academician who is unable or unwilling to appeal to the practical or the idealistic side of the American mind.

APPENDIX

The Works of Richard T. Ely

THIS LIST OF WORKS by Richard T. Ely is the most complete available. Inasmuch as Ely wrote frequently in obscure journals and newspapers, there are undoubtedly a few publications by him that I have missed. Moreover, I have not included in this list the short commentaries by Ely at the meetings of the American Economic Association which were published. He also sometimes wrote short introductions to the numerous books that he edited for Thomas Y. Crowell, Macmillan, and the Institute for Research in Land and Public Utility Economics. A complete list of these edited works is in the appendix of Richard T. Ely, *Ground Under Our Feet: An Autobiography* (New York: The Macmillan Company, 1938).

BOOKS

The Coming City. New York: Thomas Y. Crowell & Co., 1902.

(and George R. Wicker). *Elementary Principles of Economics; Together with a Short Sketch of Economic History.* New York: The Macmillan Company, 1904.

(and Samuel J. Brandenburg). *Elementary Principles of Economics.* 3rd rev. ed. New York: The Macmillan Company, 1923.

(and Edward W. Morehouse). *Elements of Land Economics.* New York: The Macmillan Company, 1924.

(and Ralph H. Hess, Charles K. Leith, Thomas Nixon Carver). *The Foundations of National Prosperity: Studies in the Conservation of Permanent National Resources.* New York: The Macmillan Company, 1917.

French and German Socialism in Modern Times. New York: Harper & Bros., 1883.

(and Frank Bohn). *The Great Change.* New York: Thomas Nelson and Sons, 1935.

Ground Under Our Feet: An Autobiography. New York: The Macmillan Company, 1938.

Hard Times—The Way In and the Way Out, with a Special Consideration of the "Seen and the Unseen." New York: The Macmillan Company, 1931.

An Introduction to Political Economy. New York: Chautauqua Press, 1889.

The Labor Movement in America. New York: Thomas Y. Crowell & Company, 1886.

(and George S. Wehrwein). *Land Economics.* Ann Arbor, Mich.: Edwards Brothers, Inc., 1928.

Monopolies and Trusts. New York: The Macmillan Company, 1900.

Outlines of Economics. New York: Flood and Vincent, 1893.

(and Thomas S. Adams, Max O. Lorenz, Allyn A. Young). *Outlines of Economics.* Rev. ed. New York: The Macmillan Company, 1908.

(and Ralph H. Hess). *Outlines of Economics.* 6th rev. ed. New York: The Macmillan Company, 1937.

(and Mary L. Shine and George S. Wehrwein). *Outlines of Land Economics.* 4 vols. Ann Arbor, Mich.: Edwards Bros, Inc., 1922.

Problems of To-day: A Discussion of Protective Tariffs, Taxation, and Monopolies. New York: Thomas Y. Crowell & Company, 1888.

Property and Contract in Their Relations to the Distribution of Wealth. 2 vols. New York: The Macmillan Company, 1914.

Science-Economic Discussion. New York: Science, 1887.

Social Aspects of Christianity and Other Essays. New York: Thomas Y. Crowell & Company, 1889.

The Social Law of Service. New York: Eaton & Mains, 1896.

Socialism: An Examination of Its Nature, Its Strength and Its Weakness, with Suggestions for Social Reform. New York: Thomas Y. Crowell & Company, 1894.

The Strength and Weakness of Socialism. New York: Chautauqua Press, 1899.

Studies in the Evolution of an Industrial Society. New York: The Macmillan Company, 1903.

(and John H. Finley). *Taxation in American States and Cities.* New York: Thomas Y. Crowell & Company, 1888.

The World War and Leadership in a Democracy. New York: The Macmillan Company, 1918.

Appendix 239

ARTICLES AND PAMPHLETS

"Address," *Consensus,* XIV (January, 1930), 8-9.

"Address before the Annual Meeting of the American Federation of Labor," *Christian Union,* XXXVII (February 9, 1888), 170-171.

"Adjusting the Tax Burden to the Tax-Paying Ability of the Tax Bearer," *Proceedings of the National Conference on Land Utilization, November 19-21, 1931.* Washington, D.C.: Government Printing Office, 1932.

"Administration," *Christian Union,* XXXIV (December 9, 16, 1886), 9-10, 10.

"Administration of the City of Berlin," *Nation,* XXXIV (March 23, 30, 1882), 245-246, 267-269.

"The Advantages of Public Ownership and Management of Natural Monopolies," *Cosmopolitan,* XXX (March, 1901), 557-560.

"America, the Land of Joy: Economic Gains of Twenty-five Years in Terms of Social Welfare," *Review of Reviews,* LXXIII (January, 1926), 37-38.

"American Boastfulness—The Oriental Congress," *Christian Union,* XL (November 28, 1889), 675.

"American Colleges and German Universities," *Harper's New Monthly Magazine,* LXI (July, 1880), 253-260.

"The American Economic Association," *Independent,* XXXIX (June 2, 1887), 681-682.

"The American Economic Association, 1885-1909," *Publications of the American Economic Association,* 3d ser., XI (1910), 47-93.

"An American Industrial Experiment," *Harper's Monthly,* CV (June, 1902), 39-45.

"American Labor Organizations," *Chautauqua Herald,* July 30, August 1, 1887.

"American Labor Organizations," *Congregationalist,* XXXIX (January 6, 13, 20, 1887), 1, 12, 20.

"An American Land Policy," in Elisha M. Friedman, ed., *America and the New Era.* New York: E. P. Dutton, 1920.

"Der Amerikanische Katheder-Socializt," Philadelphia *Tageblatt,* May 15, 1889.

"An Analysis of the Steel Trust," *Cosmopolitan,* XXXI (August, 1901), 428-431.

"Anarchy," *Harper's Weekly,* XXXVII (December 23, 1893), 1226.

"Arbitration," *North American Review,* CXLIII (October, 1886), 317-328.

"Are We Going Too Fast?" *Christian Advocate,* LXVII (March 31, 1892), 206.

"Baltimore and Ohio Employees' Relief Association," *Harper's Weekly*, XXIX (July 4, 1885), 430-431.

"Bismarck's Plan for Insuring German Laborers," *International Review*, XII (May, 1882), 504-526.

"A Brief Sketch of the Railway History of Germany," in *Papers Relating to the Foreign Relations of the United States, Transmitted to Congress, with the Annual Message of the President, December 6, 1880*. Washington, D.C.: Government Printing Office, 1880. Pp. 408-422.

"The Building and Loan Association," *Review of Reviews*, LXVIII (December, 1923), 641-645.

"The Celebration of Thanksgiving Day by the Socialists of Chicago," *Christian Union*, XXX (December 18, 1884), 594-595.

"Certain Psychological Phases of Industrial Evolution," in Howard J. Rogers, ed., *Congress of Arts and Science*. Boston: Houghton Mifflin, 1906. Vol. VII.

"The Child's Paradise: The Story of Radburn," *Child's Welfare Magazine*, XXIV (June, 1930), 527-529.

"The Christian Social Union; A Social University," *Churchman*, LV (April 2, 1892), 414-415.

"Christian Socialism in England," *Christian Union*, XXXI (May 28, June 4, 11, 1885), 7-8, 7-8, 7-8.

"Christianity as a Social Force," in John Henry Barrows, ed., *The World's Parliament of Religions*. Chicago: Parliament Publishing Co., 1893. Vol. II.

"Christianity the Remedy for Socialism," *Christian Union*, XXXI (June 26, 1884), 605.

"Christianity's Foundation: A Common Sense View of the Old Testament," *Ram's Horn*, VII (March 14, 1896), 5-6.

"Church and the Labor Movement," *Outlook*, XLIX (January 13, 1894), 60-61.

"The Church and the State," Hartford *Courant*, April 16-19, 1890.

"The Church and the Worker," *Truth Seeker*, XXXVIII (June 10, 1911), 354-355.

"City and Country," *Country Gentleman*, XC (February 21, 1925), 3-4.

"The City Housing Corporation and 'Sunnyside,' " *Journal of Land & Public Utility Economics*, II (April, 1926), 172-185.

"Commerce and Its Growth in Modern Times," in Charles E. Beale, ed., *Gately's World Progress*. Philadelphia: J. J. Cotter, 1886.

"Competition: Its Nature, Its Permanency, and Its Beneficence," *Publications of the American Economic Association*, 3d ser., II (1901), 55-70.

"Competition in the New Era," *Administration*, V (February, 1923), 129-138.

"Conditions of Industrial Peace," *Forum*, III (August, 1887), 638-644.

"Conservation and Economic Theory," in American Institute of Mining Engineers, *Bulletin* No. 109 (January, 1916), 211-226.

"The Control of Natural Monopolies," *World Today*, V (December, 1903), 1633-1634.

"Co-operation," *Chautauquan*, VIII (December, 1887), 149-152.

"Co-operation in America," *Congregationalist*, XXXVIII (February 11, 18, 25, March 4, 11, 1886), 43, 52, 62, 70, 80.

"Cooperation in Literature and the State," in William Eddy Barns, ed., *The Labor Problem*. New York: Harper and Bros., 1886.

"Cooperation, the Ultimate Solution of the Labor Problem," *Chautauqua Herald*, August 2, 3, 1887.

"Country Playgrounds," *Country Gentleman*, XC (August 15, 1925), 6, 28.

(and B. H. Hibbard and A. B. Cox). *Credit Needs of Settlers in Upper Wisconsin*. ("University of Wisconsin Agricultural Experiment Station Bulletin," No. 318), October, 1920.

"The Crime of Neglect," *Our Day*, XVI (February, 1896), 67-68.

"Debt Readjustment vs. Liquidation of Farmer's Contractual Relations," *Journal of Land & Public Utility Economics*, II (April, 1926), 254-256.

"A Decade of Economic Theory," *Annals of the American Academy of Political and Social Science*, XV (1900), 236-256.

"A Decade of Social Progress," *Christian Union*, XLIII (March 5, 1891), 303-305.

"Distribution as an Economic Problem," in R. C. Epstein, ed., *Supplementary Readings in Economics*. New York: Harper and Bros., 1929.

"Economic Aspects of Industrial Training," *Report of the Baltimore Conference on Charities*, [n.p., n.p.], 1887.

"Economic Factors Underlying Housing and the Experience of Limited Dividend Companies," *Report of President's Conference on Home Building and Home Ownership*. Washington, D.C.: Government Printing Office, 1932.

"Economic Internationalism," *Chautauquan*, X (February, 1890), 538-542.

"Economic Relationships of Construction," *Plastering Craft*, I (January 15, 1938), 9, 14, 31.

"The Economic and Social Aspects of Mormonism," *Harper's Monthly*, CVI (April, 1903), 667-668.

"The Economic Revolution," *Chautauquan*, XVI (January, 1893), 398-401.

"Economic Theory and Labor Legislation," *Publications of the American Economic Association*, 3d ser., IX (1908), 124-153.

"Economics," in Edgar Dawson, *Teaching the Social Studies*. New York: The Macmillan Company, 1927.

"Economics and Geography," *Papers and Proceedings of the American Economic Association*, 4th ser., XVI (1926), 114-115.

Economics in Its Relation to Education and Legislation for the Improvement of Individual and National Welfare, U.S. Department of Agriculture, Bureau of Markets and Crop Estimates, October 15, 1921.

"Economics in Secondary Education," *Educational Review*, XX (September, 1900), 152-158.

"Education for Farmers," *Farm, Stock and Home*, VII (March 1, 1891), 125.

"The Educational Policy of the Church," *The Churchman*, LXX (July 28, 1894), 94-95.

"Ethical Aspects of Ownership," *Cosmopolitan*, XXXII (February, 1902), 450-458.

"The Evolution of Industrial Society," Duluth *News Tribune*, October 30, 1897.

"Farm Relief and Flood Control," *Review of Reviews*, LXXVI (November, 1927), 485-487.

"The Forestry Act of 1927 of the Province of Ontario," *Journal of Land & Public Utility Economics*, IV (February, 1928), 100-102.

"The Founding and Early History of the American Economic Association," *American Economic Review, Supplement*, XXVI (March, 1936), 140-150.

"Fraternalism vs. Paternalism in Government," *Century Magazine*, LV (March, 1898), 780-784.

"The French Protestant Association for the Practical Study of Social Questions," *Virginia Seminary Magazine*, V (June, 1892), 373-378.

"Fundamental Beliefs in My Social Philosophy," *Forum*, XVIII (October, 1894), 173-183.

"The Future Organization of the Higher Education in the United States," *Journal of Proceedings and Addresses of the National Education Association*, XXXIV (1895), 645-656.

"George Mygatt Fisk—In Memoriam," Madison *Democrat*, May 17, 1910.

"George W. Childs in His Relations to His Employees," in George W. Childs, *Recollections*. Philadelphia: J. B. Lippincott, 1890.

"German Cooperative Credit-Unions," *Atlantic Monthly*, XLVII (February, 1881), 207-223.

"German Railways," *Nation*, LXVI (July 28, 1881), 67-68.

"Germany and Russia," New York *Evening Post,* November 1, 1879.

"Germany's Burdens," New York *Evening Post,* March 24, 1880.

"Germany's Dilemma," New York *Semi-Weekly Tribune,* December 21, 1885.

"Government and Business," *Papers and Discussions of the First Commercial and Industrial Congress.* ("University of Wisconsin Bulletin 800"). July, 1916, pp. 165-167.

"Government in Business and the General Welfare," *Review of Reviews,* LXXXIV (October, 1931), 44-47.

"Hard Times," *Interior,* I (December 13, 1894), 1622-1624.

"Hard Times—And a Way Out," *Review of Reviews,* LXXXIII (March, 1931), 90-92.

"Heavy Tax Burden Depreciates Value," New York *Times,* July 31, 1932, sec. x-xi, 1.

"Herbert B. Adams, A Sketch," *Review of Reviews,* XXIV (September, 1901), 321-323.

"Heredity and Circumstances," *Outlook,* XLVIII (September 16, 1893), 505-506.

Heredity and Environment, Remarks at Annual State Conference of Charities and Correction, Madison, Wisconsin, February 28–March 3, 1893.

"Higher Education: Intelligent Common Action Between the West and the South," Richmond *Dispatch,* May 7, 1893.

"The Higher Education and the Churches," *Kingdom,* VIII (June 7, 1895), 119-120.

"The Higher Education of Women in the Schools of Economics Political Science, and History of the University of Wisconsin," *Christian Union,* XLV (May 28, 1892), 1025.

"Higher Educational Work of Chautauqua," *Christian Union,* XLI (June 26, 1890), 896.

"How Do the Economic Limitations of Poorer Agricultural Sections Affect Social Conditions?" in Ezra Dwight Sanderson, ed., *Farm Income and Farm Life.* Chicago: University of Chicago Press, 1927.

"How Should Political Economy Be Taught to the Rising Generation?" *Frank Leslie's Illustrated Newspapers,* November 2, 1889.

"How to Avert Strikes," Boston *Evening Transcript,* August 3, 1901.

"How to Prevent Strikes," *Christian Union,* XXXIX (February 21, 1889), 231.

"How to Spoil a City—Railway Openings in the Streets and Lots," Baltimore *Sun,* April 11, 1890.

"If You Can't Go to College," *Success Magazine,* VI (February, 1903), 85, 102.

244   *Appendix*

"Important New Social Movements in England," *Christian Union,*
XLII (November 6, 1890), 593-594.
"The Improvement of Municipal Government," *Christian Union,*
XLII (October 9, 1890), 460-461.
"Industrial Betterment," *Harper's Monthly,* CV (September, 1902),
548-553.
"Industrial Democracy in American History," Madison *Democrat,*
December 11, 1906.
"Industrial Liberty," *Publications of the American Economic As-
sociation,* 3d ser., III (1902), 59-79.
"The Inheritance of Property," *North American Review,* CLIII
(July, 1891), 54-66.
"Institute for Research in Land Economics and Public Utilities,"
Sewanee Review, XXXII (February, 1924), 313-316.
(and Edward D. Jones). "Instruction in Charities and Correction
in the University of Wisconsin," *Lend-a-Hand,* XIV (June,
1895), 406-411.
"John Stuart Mill," in Charles D. Warner, ed., *Library of the
World's Best Literature.* New York: R. S. Peale and J. A. Hill,
1897. Vol. XVII.
"The Johns Hopkins University," *Christian Union,* XXVI (August
24, 1882), 146.
"Knights of Labor and Administrative Reform," *Civil Service Re-
former,* II (April, 1886), 57-59.
"Labor Movement and International Peace," *Our Day,* XVI (April,
1896), 194-195.
"The Labor Movement: A Reply to the Editor of the Christian
Register," *Christian Register,* LXVI (October 27, 1887), 675.
"Labor Organizations," *Chautauqua Herald,* July 30, 1887.
"Labor Organizations," *Forum,* III (March, 1887), 50-58.
(and George S. Wehrwein). "Land Colonization, Private," in
Edward M. Tuttle, ed., *Book of Rural Life.* Chicago: Bellows-
Durham, 1925.
"Land as an Economic Concept: A Fragment," in *Economia
Politica Contemporanea Saggi di Economia Finanza in Onore
del Professor Camillo Supino.* Milan: A. Padova, 1930.
"Land Economics," in Jacob H. Hollander, ed., *Economic Essays,
Contributed in Honor of John Bates Clark.* New York: The
Macmillan Company, 1927.
"Land Economics," *Papers and Proceedings of the American Eco-
nomic Association,* 4th ser., XVI (March, 1926), 297-299.
"Land Economics and Business Executives," *Administration,* II
(December, 1921), 721-728.
"Land Economics as a Science and the Real Estate Business as a
Profession," *Krenn and Dato Times,* December, 1927,

"Land Income," *Political Science Quarterly*, XLIII (September, 1928), 408-427.

"Land Speculation," *Journal of Farm Economics*, II (July, 1920), 121-135.

"Landed Property as an Economic Concept and as a Field of Research," *Papers and Proceedings of the American Economic Association*, 4th ser., VII (1917), 18-33.

"Landlord and Tenant Problems," *Breeder's Gazette*, LXXXVII (December 3, 1925), 658-659.

The Larger Aspects of Civil Service Reform," *Independent*, XLVI (April 26, 1894), 520.

"Leadership in a Democracy," *Chinese Students' Monthly*, XIII (November, 1917), 28-38.

"Lessons to be Drawn from the Year's Labor Troubles," *Interior*, XXXII (December 26, 1901), 1653-1654.

Letter to H. A. Schauffler, in "Address of Rev. Virgin," *Home Missionary*, LVII (October, 1884), 227-229.

Letter to the Editor, Buffalo *Courier*, November 25, 1888.

"Liberty a Social Product," *Our Day*, XVI (December, 1886), 671-672.

"Life and Services of Herbert Baxter Adams," in *Herbert B. Adams: Tributes of Friends, 1876-1901*. Baltimore, Md.: Johns Hopkins Press, 1902.

"Luck and Chance in Success and Failure," *Administration*, I (May, 1921), 577-584.

"Memorial to Former President Henry C. Adams," *American Economic Review*, XII (September, 1922), 401-416.

"Merchandising of Offices," *Journal of Land & Public Utility Economics*, II (October, 1926), 479.

"Model Towns," *Christian Union*, XLII (November 27, 1890), 708.

"Money and Its Functions," *Banker's Magazine*, XXXVII (January, 1883), 490-501.

"Municipal Ownership of Natural Monopolies," *North American Review*, CLXXII (March, 1901), 445-455.

"Municipal Ownership of Waterworks: A Corporation Canard," Baltimore *Sun*, December 22, 1890.

"The National Agricultural Conference," *Review of Reviews*, LXV (March, 1922), 271-274.

"A National Policy for Land Utilization," in *Report of the National Agricultural Conference, January 23-27, 1922*, 67th Cong., 2nd Sess., H. R. Doc. 195 (1922).

"National Problems: Revision of the Tariff," Boston *Sunday Times*, February 7, 1886.

"Natural Monopolies," in Herbert B. Dorau, *Materials for the*

Study of Public Utility Economics. New York: The Macmillan Company, 1930.

Natural Monopolies and Local Taxation: An Address before the Boston Merchants Association, January 8, 1889. Boston: Robinson and Stephenson, 1889.

"Natural Monopolies and the Workingman," *North American Review,* CLVIII (March, 1894), 294-303.

"The Nature and Significance of Monopolies and Trusts," *International Journal of Ethics,* X (April, 1900), 273-288.

"The Nature of Socialism," Duluth *News Tribune,* November 13, 1897.

The Needs of the City: An Address Delivered Before the Boston Conference of the Evangelical Alliance, December 4, 1889. New York: [n.p.], 1889.

"Neglected Aspects of Municipal Reform," Duluth *News Tribune,* December 18, 1897.

"The Negro Question," in William I. Haven, ed., *My Brother and I.* New York: Hunt and Eaton, 1895.

"The New Economic World and the New Economics," *Journal of Land & Public Utility Economics,* V (November, 1929), 341-353.

"The Next Things in Social Reform," *Christian Union,* XLIII (April 23, 1891), 531-532.

"Objections to Socialism," *Harper's Weekly,* XXXVIII (January 6, 13, 26, 1894), 15, 31, 58.

"Oliver Goldsmith," *Acta Columbiana,* November, 1876, pp. 23-26.

"On Methods of Teaching Political Economy," in G. Stanley Hall, ed., *Methods of Teaching History.* 2nd ed. Boston: D. C. Heath, 1902.

"Ought Church Seats to be Free?" *Christian Union,* XXXVIII (July 19, 1888), 69-70.

"Our Common Schools," *Lippincott's Magazine,* III (January, 1882), 89-95.

"Parsimony in Public Finance," *Harper's Weekly,* XXXVII (September 2, 1893), 46.

"The Past and the Present of Political Economy," in Herbert B. Adams, ed., *Johns Hopkins University Studies in Historical and Political Science.* Vol. II. Baltimore, Md.: Johns Hopkins Press, 1884.

"The Past and the Present of Political Economy," *Overland Monthly,* II (September, 1883), 225-235.

"Pauperism in the United States," *North American Review,* CLII (April, 1891), 395-409.

"Philanthropy," Baltimore *Sun,* March 9, 1887.

"Philanthropy," *Chautauquan*, IX (October, 1888), 16-18.

"The Place of Research in Graduate Training," in *Proceedings of the Northwestern University Conference on Business Education Held in Connection with the Dedicatory Exercises of Wieboldt Hall . . . June 16 and 17, 1927*. Chicago: Northwestern University, 1927.

"Political Economy in America," *North American Review*, CXLIV (February, 1887), 113-119.

"Political Economy in Germany in 1882," *Johns Hopkins University Circulars*, II (December, 1882), 27-28.

"Political Economy in the High School," *School Education*, XIV (March, 1896), 9-11.

"Political Economy in the Schools of the South," Charlotte (North Carolina) *Evening Chronicle*, May 20, 1906.

"The Population Bugaboo," *Country Gentleman*, XC (May 16, 1925), 3-4.

"The Practical Approach to the World," in Bertrand Russell, *et al.*, *The World Man Lives In*. New York: D. Van Nostrand, 1929.

"The Price of Progress," *Administration*, III (June, 1922), 657-663.

"Private and Public Colonization or Organized Settlement of the Land," *National Real Estate Journal*, XXIV (March 12, 1923), 46-49.

"Private Colonization of the Land," *American Economic Review*, VIII (September, 1918), 522-548.

"Proceedings of the Second Annual Meeting of the American Economic Association," *Publications of the American Economic Association*, III (1888), 193-225.

"Professor Ely and Socialism: An Explanation of His Views," Baltimore *American*, February 10, 1886.

"Professor Ely Asks for a Religious Reform," New York *Mail and Express*, April 13, 1889.

"Professor Richard T. Ely Makes a Personal Statement in Reply to Accusations Affecting His Conduct as a University Professor, His Teaching and Writings," *Chautauqua Assembly Herald*, August 15, 1894.

(and Seth Low). "A Programme for Labor Reform," *Century Magazine*, XXXIX (April, 1890), 938-951.

"The Progress of Cooperation in England," *Congregationalist*, XXXVII (March 12, 1885), 87.

(and Thomas K. Urdahl). "Progress of Socialism Since 1893," *Chautauquan*, XXX (October-December, 1899), 77-84, 186-193, 294-299.

"Progressivism, True and False—An Outline," *Review of Reviews*, LI (February, 1915), 209-211.

"The Proper Aims of Schools of Economics and Politics," *Independent*, XLIV (May 19, 1892), 682-683.

"Prophecy of German Domination of Russia," Chicago *Tribune*, March 31, 1918.

"Prussian Civil Service," *Overland Monthly*, I (May, 1883), 451-458.

"Psychical Forces of Industry," *International Quarterly*, XI (July, 1905), 301-315.

"Public Control Begins Where Private Competition Ends," Toledo *Sunday Journal*, February 15, 1891.

"Public Control of Private Corporations," *Cosmopolitan*, XXX (February, 1901), 430-433.

"Public Ownership: What Shall Be Done With the Natural Monopolies?" Portland (Maine) *Advertiser*, August 25, 1894.

"Public Service Research and Education," in *National Electrical Light Association Proceedings*, LXXIX (1923), 134-135.

"Public Utilities and Corporations in Wisconsin," *Publications of the American Economic Association*, 3d ser., X (1909), 423-425.

"Pullman: A Social Study," *Harper's New Monthly Magazine*, LXX (February, 1885), 452-466.

"Questions of the Day: IV—Social Progress," *Cosmopolitan*, XXXI (May, 1901), 61-64.

"Real Estate Education in the Future," *Annals of Real Estate Practice*, I (1925), 228-241.

"Real Estate in the Business Cycle," *American Economic Review, Supplement*, XXII (March, 1932), 137-143.

[Real Estate Problems], New York *Times*, September 11-October 23, 1932. Seven weekly articles in Sections X and XI.

"Recent American Socialism," in Herbert B. Adams, ed., *Johns Hopkins University Studies in Historical and Political Science*. Vol. III. Baltimore, Md.: Johns Hopkins Press, 1885.

"Recent Phases of Socialism in the United States," *Christian Union*, XXIX (April 24, May 1, 1884), 389-390, 438-439.

"Recollections of the Life and Work of Professor Simon N. Patten," *Papers and Proceedings of the American Economic Association*, 4th ser., XIII (1923), 259-266.

"Recovery Program for a State," *Review of Reviews*, XC (August, 1934), 39, 62.

"Reform in Taxation," *Cosmopolitan*, XXX (January, 1901), 307-309.

The Relation of Temperance Reform to the Labor Movement. Chicago: National W.C.T.U., 1889.

(and George S. Wehrwein). "The Relation of the Engineer to Land Economics," *Professional Engineer*, X (October, 1925), 8-10, 23.

"The Religious Press and the Labor Movement," *Central Christian Advocate*, XLVI (September 3, 1902), 1130-1131.

Report of the Baltimore Tax Commission. Baltimore, Md.: King, 1885.

"Report of the Industrial Commission: Labor," *Yale Review*, XI (November, 1902), 229-250.

"Report of the Organization of the American Economic Association," *Publications of the American Economic Association*, I (1887), 5-46.

"Report of the Proceedings at the Third Annual Meeting," *Publications of the American Economic Association*, IV (1889), 269-321.

"Report of the Second Annual Meeting of the American Economic Association," *Publications of the American Economic Association*, III (1888-1889), 43-70.

"Report of the Tax Commission and Tax Reform in Wisconsin," Milwaukee *Sentinel*, February 18, 1901.

(and L. S. Merriam). "Report on Social Legislation in the United States for 1889-1890," *Economic Review*, I (April, 1891), 234-256.

"Robber Taxes," *Country Gentleman*, LXXXIX (July 12, 1924), 1-2.

"Russian Land Reform," *American Economic Review*, VI (March, 1916), 61-68.

"The Scaffold in Switzerland," New York *Evening Post*, June 11, 1879.

"School and Postal-Savings Banks," *Our Continent*, I (April 26, May 3, 1882), 163, 179.

"The School of Economics, Political Science and History," in R. G. Thwaites, ed., *The University of Wisconsin: Its History and Its Alumni*. Madison, Wis.: University of Wisconsin Press, 1900.

"Schools and Churches in Their Relation to Charities and Correction," *Charities Review*, IV (December, 1894), 57-64.

"Science and the Practical Problems of Life," Schenectady (New York) *Citizen*, July 31, 1925.

(and H. D. Simpson). *Scientific Research in Public Finance and Taxation and the Practical Application of the Results.* Northwestern University Associates, Union League Club, Chicago, 1930.

"Senior's Theory of Monopoly," *Publications of the American Economic Association*, 3d ser., I (1900), 89-102.

"Shall We Have Public Ownership or Public Control?" *World Today*, V (November, 1903), 1439-1443.

"Should the Government Control the Telegraph? I. Why the Government Should Own the Telegraph," *Arena*, XXV (December, 1895), 49-53.

"Should the University of Wisconsin Aim to Attract Students From Every Part of the United States and Even From Foreign Countries?" *Aegis,* VII (February 3, 1893), 121-123.

"The Single Tax," *Christian Advocate,* LXV (December 25, 1890), 856.

"The Situation and the Remedy," *Independent,* XLIX (March 4, 1897), 268-271.

"Smaller and Better Taxes," *Farm Journal,* LIII (November, 1929), 7-8.

"Social Aspects of Insurance," *Views,* XI (February, 1899), 4-6.

"Social Observations in Germany," *Congregationalist,* LXXVII (June 9-July 28, 1892), 182, 190, 198, 206, 214, 222, 230, 238.

"Social Progress," Duluth *News Tribune,* December 19, 1897.

"Social Reform Versus War," *Our Day,* XVIII (June, 1896), 313-314.

"Social Studies—[Corporations]," *Harper's New Monthly Magazine,* LXXIV (May, 1887), 970-977, LXXV (June, 1887), 71-79, and LXXV (July, 1887), 259-266.

"Social Studies—[Railroads]," *Harper's New Monthly Magazine,* LXXIII (July, 1886), 250-57, (August, 1886), 450-457, and (September, 1886), 571-578.

"Social Studies in Europe," *Christian Union,* XL (November 28-December 19, 1889), 691, 711-712, 763, 798-799.

"Socialism," *Andover Review,* V (February, 1886), 146-163.

"Socialism," *Proceedings of the Inter-Denominational Congress,* (1885), 89-90.

"Socialism [Its Nature, Its Strength, and Its Weakness]," *Independent,* XLIII (February 5-July 2, 1891). A series of twenty-one consecutive weekly articles which were reprinted with revison as *Socialism: An Examination of Its Nature, Its Strength, and Its Weakness, with Suggestions for Social Reform.*

Socialism: Syllabus of a Course of Six Lectures. Syllabus No. 4. Madison, Wis.: University of Wisconsin Extension Department, 1892.

"Socialism in America," *North American Review,* CXLII (June, 1886), 519-525.

(and Thomas K. Urdahl). "Socialistic Propaganda," *Chautauquan,* XXX (January, 1900), 381-382.

"Soil Deterioration and Public Land Policy," *Journal of the American Socety of Agronomy,* XVIII (February, 1926), 161-165.

"Some Applications of Laissez-Faire," *Harper's Weekly,* XXVIII (April 26, 1884), 271.

"Some Ethical Aspects of Ownership," *Cosmopolitan,* XXXII (February, 1902), 456-458.

"Some Recent Theories Regarding the Stages of Economic Development," *Publications of the American Economic Association,* 3d ser., VIII (1907), 133-136.

"Eine Stadt der Arbeiterwohlfahrt," in Leopold Katscher, ed., *Mit, Nicht Gegen Einander!* Dresden: Albanus, 1905.

"The State Unversities," *Cosmopolitan,* XIX (October, 1895), 648-653.

"The State University: It Should Rank Second to None in the Country," Milwaukee *Sentinel,* October 26, 1892.

"The Strength and Weakness of Socialism," Duluth *News Tribune,* November 14, 1897.

"Street Cleaning in Berlin," New York *Evening Post,* April 6, 1881.

"Studies in the Evolution of Industrial Society: A Statement from Professor Ely," *Charities,* XII (February 6, 1904), 166-169.

"The Study of Social Science and the Christian Minister," *Northwestern Congregationalist,* V (October 7, 1892), 4-5.

"A Study of the 'Decreed' Town," *Harper's Monthly,* CVI (February, 1903), 390-411.

"Suggestions for Social Topics," *Christian Advocate,* LXVI-LXVII (February 12, 1891–February 18, 1892), 103, 186-187, 257-258, 321-322, 386, 465-466, 538, 602, 764, 824, 100-101. A series of eleven articles published monthly except October, 1891, and January, 1892.

Suggestions for Speakers on the United States and the World War. ("Patriotism Through Education Series," Pamphlet No. 13.) New York: National Security League, [n.d.].

"Suggestions to Teachers of General Economics," *Journal of Political Economy,* XVIII (June, 1910), 437-440.

"Supplementary Report on Taxation in Maryland," in *Report of the Maryland Tax Commission to the General Assembly.* Baltimore, Md.: King, 1888.

"Systematic Charity," Baltimore *Sun,* March 9, 1887.

"The Tariff," New York *Evening Telegram,* December 13, 1884.

"The Tariff and the Trusts—Expenditures for Internal Revenues," in Albert Shaw, ed., *The National Revenues.* Chicago: A. C. McClurg, 1888.

"Taxation in Hard Times," *Review of Reviews,* LXXXIV (August, 1931), 67-68.

The Taxation of Farm Lands. St. Paul, Minn.: Webb, 1924.

"The Taxation of Land," *Ohio Journal of Commerce,* XX (August 1, 1924), 122-124.

"The Taxation of Land," *Proceedings of the National Tax Association, 1921* (1922), 228-281.

"Taxing Land Values and Taxing Building Values," *Annals of the American Academy of Political and Social Science,* CXLVIII (March, 1930), 165-169.

"The Telegraph Monopoly," *North American Review,* CXLIX (July, 1889), 44-53.

"Tenancy in an Ideal System of Land Ownership," *American Economic Review, Supplement,* IX (1919), 180-212.

"Thou Art the Man," in *Luxury and Responsibility.* (Women's Education and Industrial Union, Leaflet No. 4.) Boston: [n.p], 1897.

"Thoughts on Immigration," *Congregationalist,* LXXIX-LXXX (June 28, June 9, 1894), 889-890, 13-14.

"The Three G's: A Program for Prosperity," *Country Gentleman,* LXXXIX (August 30, 1924), 1-2, 28.

"Training for the Real Estate Profession," *Ex Libris,* I (November, 1925), 5-8.

"Two Kinds of Optimism," *Our Day,* XVII (June, 1897), 275-276.

"Ulm on the Danube: A Study in Municipal Land Policy, and Its Provision for Workingmen's Homes," *Survey,* XXXI (December 6, 1913), 253-258.

"Under All, the Land," Schenectady (New York) *Citizen,* July 31, 1925.

"Unemployed," *Harper's Weekly,* XXXVII (September 2, 1893), 845.

"Unemployment and Our Civil Service," in Arthur O. Taylor, ed., *Persistent Public Problems.* Boston: [n.p.], 1916.

The Universities and the Churches: An Address Delivered at the Thirty-first University Convocation . . . July 5, 1893. Albany, N.Y.: University of the State of New York, 1893.

"The University as a Commercial Asset of Wisconsin," Madison *Wisconsin State Journal,* February 19, 1915.

"A Valuable Privilege: The Purchase Clause in the City Passenger Charter," Baltimore *Sun,* March 5, 1890.

"A View from Abroad: Learned Germans on the Coolie Immigration," San Francisco *Chronicle,* August 10, 1882.

"Views of Professor Ely," Baltimore *Sun,* January 26, 1885.

"Views on the Street-Car Question," Baltimore *Sun,* March 9, 1886.

"A Vision of Real Estate Education in the Future," *School Life,* XI (September, 1925), 12-13.

"What are the Trusts? A Study of Their Uses and Their Dangers," Boston *Evening Transcript,* January 30, 1901.

"What is Bolshevism?" *Review of Reviews,* LXII (November, 1920), 497-506.

"What is the Remedy?" *New Occasions,* III (February, 1895), 8-12.

"Die Wirtschafts-Theorie der Gegenwart," *Kosten und Einkommen bei der Bodenverwertung.* Vienna: Julius Springer, 1928.

"Worthless Land: What Can We Do for the Men on It?" *Country Gentleman,* LXXXIX (October 25, 1924), 1-2, 16.

Appendix 253

BOOK REVIEWS

Allotments and Small Holdings in Oxfordshire, by Arthur W. Ashby. *American Economic Review,* XVIII (March, 1918), 114-116.

American Political Ideas, by John Fiske. *Dial,* VI (May, 1885), 16-17.

The Colonization of Australia, 1829-1842: The Wakefield Experiment in Empire Building, by Richard Charles Mills. *American Economic Review,* VI (December, 1916), 874-876.

Contemporary Socialism, by John Rae. *Science,* IV (December 12, 1884), 534-535.

Cyclopedia of American Government, by Andrew C. McLaughlin and A. B. Hart, eds. *Dial,* LX (February 17, 1916), 169-171.

The Economics of Tenancy Law and Estate Management, by H. Stanley Jevons. *American Economic Review,* XIII (March, 1923), 110-111.

English Farming Past and Present, by Rowland E. Prothero. *American Historical Review,* XXIX (July, 1914), 860-865.

Excess Condemnation, by Robert Eugene Cushman. *American Economic Review,* VIII (June, 1918), 385-386.

Faith and Social Service, by George Hodges. *Expositor,* I (February, 1897), 85-89.

Icaria: A Chapter in the History of Communism, by Albert Shaw. *Science,* V (January 9, 1885), 34-35.

Joseph Warren: The First American Anarchist, by William Bailie. *American Political Science Review,* II (1906), 125-126.

Land Tenure in the United States with Special Reference to Illinois, by Charles Leslie Stewart. *American Economic Review,* VII (September, 1917), 614-617.

Land-Value Policy, by James Dundass White. *American Economic Review,* XIV (December, 1924), 776.

Merchandising Fruits and Vegetables, by Wells A. Sherman. *Journal of Land & Public Utility Economics,* VI (February, 1930), 109.

Principles of Economics, by F. W. Taussig. *American Economic Review,* II (September, 1912), 601-606.

Rich and Poor, by Mrs. Bernard Bosanquet. *Expositor,* 1 (February, 1897), 85-89.

The Right to the Whole Produce of Labor, by Anton Menger. *Annals of the American Academy of Political and Social Science,* XVI (September, 1900), 309-311.

Studies in Socialism, by Jean Jaures. *American Political Science Review,* II (November, 1907), 128-130.

University Addresses, by William Watts Folwell. *Yale Review,* XIX (August, 1910), 197-199.

BIBLIOGRAPHICAL NOTE

To LIST ALL of the works that treat Ely's career and influence would make an inordinately long bibliography. The reader will find in the footnotes of this work the use that I have made of secondary sources, newspapers, and magazines. This essay serves to bring together the lesser known materials for the researcher who wants to delve deeper into aspects of Ely and those closely associated with him.

The State Historical Society of Wisconsin in Madison has several voluminous collections of personal papers that are indispensable. The Ely manuscripts comprise 254 boxes of personal correspondence, lecture notes, occasional pamphlets, announcements, press releases, and the manuscripts of a few unpublished speeches. In addition, the collection includes two typewritten manuscripts by Richard's sister, Frances Mason Ely, "Story and Life of Harriet Gardner Ely," and "In Memoriam, Ezra Sterling Ely, 1825-1899," which contain several letters not found elsewhere. Ely compiled four scrapbooks over the years: "Miscellaneous Writings, 1876-1930," "Personal Scrapbooks, 1873-1908," "Scrapbook of the Institute for Research in Land Economics and Public Utilities," and "Scrapbook of the American Economic Association, 1885-1910," all located in the State Historical Society. The society has also obtained a microfilm copy of the Transcript of the Ely Trial of 1894. The papers of Edward A. Ross, John R. Commons, Theodore Herfurth, Henry D. Lloyd, Balthasar H. Meyer, Paul Reinsch, Algie M. Simons, and Henry C. Taylor, also located in the society, have less value since the Ely manuscripts contain duplicate letters of most of the correspondence with these men. The papers of Daniel Coit Gilman and Herbert Baxter Adams at the Johns Hopkins University are important for the study of Ely's early academic career. For the same period the candid, if somewhat sarcastic, diary of J. Franklin Jameson in the Library of Congress is revealing.

Published correspondence and memoirs of Ely's contemporaries are of considerable value. For life at Johns Hopkins in the 1880's as seen by the students see Ray Stannard Baker, ed., *Woodrow Wilson, Life and Letters: Youth, 1856-1890* (Garden City, N.Y.: Doubleday, Page & Co., 1927), and Elizabeth Donnan and Leo F. Stock, ed., *An Historian's World: Selections from the Correspondence of John Franklin Jameson* (Philadelphia: American Philosophical Society, 1956). Published letters by Ely are in Joseph Dorfman, ed., "The Seligman Correspondence," *Political Science Quarterly,* LVI (March, 1941), 107-124, (June, 1941), 270-286; Sidney Fine, ed., "The Ely-Labadie Letters," *Michigan History,* XXXVI (March, 1952), 1-32; and Benjamin G. Rader and Barbara K. Rader, "The Ely-Holmes Friendship, 1901-1914," *The Journal of American Legal History,* X (April, 1966), 128-147. Apart from manuscript sources, autobiographies occasionally provide material not found elsewhere. See especially the memoirs of Louis Brownlow, John R. Commons, Frederic C. Howe, Robert M. La Follette, Edward A. Ross, and Ida Tarbell. For the Ely family genealogy see Moses E. Beach and William Ely, *The Ely Ancestry* (New York: Calumet, 1902).

While this study is the first to be devoted exclusively to him, Ely has long been recognized by other authors as a pivotal figure in the history of reform ideology. Almost all works on the history of recent American reform give some attention to Ely's role, particularly the students of the Social

Gospel Movement. Ely's economic ideas are summarized in Sidney Fine, *Laissez-Faire and the General-Welfare State* (Ann Arbor: University of Michigan Press, 1956); David Noble, *The Paradox of Progressive Thought* (Minneapolis: University of Minnesota Press, 1958); and Joseph Dorfman, *The Economic Mind in American Civilization* (5 vols.; New York: Viking Press, 1946-1959). The tension between Ely's desire for professional recognition and his urge to reform which helps to explain the tortuous path that he pursued receives inadequate attention from all of these works. Ely's important influence in the twentieth century has been all but ignored, but Henry C. Taylor and Anne Dewees Taylor, *The Story of Agricultural Economics in the United States, 1840-1932* (Ames: Iowa State College Press, 1952) provides useful information on his contribution to the study of land economics. The unpublished theses of Samuel Elliot Cranfill, "The Contributions of Richard T. Ely to Economic Thought," Ph.D. Dissertation, Louisiana State University, 1941, and Bertha Mae Hancock, "The Economic Thought of Richard T. Ely," M.A. Thesis, University of Southern California, 1924, suffer from the inaccessibility of the Ely manuscripts at the time they were written.

INDEX

Abbott, Lyman: 59, 62, 134; reviews *Labor Movement in America*, 70; on Pullman strike, 136

Academic freedom: at Johns Hopkins University, 71; and depression of 1890s, 135-136; German conception of, 143; "sifting and winnowing" statement, 149-150. *See also* Ely: academic freedom

Adams, Charles Francis: 34

Adams, Charles Kendall: 36, 115, 138-139, 140, 142, 144, 148, 149, 154-155; as author of "sifting and winnowing" statement, 149; and reorganization of School of Economics, Political Science and History, 162

Adams, Henry C.: 20, 34, 38, 69; teaches political economy at Johns Hopkins University, 16-17; on platform of American Economic Association, 37; as author of "Relation of the State to Industrial Action," 88; and natural monopolies, 91

Adams, Herbert Baxter: 16, 18, 19, 26, 36, 37, 69, 70, 106-110 *passim;* renews friendship with Ely, 162-163

Adams, Thomas S.: 162, 178; as author of *Outlines of Economics*, 161; and progressive movement in Wisconsin, 174

Addams, Jane: 116, 127, 128

Administration: Ely study of in Berlin, 15. *See also* Ely: administration

Agricultural Adjustment Act: 232

Agricultural Atlas: 203

Agricultural economics. *See* Ely: agricultural economics

Agriculture, United States Department of: 202-203

Alden, H. M.: 54

Allen, William H.: 178

Alliance movement: 124-125, 154. *See also* National Farmer's Alliance

American Academy of Political and Social Science: 156-157

American Association for Agricultural Legislation: Ely helps to organize, 201-202

American Association for Labor Legislation: 168; Ely advocates peacetime army to, 231

American Association of University Professors: 171; and World War I, 183; investigation of utility propaganda and universities, 226-227

American Bureau of Industrial Research: 167-168

American Charities, by Amos G. Warner: 123

American Economic Association: 26, 28, 88, 121, 122, 156-157, 168, 169, 201, 213; founding of, 32-38; influence in foreign countries, 39-40; dispute over scheduling 1892 convention, 118-120; investigates Ross's dismissal, 171. *See also* Ely: American Economic Association

American Federation of Labor: Ely addresses, 24; and Ely's Institute, 213
American Federation of Teachers: condemns Ely's Institute, 213
American Historical Association: 36, 37
American Home Missionary Society: 58, 59
American Institute of Christian Sociology: 65, 121, 133-134
American Journal of Sociology: 90
Anarchism: 23, 60. *See also* Ely: labor
Anderson, Anna Morris. *See* Ely, Anna Anderson
Andrews, E. Benjamin: 148
A priori economics. *See* Classical economics
Arbitration. *See* Ely: labor
Armstrong, Robert H.: 233
Army, peacetime: Ely advocates during depression, 231-232
Associated Charities: 23, 123-124
Athenaean Joint Debate Team: 126
Atkinson, Edward: 34
Aylesworth, M. H.: 224
Ayres, Philip W.: 23; and Associated Charities, 123-124

Baker, Newton D.: 26, 90
Baker, Oliver E.: on Ely as teacher, 125; on Ely, 202
Baker's case: 169
Baltimore, Maryland: Ely residence in, 19; "How to Obtain a Home in Baltimore," by John R. Commons, 25; tax commission of, 26, 84-85; assessment practices in, 85; street railways of, 93
Baltimore *American*: on Ely leaving Johns Hopkins, 114
Baltimore and Ohio Railroad: 85
Baltimore and Ohio Telegraph: 92
Baltimore *Sun*: Ely's letter in, 24; on *Problems of To-day*, 89
Baptist Pastor's Conference: 62
Bartlett, William P.: 140-141
Bascom, John: 172, 175
Bates, Helen P.: 124

Bayview Summer School: 65
Beard, Charles A.: 200
Bell, Alexander Graham: 123, 127
Bellamy, Edward: 90, 97
Bemis, Edward H.: 21, 26, 117, 128, 132, 135, 152, 167, 171, 199; on Ely's trial for heresy, 143; on Ely and reform, 154
Bennett Act: 137
Bent, Mattie: 215, 224
Berle, Jr., A. A.: 53
Berlin, Germany: compared with New York City, 1; administration of, 15, 17
Berlin, Congress of (1878): 14
Bible: 97
Bing, Alexander M.: organizes City Housing Corporation, 219
Bird, George W.: 145, 146
Birge, Edward A.: 162, 186; and private contributions to university research, 212
"Bishop Hill," by M. A. Mikkelson: 25
Bismarck, Otto von: 55
Black, John D.: 193, 217
Blaine, James G.: 54
Bliss, William D. P.: 62, 66
Board of Regents of University of Wisconsin. *See* Wisconsin, University of
Bohn, Frank: with Ely as author of *The Great Change*, 232
Bolshevism: 183, 188, 189, 190, 205
Brandenburg, Samuel J.: 160, 224
Brentano, Ludwig J.: criticism of commodity labor thesis, 73
British Economic Association: 40
Brown, George W.: on Ely, 17; on review of "The Past and the Present of Political Economy," 31
Brown, T. Edwin: 62; on review by *Nation*, 72
Brownlow, Louis: 233
Bulletin of Manufacturers and Merchants Federal Tax League: carries attacks on Ely's Institute, 209-210, 211

Bulletin of the Christian Social Union of the United States and Canada: 66
Bullock, Charles J.: 65, 116, 127, 159, 163; on Ely, 89
Bureau of Farm Management and Farm Economics: 203

Call of the Cross, The, by George D. Herron: 133
Cannon, "Uncle Joe": 163
Capper, Arthur: 202, 203
Carew Lectures: 62
Carnegie, Andrew: 132; on Ely, 40
Carnegie Corporation: 205, 208; and support of Ely's Institute, 207
Carnegie endowments: La Follette on, 211
Carnegie Foundation: 167, 168
Carter, John: 63
Carver, Thomas Nixon: 26
Cassidy, J. M.: on Ely as a student, 8
Central Labor Union of New York: 80
Chamberlin, Thomas C.: 110, 115, 137; on Ely, 111; rift with Ely, 111-114
Charities and corrections. *See* Ely: University of Wisconsin
Chautauqua, New York: 165
Chautauqua Assembly Herald: 65
Chautauqua County, New York: 3, 7
Chautauqua Literary and Scientific Circle: 97
Chautauqua movement: 64-65, 118-119, 130, 133
Chautauquan Magazine: 65
Chautauqua Summer School: 7. *See also* Chautauqua movement
Chicago, Illinois: real estate taxation in, 221
Chicago Association of Commerce: sponsors study of Chicago real estate taxation, 221
Chicago Conference on Trusts: 154
Child labor. *See* Labor
Childs, George W.: 132

Chippewa *Herald*: on Ely and economic heresy, 139
Christian Social Union: 61, 63, 66, 133, 138, 142, 147, 175
Christian sociology: 134. *See also* Ely: sociology; Ely: churches
Christian Union: 59, 70
Church. *See* Ely: churches
Churchman: on Ely leaving Johns Hopkins University, 114
Chynoweth, H. W.: 141, 146
"Citizens Library, The": edited by Ely, 156, 157, 172, 194
City Housing Corporation: 219
Civilian Conservation Corps: 232
Civil service reform: 104, 158. *See also* Ely: natural monopolies
Clark, John Bates: 13, 38, 150, 163, 167; on *An Introduction to Political Economy,* 63; and platform of American Economic Association, 117
Clark, John Maurice: and influence of *Property and Contract* on, 199
Class conflict. *See* Ely: labor
Classical economics: 28, 52; and new economics, 29-32. *See also* Ely: new economics
Cleveland, Grover: 54; retrenchment and hard money, 135
Cliffe-Leslie, T. E.: 29
"College Anarchist, The": by O. E. Wells, 137
Collier's: and University of Wisconsin, 176
Columbia College. *See* Columbia University
Columbia University: 9-11; appoints Ely as honorary associate, 233
Committee on Cooperation with Educational Institutions. *See* National Electric Light Association
Commons, John R.: 20, 23, 25, 26, 53, 65, 72, 117, 121, 128, 132, 134, 135, 152, 160, 171, 172, 180, 211-212, 225; and labor project of, 166-168, 169-170; as author of *A Documentary History of Industrial Society,* 169;

Commons, John R. (*continued*):
and dispute with Ely, 169-170;
and La Follette, 173-174; and in-
fluence of *Property and Contract*
on, 199; defends Ely, 211, 213
Commonsense philosophy: 9, 12
Communal societies: 25
Competition: 103-104; and natural
monopolies, 91-92. *See also* Ely:
new economics
Congregationalist: 23, 151
Congress of Berlin. *See* Berlin,
Congress of
Conrad, Johannes: 11-12
Constitution, United States: Ely
on, 223
Consumption, law of: Engel's, 14
Cook County, Illinois: real estate
taxation of, 221
Cook County Joint Commission of
Real Estate Valuation: 221
Cooperation: 21. *See also* Ely:
labor
Cooperative Commonwealth, by
Lawrence Gronlund: 57
Cooperatives: 25
Cooper Union: 176
Corporations: 89; municipal fran-
chises to, 84. *See also* Ely:
corporations
Council of Defense: in Wisconsin,
189
Crowell, Thomas Y.: 89; on Ely,
40; on labor, 67-68
"Crowell Library of Economics
and Politics": 97, 128

Dale, H. B.: 141, 146
Dartmouth College: 8-9
Darwin, Charles: 46
Darwinism: 33
Debs, Eugene: 136, 170
Deductive method: 45-46
Deibler, Frederick S.: 222
De Lavéleye, Émile. *See* Lavéleye,
Émile de
Democratic party: and free silver,
154
Depression of 1890s: 97; and
academic freedom, 135-136

Dewey, Davis R.: 21, 26
Dial: 33, 70, 151
*Documentary History of Industrial
Society, A*, by John R. Com-
mons *et al.*: 169
Dodge, William: 113
Dolliver, Jonathan P.: 164
Dorau, Herbert B.: and urban
land economics, 221
Drisler, Henry: 9
Dunbar, Charles: 34, 150; attacks
new economics, 120-121

Economic Crises, by Edward D.
Jones: 128
Economic Review: 63
Economics: history of American
economic ideas, 21. *See also*
Classical economics; Ely: agri-
cultural economics; Ely: land
economics; Ely: new economics;
Historical School; Institutional
economics
Economics of Distribution, The, by
John Hobson: 230
Education: in Germany, 13, 14-15
Education Protective Association:
213
Eight-hour day law: 66
Election of 1890: Democratic upset
in Wisconsin, 137
Election of 1896: 154
Election of 1912: 179
Electric power companies. *See* Na-
tional Electric Light Association
*Elementary Principles of Econom-
ics*, by R. T. Ely and George
Ray Wicker: 160
Elements of Land Economics, by
R. T. Ely and Edward More-
house: 216
Ely, Anna (daughter): 164, 165;
marries Edward W. Morehouse,
214
Ely, Anna Anderson (wife): 54,
55, 135, 192; as hostess, 19;
description of, 127; illness of,
164-165; death of, 213-214
Ely, Ezra Sterling (father): 2, 12,
135; and farming, 2-3; religious

Ely, Ezra Sterling (*continued*): beliefs of, 4-5; lost money in 1880s, 7; assumes job with Warren and Venango Railroad, 9

Ely, Ezra Stiles (ancestor): 4; and reform, 6

Ely, Frances Mason (sister): 3

Ely, George Stetson (brother): 3, 18

Ely, Harriet Gardner Mason (mother): 2; influence of, 6-7; on Ely winning fellowship at Columbia, 10-11

Ely, John (son): 165, 214; fights in World War I, 183

Ely, Josephine (daughter): 135

Ely, Margaret Hahn (wife): 233; courtship and marriage, 222

Ely, Mary (daughter): 222

Ely, Richard (ancestor): 4

Ely, Richard Sterling (son): 19, 165, 214

ELY, RICHARD THEODORE:
—academic freedom: at Johns Hopkins University, 71; conception of, 136, 171-172. *See also* Ely: trial for economic heresy
—administration: study of Berlin, 15; public, 84-87. *See also* Ely: natural monopolies
—agricultural economics: 192-194; and irrigation economics, 194-195; organizes American Association for Agricultural Legislation, 201-202
—American Economic Association: secretary of, 21, 26, 38-40, 132; founding of, 32-38; draws platform of, 35; views as reform organization, 35-36; defense of platform, 37; controversy over platform, 117-118; resigns secretaryship, 118-120; encouraged to remain active in, 122; as president appoints committee to investigate dismissal of Ross, 171
—author of: "Oliver Goldsmith," 10; "The Scaffold in Switzerland," 14; "The Past and the Present of Political Economy,"

ELY: author of (*continued*): 31, 41; *French and German Socialism in Modern Times*, 57; "Recent American Socialism," 59; *Social Aspects of Christianity and Other Essays*, 60-61; *The Social Law of Service*, 61; *Outlines of Economics*, 65, 160-161; *The Labor Movement in America*, 67-68; *Socialism and Social Reform*, 84, 96-97; "Supplementary Report on Taxation in Maryland," 85; *Taxation in American States and Cities*, 85; *Problems of Today*, 89; editor of "Crowell Library of Economics and Political Science," 128; *Monopolies and Trusts*, 155; editor of Macmillan's "Citizens Library," 156, 157, 172, 194; *Studies in the Evolution of an Industrial Society*, 159; *An Introduction to Political Economy*, 160; *Elementary Principles of Economics*, 160; *Property and Contract*, 196-200; *Elements of Land Economics*, 216; *Land Economics*, 216; *Hard Times—The Way In and the Way Out*, 230-232; *The Great Change*, 232
—Chautauqua. *See* Ely: churches
—churches: and labor, 56; popularity of writings, 59, 61, 62; influence on Catholics, 60-61; secretary of Christian Social Union, 63, 66; and Chautauqua, 64-65; principal of Bayview Summer School, 65; joins Grace Episcopal Church in Madison, 116; and American Institute of Christian Sociology, 133-134; dropped by Chautauqua, 152-153; attitude toward in twenties, 223-224
—corporations: 83-84; regulation of, 94-96, 105; and monopolies, 104-105; consolidation of, 229. *See also* Ely: natural monopolies
—courtship and marriage: Anna Morris Anderson, 19; Margaret Hale Hahn, 222

Ely (*continued*):
—depressions: 104; and public works, 104. *See also* Ely: Great Depression
—early life: birth, 2; on farm, 2-3; ancestry of, 2-3; father's concern about religious beliefs of, 5; joins Protestant Episcopal Church, 6; at Dartmouth College, 7-8; impressions of men of wealth, 10; wins fellowship at Columbia, 10-11; studies at Halle, 11-12; education in Germany, 11-14; decides to study economics, 12; influence of Knies on, 13; in Berlin, 14; influence of Andrew D. White on, 14; views on German education, 15; seeks academic post, 16
—Great Depression: causes of, 228-230; solutions, 230-232; testifies to Wisconsin legislative committee, 232; views on New Deal, 232
—Institute for Research in Land Economics and Public Utilities: raising funds for, 204-208; criticism of, 209-213; moves to Northwestern University, 212, 213-214; publicity of, 214-215; and utility "education," 224-227; retires as director, 227-228. *See also* Ely: land economics
—Johns Hopkins University: appointment at, 16-17; and Seminary of, 18; residence in Baltimore, 19; as teacher, 19-23, 26-27; interest in Japanese students, 22; encourages use of "look and see" method, 23; influence on students, 26-27; controversies with Simon Newcomb, 31-33, 69-71; promotion to associate, 70-71; serves on Baltimore and Maryland tax commissions, 84-85; difficulties at, 106-110; position offered at University of Chicago, 109; press reaction to leaving for University of Wisconsin, 114-115

Ely (*continued*):
—labor: on anarchism and Johann Most, 23; addresses the American Federation of Labor, 24; letter to Baltimore streetcar workers, 24; studies Pullman, 54-56; and role of churches, 56, 58-59, 82; danger of radicalism of, 58-60; and anarchism, 60; on Knights of Labor, 67; and self-made man, 68; influence of *Labor Movement in America*, 72; commodity labor thesis criticized, 72-76; and class conflict, 76, 82; and arbitration 77-78; unions, 77-82, 152; and war, 81-82; and cooperation, 83-84; project with John R. Commons, 166-168, 169-170; addresses American Association for Labor Legislation, 168-169. *See also* Ely: socialism
—land economics: early interest in, 193-194; and landed property, 195-200 *passim*; study of cutover lands in northern Wisconsin, 200; and tenancy, 201; association with U.S. Department of Agriculture, 202-203; appointment to Committee of Fifteen (Wisconsin), 203; and land settlement, 203-204; land utilization, 216-218; and theory of ripening costs, 218; and planned communities, 219; and Montana Fairways Farms, 219-220. *See also* Ely: Institute for Research in Land Economics and Public Utilities
—last years: forms Institute for Economic Research, 228; appointed honorary associate at Columbia, 233; death of, 233-234. *See also* Ely: Great Depression
—natural monopolies: early views of, 13; street railways, 24; writings on, 87-88; influence of H. C. Adams on, 88; and municipal reform, 90-91; economics of, 91-92; advantages of government

ELY: natural monopolies (*cont.*): ownership of, 92-96; and depressions, 94; and civil service reform, 95; speech at Minneapolis on, 124-125; government ownership of, 151-152; change of views on, 224. *See also* Ely: railroads

—new economics: and classical economics, 28, 29-32, 41-46 *passim;* personal meaning of, 41; inductive and deductive method, 45-46; and social nature of man, 46-47; and ideal of brotherhood, 48-49, 53; and state, 49-50; and individual liberties, 51; and institutional economics, 53

—Northwestern University: moves Institute to, 212, 213-214; graduate work at, 221-222

—personal business: 135; real estate, 107-108, 166; sale of library, 165-166

—personal characteristics: sensitivity of, 2, 7-8; early maturity, 3; physical description of, 7; personality of, 18; capacity for work, 40, 214, 215; as teacher, 125

—personal relationships: with father, 5; with A. D. White, 14; with students, 18; with H. B. Adams, 106-110 *passim;* with Chamberlin, 111-114; with C. K. Adams, 115; with Herron, 132-134; with Commons, 169-170

—politics: views of civil service reform and, 104; and political parties, 132; elected town supervisor, 163; seeks appointment as special investigator with federal government, 163-164; considers running for Congress, 183-184

—railroads: study of Prussian ownership of, 15, 16; writings on, 87-88, 92-93. *See also* Ely: natural monopolies

—reform: and competitive order, 103-104; and money and banking, 104; views on initiative,

ELY: reform (*continued*): referendum, proportional representation, and recall, 104; activities in Madison, 115-116; as president of American Institute of Christian Sociology, 121; appointment to State Conference on Charities and Corrections (Wisconsin), 123; retreat from, 131-134; and tariff, 132; Gates and Herron, 151; increasing conservatism of, 151-158; role in Wisconsin Progressive Movement, 173,175,190-191; attitude toward in twenties, 223-224; changing views on, 234-235

—socialism: and professorial socialism, 23; French and German, 56-57; sympathy for, 57; views on, 96-103; personal position of, 103; public lectures on, 123-124; accused of teaching, 138. *See also* Ely: labor; Ely, natural monopolies

—sociology: interest in, 63-65, 123-124

—Spanish-American War: 181-182

—statements concerning others: on Haym, 12; on Anna Anderson, 19; on Newcomb, 33; on Pullman, 56; on Meyer, 173; on La Follette, 179; on Beard and Hand, 200

—statements of others concerning: Cassidy, 8; Godkin, 17; G. W. Brown, 17; Jameson, 20, 108; Howe, 22; Crowell, 40; Carnegie, 40; Small, 63-64; Gladden, 70; Bullock, 89; Peffer, 89; Tracy, 90; Chamberlin, 111; Walker, 119; O. E. Baker, 125; Bemis, 154; Fish, 160; New York *Times* obituary, 233-234

—taxation: 84-87 *passim*

—trial for economic heresy: 129, 135; charges against, 136-138; reaction to charges, 139-141; advice of friends, 140; appointment of investigating committee, 140-141; and Madison printers'

ELY: trial (*continued*):
strike, 141-142; denial of charges, 142-143; support of friends, 148-149; "sifting and winnowing" statement, 149-150; exoneration of charges, 149-150; personal effects on Ely, 152
—University of Wisconsin: applies for position at, 110-111; rift with Chamberlin, 111-114; and School of Economics, Political Science and History, 111, 112, 116, 127-128; charities and corrections, 122-124; and students, 125-128; as teacher, 125; residence on University Heights, 127; seeks eastern post, 157; administrative difficulties at, 162; seeks post at Johns Hopkins or Harvard, 162-163; labor project with Commons, 166-168, 169-170; conservative criticism of political economy department at, 177, 178-181; offers course on "Landed Property and Rent," 193-194; establishes scholarship in memory of wife, 214
—World War I: view of Germany, 182; opponents of, 183-188 *passim;* and League of Nations controversy, 188-189; organizes Wisconsin Society for Civic and Industrial Improvement, 190; and postwar Red scare, 190
Ely, William Brewster (son): 222
Ely Economic Foundation: 228
Engel, Ernst: 14
English political economy. *See* Classical economics
Episcopal church. *See* Protestant Episcopal church
Epworth Youth League: 61
Equitable Tax Association: 227
Esch, John J.: condemns La Follette, 185
Espionage Act of 1918: 184, 185
Evangelical Alliance: 62
Eve, H. Trustram: 196
Everest, Kate: 124
Evolution, theory of: 44, 46
Experimentalism: 53

Fabian Society: 97
Fairchild, Lucius: 116
Fairways Farms. *See* Montana Fairways Farms
Farm bloc: denounced by Harding, 216
Farm Economic Association: 202
Farm Mortgage Bankers Association: supports research in land economics, 206; and Ralston-Nolan bill, 207
Farm, Stock and Home: 90
Farnam, Henry: 34, 168, 171; on 1892 American Economic Association Convention, 120
Farrer, T. H.: as author of *The State and Its Relation to Trade*, 91
Fawcett, Millicent G.: as author of *Political Economy for Beginners*, 9
Federal Reserve System: 232
Federal Trade Commission: hearings on utility propaganda, 226
Federated Trades Council of Madison: 151
Fernow, Bernard: 127; gives course in forestry at Wisconsin, 193
Fetter, Frank: 171
Fifteen, Committee of: frames postwar land policy for Wisconsin, 203; opposes Mead plan, 204
Finley, John H.: 21, 85, 160
Finley, Robert: 127
First Wisconsin Commercial and Industrial Congress: 180
Fish, Carl Russell: 186; on Ely as administrator, 160
Fisher, Ernest M.: 208
Folwell, William W.: 36, 122
Ford, Guy Stanton: 187
Forum: 90, 121
Four Lakes Kindergarten Association: 116
Franco-Prussian War of 1870: 82
Fredonia, New York: religious life of, 5
Fredonia Academy: 8
Fredonia Normal School: 7
Free Silver: and Democratic party, 154

Fremantle, Bishop Canon: 62
French and German Socialism in Modern Times, by R. T. Ely: 57
Fuller, Homer: 8

Galbraith, John Kenneth: 53
Gamble, W. W.: recommends Ely's books on natural monopolies, 89-90
Gardner, Henry: 171
Gates, George: 23, 134-135, 151, 153
Geneva, University of: 13
Genteel reformers: 157
George, Henry: 96; speech in Baltimore, 23; as author of *Progress and Poverty,* 80
German Historical School of economics. *See* Historical School of economics
German Society for Social Policy: 33
Gibbons, James Cardinal: 61
Gide, Charles: 96
Gifford, Walter: 183
Gilded Age: 157
Gilman, Daniel C.: 16, 17, 19, 31, 32, 36, 70, 71, 107, 108, 109
Gladden, Washington: 38, 62, 65; on Ely, 70
Glaeser, Martin: prepares textbook on utilities, 208; and utility "education," 225, 226
Godkin, E. L.: 34, 71, 158; on Ely, 17
Golden Mean: 82, 89, 103. *See also* Ely: natural monopolies
Goldman, Emma: 176, 177, 180
Goldsmith, Oliver: 10
Gompers, Samuel: 68
Goucher College: 19
Gould, E. R. L.: 153
Gould, Jay: 66
Grace Episcopal Church of Madison: 116, 224
Gray, Lewis C.: 193, 217; heads division of land economics, 203; directs program of land retirement in New Deal, 218
Great Change, The, by R. T. Ely and Frank Bohn: 232

Great Depression. *See* Ely: Great Depression
Greeley, Horace: 6
Green, William: 213
Gregory, Charles W.: 115-116, 140, 142
Gronlund, Lawrence: 57

Hadley, Arthur T.: 117, 120, 122; reviews *Socialism and Social Reform,* 121
Hahn, Margaret Hale. *See* Ely, Margaret Hahn
Hall, A. B.: 188
Halle, University of: 11-12
Hamilton, William: 9
Hand, Learned: 200; on *Property and Contract,* 197
Handbuch der Politischen Oekonomie, by G. V. Schönberg: 73
Harding, Warren G.: 216
Hard Times—The Way In and the Way Out, by R. T. Ely: 230-232
Harper, William Rainey: 64; offers Ely and H. B. Adams positions at Chicago, 109, 110; dismisses Ely from Chautauqua, 153
Harper and Brothers: 57
Harper's New Monthly Magazine: 14, 54, 87, 89
Hart, Albert Bushnell: 150
Harvard University: Ely seeks post at, 162, 163
Harvard University Graduate School of Business Administration: 226
Haskins, Charles: 27, 112
Haym, Rudolph: 12
Healy, Robert E.: 226
Hearst newspapers: attack Ely's Institute, 226
Hegel, Georg: 12
Heidelberg, University of: 12
Heilman, Ralph E.: 212, 214
Henry Strong Foundation: 222
Herron, George: 61, 62, 65, 117, 121, 132-134, 151, 153; as author of *The Call of the Cross,* 133
Hibbard, Benjamin, 193, 200, 213, 220; criticizes Ralston-Nolan bill, 207

Hildebrand, Bruno: 13, 47
Hinman, Albert S.: and urban land economics, 221
Historical and Political Science Association of Madison: 115-116
Historical School of economics: 11, 13, 20, 29-34 *passim*, 47, 52, 148, 203. *See also* Ely: new economics
History, Organization, and Influence of the Independent Treasury of the United States, by David Kinley: 127
Hobson, John: as author of *The Economics of Distribution*, 230
Hollander, Jacob: 163, 167
Holmes, Jr., Oliver Wendell: 172; on Ely's address to American Association for Labor Legislation, 169; assists Ely on *Property and Contract*, 197
Homestead Steel Works: 135
Hoover, Herbert: 231-232
Hough, Eugene: 9
Howe, Frederic C.: 26, 90, 128, 150; on Ely as teacher, 22; as author of *Wisconsin: An Experiment in Democracy*, 174
Hubbard, Charles M.: and Associated Charities, 124
Hughes, Thomas: 62
Hull, Charles H.: and Ross affair, 171
Hull House (Chicago): 124
Hunt & Eaton: 65
Hunter, Robert: 167
Huntington, J. O. S.: 62
Hyde, Arthur M.: calls National Land Utilization Conference, 217

Ideal of brotherhood: 48-49. *See also* Ely: new economics
Illinois State Tax Commission: orders reassessment of Cook County, 221
Income tax. *See* Ely: taxation
Increasing returns, law of: for natural monopolies, 91
Independent: 126
Inductive method: 25, 45-46
Industrial Commission: 167

Initiative: 104
Institute for Economic Research: 228
Institute for Research in Land Economics and Public Utilities: 196; urban land studies, 220. *See also* Ely: Institute for Research
Institute News: 214-215
Institutional economics: 53
Insull, Martin: 208, 212
Insull, Samuel: 208
Intellectuals: and farmer-labor reformers, 157-158; as reformers, 157-158
Interchurch World Movement: supports research in land economics, 206
Interdenominational Conference: 62
International Working People's Association: 59-60
Interstate Commerce Act of 1887: 88
Introduction to Political Economy, An, by R. T. Ely: 22, 61, 63, 65, 89, 160; Sato on, 22
Irrigation economics. *See* Ely: agricultural economics
Irving, Washington: 10

Jackson, Carl D.: and Glaeser textbook, 226
James, Edmund J.: 11, 34, 35, 36, 108
James, William: as author of *The Moral Equivalent of War*, 231
Jameson, J. Franklin: 18, 27, 42; on Ely as teacher, 20; on Ely and classical economics, 29-30; on Ely, 108
Japan: influence of Ely in, 22
Jastrow, Joseph: 111-112
Jesse, R. H.: on Elys as hosts, 127
John Crerar Library: Ely sells personal library to, 166
Johns Hopkins University: 16; Seminary in History and Political Science, 18; policy toward political economy and history department, 106, 108. *See also* Ely: Johns Hopkins University

Johns Hopkins University Studies in Historical and Political Science: 18, 31
Johnson, Joseph F.: 11
Johnson, Tom L.: 167
Johnston, Alexander: 38
Johnston, John: 141, 146-147
Jones, Alton: 222
Jones, Burr: 148; defends Ely in trial for economic heresy, 144, 145
Jones, Edward D.: as author of *Economic Crises*, 128
Jones, Granville D.: on radicalism in University of Wisconsin, 180
Jones, Richard Lloyd: 184
Jones, Sam: 65
Jordan, David Starr: 170
Jorgensen, Emil O.: attacks Ely's Institute, 209-211, 212
Journal of Land & Public Utility Economics: 125, 226, 228
Journeymen Baker's National Union: 58

Kant, Immanuel: 12
Kemmerer, Edwin W.: 213
Kies, William S.: 222, 233; supports research in land economics, 206
Kingdom, The: 23, 151, 153
Kinley, David: 65, 113, 116, 122, 141-150 *passim*, 154, 184, 199; as author of *History, Organization, and Influence of the Independent Treasury of the United States*, 127; takes charge of Ely's defense, 143-144
Klunk, Frank: and Ely trial for economic heresy, 144, 147
Knies, Karl: 30, 47, 175; influence on Ely, 13; on changing economic theory, 46
Knights of Labor: 60, 66-67, 68, 69, 78, 82, 84; encourage temperance, 81; and cooperation, 83

Labor: Baltimore streetcar workers, 24; twelve-hour day law, 24; contract, 51; women, 51; attitude of churches toward, 58; commodity thesis of, 72-76; re-

Labor (*continued*):
search project of Ely and Commons, 166-168, 169-170. *See also* Ely: labor
Labor Movement in America, The, by R. T. Ely: 20, 67-68, 72, 83, 152, 166, 168
Labor unions: strikes in 1890s, 135-136. *See also* Ely: labor
La Follette, Robert M.: 178, 181, 190; elected governor of Wisconsin, 172-173; Ely on, 179; and World War I, 183-188 *passim*; attacks private support of university research, 210, 211
Laissez faire. *See* Classical economics
Land, utilization of: 216-218
Land economics. *See* Ely: land economics
Land Economics, by R. T. Ely and George Wehrwein: 216
"Landed Property and Rent": course offered by Ely, 193-194
Laughlin, J. Laurence: 34, 117, 157
Laura Spelman Rockefeller Memorial: 220
Lavéleye, Émile de: 30
League of Nations: 188, 189, 190
League to Enforce the Peace: Wisconsin branch, 187-189
Lee, H. W.: 96
Legal Foundations of Capitalism, The, by J. R. Commons: 199
Legislative Reference Library (in Wisconsin): 174
Lehrfreiheit und Lernfreiheit: 136. *See also* Ely: academic freedom
Lenroot, Irvine: 189, 203; condemns La Follette, 185
Levermore, Charles H.: on "Newcomb on Mathematical Economy," 32
Liberty, industrial: 51
Literary and Scientific Circle of Chautauqua. *See* Chautauqua movement
Liverpool, England: compared with New York City, 1
Living Wage, A, by John A. Ryan: 62

Lloyd, Henry Demarest: 117, 126, 168
Lloyd George, David: 195
"Look and see" method: 23, 148. *See also* Inductive method
Lorenz, Max O.: as author of *Outlines of Economics,* 161
Loucks, H. L.: 89
Love, Jonathan: 132
Lovejoy, Arthur: 171
Lowell, A. Lawrence: 189

Mabie, Hamilton W.: 153
MacChesney, Nathan W.: 212
Macmillan Company: 156, 165. *See also* "Citizens Library"
Macy, V. Everit: 167
Madison Civil Service Reform Association: 115
Madison *Democrat*: on Ely and economic heresy, 139
Madison Park Corporation: 166
Malthus, Thomas: 42, 73; population theory, 169
Manchester School of Economics: 22. *See also* Classical economics
Manufacturers and Merchants Federal Tax League: attacks Ely's Institute, 209-210, 211
Marburg Company: 166
Marginal utility, theory of: 32
Marx, Karl: 97, 98
Maryland Tax Commission: 26, 84-85, 89
Materialism: 98. *See also* Socialism
Mathematics: and political economy, 31-32
Maurice, Frederick D.: 62
McCarthy, Charles: and progressive movement in Wisconsin, 174; author of *The Wisconsin Idea,* 174-175; and conservatism of University of Wisconsin, 181
McCormick, Stanley: 167
McGovern, Francis: 174, 175
Mead, Elwood: 194; land settlement proposal of, 203-204
Means, Gardner C.: 53
Meriwether, Charles: on Ely's influence in Japan, 22

Methodist Episcopal church: 61
Meyer, Balthazar H.: and economics of transportation, 128; appointed to Interstate Commerce Commission, 173
Mikkelson, M. A.: 25
Mill, James: 42
Mill, John Stuart: 42; Ely and, 29, 30; and wages fund theory, 78-79
Milwaukee *Advance*: 125
Milwaukee Electric Railway and Light Company: study of, 225
Milwaukee *Journal*: on Ely and economic heresy, 140
Milwaukee Settlement House: 124
Milwaukee *Wisconsin*: on Ely and economic heresy, 139-140
Mitchell, Wesley Clair: 53
Monopolies: 104-105. *See also* Ely: corporations
Monopolies and Trusts, by R. T. Ely: 155
Montana Fairways Farms: and Ely's Institute, 219-220
Moral Equivalent of War, The, by William James: 231
Morehouse, Edward W.: marries Anna Ely, 214; edits *Journal of Land & Public Utility Economics,* 215; as author with Ely of *Elements of Land Economics,* 216
Morganthau, Henry: 189
Morris, George P.: 23
Most, Johann: 23
Municipal reform: 90-91. *See also* Ely: natural monopolies

Nairne, Charles Murray: 9; influence on Ely, 10
Nation: 16, 69, 70, 72, 115, 131, 136, 138-139, 140, 141, 146, 150; on *The Labor Movement in America,* 20; review of "The Past and the Present of Political Economy," 31; review of *Taxation in American States and Cities,* 85
National Agricultural Conference: Ely speaks at, 216-218

National Association of Real Estate Boards: 217; and real estate education, 207-208; and Ralston-Nolan bill, 207, 210
National Civic Federation: 167
National Conference on Land Utilization: 193
National Electric Light Association: support of Ely's Institute, 208; on utility textbooks, 225, 226; discontinues contribution to Ely's Institute, 227
National Farmer's Alliance: 89-90
National Industrial Recovery Act: 232
National Irrigation Congress: 194
National Land Use Planning Commission: 218
National Land Utilization Conference: 217-218
National League for Promoting Government Ownership of Monopolies: 154
National Resources Commission: 218
National Security League: 182
Natural law: 44. *See also* Classical economics
Natural monopolies. *See* Ely: natural monopolies
Neale, Vansittart: 62
Negroes: 235; and tenancy in the South, 201
Nelson, John M.: 183-184
Newcomb, Simon: 34, 131; on Ely and new school, 31-32; as author of *Principles of Political Economy*, 33; view of American Economic Association, 36; reviews *Labor Movement in America*, 69; controversy with Ely, 69-71; as author of *A Plain Man's Talk on the Labor Question*, 70
New Deal: 103, 202, 235; community programs of, 195, 219; agricultural programs of, 217, 218
New economics. *See* Ely: new economics
Newell, F. H.: 194

New school of economics. *See* Ely: new economics
Newton, Isaac: 44
Newton, R. Heber: 57, 62
New York, New York: compared with Berlin and Liverpool, 1
New York *Evening Post*: 14, 16, 138, 140
New York *Times*: review of *Hard Times—The Way In and the Way Out*, 231; obituary of Ely, 233-234
New York Times Book Review: on *Property and Contract*, 197
Nonpartisan League: 184
Northern California Alumni Association: 185
Northwestern Congregationalist: 151
Northwestern University: 212; graduate work at, 221-222. *See also* Ely: Northwestern University
Noyes, George H.: 149

O'Connell, Friend: and Ely trial for economic heresy, 144
Old Lyme, Connecticut: Ely resides in, 233
Olin, John M.: suggests idea of "sifting and winnowing" statement, 149
Omaha *Bee*: 90
Oshkosh *Northwestern*: on Ely and economic heresy, 139
Outlines of Economics, by R. T. Ely *et al.*: 65, 160-161, 177
Outlook: 126, 142-143, 151; on Herron, 134

Page, Walter Hines: 121, 196
Parker, John C.: 212
Parkinson, John B.: 110, 113, 114
"Past and the Present of Political Economy, The," by R. T. Ely: 115; review in *Nation*, 31
Patten, Simon N.: 11, 34, 35, 36
Peck, William: 9
Peffer, William A.: on Ely, 89
People's Institute of Milwaukee: 124

Perlman, Jacob: 220-221

Perry, Arthur: 34

Philipp, Emmanuel L.: 173, 178, 179, 181; appoints Ely to Committee of Fifteen, 203

Pinchot, Gifford: 195; attacks Ely's Institute, 226

Pinkerton detectives: 135

Plain Man's Talk on the Labor Question, A, by Simon Newcomb: 70

Plunkett, Horace: 196

Political economy: and mathematics, 31-32. *See also* Ely: new economics; Classical economics

Political Economy Club: 34; at University of Wisconsin, 181

Political Economy for Beginners, by Millicent G. Fawcett: 9

Politics. *See* Ely: politics

Populist movement: 89-90, 135

Porter, Noah: 11

Pound, Roscoe: 225; on *Property and Contract*, 199

Powderly, Terrance V.: 68, 81

Powell, William W.: campaigns in Wisconsin for League of Nations, 189

Powers, H. H.: 144

Presbyterianism: 5

Principles of Economics, by John Stuart Mill: 30

Principles of Political Economy, by Simon Newcomb: 33; reviewed by Albert Shaw, 33

Problems of To-day, by R. T. Ely: 89

Professorial socialism. *See* Socialism

Professors, western: reaction to conservatism of the East, 116-117, 121-122

Progress and Poverty, by Henry George: 80

Progressive movement: 91, 103, 168, 183, 209, 223; in Wisconsin, 128, 160, 173-175, 178, 190-191

Property and Contract, by R. T. Ely: 195, 196-200

Property tax. *See* Ely: taxation

Proportional representation: 104

Protestant Episcopal church: 61

Protestant Episcopal Divinity School: 62

Public utilities. *See* Utilities

Public works: 104

Pullman, George M.: 54, 56, 135-136

Pullman, Illinois: 19, 54, 55, 152

Pullman Palace Car Company: 54

Pullman strike: 135-136, 152

Radburn, New Jersey: 219

Railroads: 87-88, 92-93, 99; government ownership in Prussia, 15; contributions to Ely's Institute, 207. *See also* Ely: natural monopolies

Ralston-Nolan bill: 207, 210, 211

Rauschenbusch, Walter: 62

"Reaction in Political Economy," by Charles Dunbar: 121

Reagen bill: 88

Realtors. *See* National Association of Real Estate Boards

Recall: 104

"Recent American Socialism," by R. T. Ely: 59

Red scare: 190

Referendum: 104

Reichstag: 14

Reifseirder, Charles S.: on Ely's influence in Japan, 22

Reinsch, Paul: as author of *World Politics at the End of the Nineteenth Century*, 128; and La Follette, 173

"Relation of the State to Industrial Action," by Henry C. Adams: 88

Remsen, Ira: 162, 163

Review of Reviews: 26, 90, 126, 151, 155-156, 162, 231; on Ely, 131; on Herron, 134; on *Property and Contract*, 197

Rew, R. Henry: 196

Reynolds, Thomas: 147

Ricardo, David: 42; and subsistence wage, 73, 77; and land economics, 218

Riis, Jacob: 116, 127
Ripening cost, theory of: 218
Robbins, Kingman N.: 206
Rockefeller, Jr., John D.: 219, 220
Rockefeller General Education
Board: La Follette on, 211
Rockefeller Memorial: 211-212
Roman Catholic church: and
reform, 60-61
Roosevelt, Franklin Delano: 229,
232
Roosevelt, Theodore: 26, 127, 179,
185, 186, 189; considers Ely for
appointment, 163, 164; on Ely's
address to American Association
for Labor Legislation, 169; on
La Follette, 184
Root, Winfred T.: 186
Roscher Wilhelm: 13, 30, 47
Ross, Edward A.: 26, 38, 116, 117,
120, 125, 152, 160, 180, 199,
213, 235; on Ely as a teacher,
21; on Ely's methodology, 24-25;
dismissal at Stanford and hiring
at Wisconsin, 170-172; as author
of *Social Control*, 172; and Gold-
man-Sercombe affair, 176-177
Round Table: Engel's, 14; Ely's,
214, 222
Royal Statistical Bureau: 14
Russell Sage Foundation: 195
Ryan, John A.: 61-62

Sato, Shosuke: 22
Say, John Baptiste: law of, 44
Schauffler, H. A.: 58, 59
Schönberg, Gustav: 30; as author
of *Handbuch der Politischen
Oekonomie*, 73
School of Economics, Political Sci-
ence and History (University of
Wisconsin): 162. *See also* Ely:
University of Wisconsin
School of Commerce (University
of Wisconsin): 162
School of History (University of
Wisconsin): 162
Schurz, Carl: reviews Ely's study
on Prussian railroads, 16
Schwedtman, F. C.: 205

Science: 33
Scientific Association: 32
Scott, Walter Dill: 212
Scott, William A.: 113, 128, 140,
150; and School of Commerce,
162
Securities and Exchange
Commission: 232
Seelye, Julius: 59
Self-interest, theory of: 43, 45. *See
also* Classical economics
Seligman, Edwin R. A.: 35, 38,
119, 120, 150, 163, 171, 172; on
platform of American Economic
Association, 37, 117; prepares
American Association of Univer-
sity Professors report, 227
Seligman, Eugene: 10
Seminary. *See* Round Table
Senate, United States: 87
Senior, Nassau: 42; theory of
monopoly, 157
Sercombe, Parker: 176-177, 180
Shaw, Albert: 21, 26, 56, 90, 134,
140, 141, 148, 150, 154, 162,
168, 187; review of Newcomb's
Principles of Political Economy,
33; reviews *Labor Movement in
America*, 70; supports Ely's ap-
pointment to federal post, 164
Sherman Act: 229
Shine, Mary L.: 215
Short, Henry A.: 9
"Sifting and winnowing" statement:
controversy over plaque, 178.
See also Ely: Trial for economic
heresy
Simpson, Herbert D.: study of
taxation in Chicago, 221
Single tax: 205, 209; theory of,
218. *See also* George, Henry;
Jorgensen, Emil O.
Small, Albion: 20, 26, 90, 148,
150, 172; on Christian sociology,
63-64; on Herron and Gates,
134-135
Smith, Adam: 42, 73, 75; as author
of *Wealth of Nations*, 161
Smith, Asa Dodge: 9
Smith, Charles Lee: 150

Social Aspects of Christianity and Other Essays, by R. T. Ely: 60-61, 126
Social Control, by Edward A. Ross: 172
Social gospel movement: 23; and Ely, 60-66. *See also* Ely: churches
Socialism: 135; in western states, 90. *See also* Ely: socialism
Socialism and Social Reform, by R. T. Ely: 61-62, 84, 89, 96-97, 103, 121
Social Law of Service, The, by R. T. Ely: 61
"Society for the Study of National Economy": 34
Society of Land Economics: 196
Sociology. *See* Ely: sociology
Spanish American War: Ely's view of, 181-182
Sparling, Samuel E.: 128, 174
Speirs, Fred H.: 125
Spencer, Herbert: 33, 46; and individual liberty, 51
Spooner, John: 172; and Ely appointment with federal government, 163-164
Stalwarts: 163, 173, 181, 184, 186
Standard Oil trust: 93
Stanford, Mrs. Leland: 170
State Board of Public Affairs: investigates University of Wisconsin, 178
State Conference on Charities and Corrections (in Wisconsin): 123
State in Its Relation to Trade, The, by T. H. Farrer: 91
Steffens, Lincoln: and "sifting and winnowing" statement, 178
Stevens, Breese J.: 140, 141
Streetcar workers: in Baltimore, 61
Strong, Josiah: 62, 134
Studies in the Evolution of an Industrial Society, by R. T. Ely: 159
Suburban and Country Homes Company: 195
Sumner, William Graham: 32, 33, 34, 36, 117, 118, 120, 131
Sundry Civil bill: 163-164
Sunnyside, New York: 219

"Supplementary Report on Taxation in Maryland": 85
Supreme Court, United States: 87, 169; uses Ely's definition of monopoly, 105
Swan Sonnenschein and Company: 97

Taft, William Howard: 179, 187, 189; on La Follette, 184; addresses Wisconsin Win the War for Permanent Peace Convention, 188
Tarbell, Ida: 65
Taussig, Frank: 150
Taxation. *See* Ely: taxation
Taxation in American States and Cities, by R. T. Ely and John H. Finley: 21, 85, 89
Taylor, Henry C.: 200, 209, 212, 215, 219-220; and agricultural economics, 192, 193, 194; and irrigation economics, 195; helps form American Association for Agricultural Legislation, 201-202; joins Department of Agriculture, 202-203; and National Agricultural Congress, 216; joins Ely's Institute, 220-221
Taylor, Graham: 134
Teale, R. P.: 195
Telegraph: 92-93. *See also* Ely: natural monopolies
Tenancy: 201
Ten-hour day law: 58
Tracy, W. A.: 142, 143, 147
Treaty of Versailles: 188-189
Trial for economic heresy. *See* Ely: trial for economic heresy
Trusts. *See* Monopolies
Turner, Frederick Jackson: 27, 110, 112, 113-114, 141, 148, 150; and School of History, 162; takes post at Harvard, 176
Twelve-hour day law: 61

Ulrici: 11
"Unearned increment." *See* George, Henry
United Brethren of Christ church: 61

Universities: in western states, 116-117
University Association of Chicago: 165
University Heights, Madison, Wisconsin: 165
University of Wisconsin. *See* Wisconsin, University of
Utilities: support of Ely's Institute, 208, 226-227. *See also* Ely: and natural monopolies; National Electric Light Association

Van Dyke, Henry: 189
Van Hise, Charles R.: 162, 172, 173, 176, 180, 184, 186, 188, 212; and Ely-Commons dispute, 170; recommends censure of Ross, 177
Veblen, Thorstein: 20, 21, 53, 100
Vested rights, theory of: 198
Vincent, John H.: 62, 64, 65, 152-153; reads Ely's denial of heresy charges, 130
Virgin, Samuel H.: 58
Vrooman, Carl: 209

Wages: subsistence thesis of Ricardo, 73, 77; fund theory of, 78-79, 169
Wagner, Adolph: 14, 23, 30, 175
Walker, Francis A.: 30, 32, 38, 120, 122; on Chautauqua, 119; on Ely, 119
Warner, Amos G.: 21, 127, 128; on organized charities in Baltimore, 25; as author of *American Charities*, 123
Warner, Charles D.: 23
Warren and Venango Railroad: 9
Washington School for Secretaries: 214
Wealth of Nations, by Adam Smith: 161
Webb, Sidney: 40, 96, 97
Wehrwein, George: 193, 215, 220; as author with Ely of *Land Economics*, 216
Wells, Oliver E.: and Ely's trial for economic heresy, 136-150 *passim*

Western Union: 92
Wharton School of Finance, University of Pennsylvania: 110
White, Andrew D.: 17, 36, 56; influence on Ely, 14, 15
White, William Allen: 189
Whitehead, John M.: 188
Williams, Leighton: 62, 134
Williams, Roger: 72
Willoughby, W. F.: 27
Willoughby, William W.: 26, 27
Wilnn, S. Robert: on Ely and socialism, 57
Wilson, George S.: and Associated Charities, 124
Wilson, James: refuses to publish Ely's irrigation report, 195
Wilson, Milburn L.: 193, 202, 217, 218, 232
Wilson, Woodrow: 21, 26, 27, 127, 179, 183, 186, 188, 189
Wines, Frederick H.: 122, 128
Wisconsin, University of: establishes chair of Finance and Statistics, 110; Board of Regents of, 131, 137; social sciences in, 111; special investigating committee, 140-141; and progressive movement, 175-176; investigation by State Board of Public Affairs, 178; McCarthy on conservatism at, 181; war committee and La Follette petition, 185-186; establishes division of land economics, 206; and Ely's Institute, 207; resolution of Board of Regents, 212
Wisconsin: An Experiment in Democracy, by Frederic C. Howe: 174
Wisconsin Idea: 181
Wisconsin Idea, The, by Charles McCarthy: 174-175
Wisconsin Loyalty Legion: 189; Madison chapter, 185-186
Wisconsin Peace Society: 182
Wisconsin Society for Civic and Industrial Improvement: organized by Ely, 190
Wisconsin State Journal: 142, 180, 184; on Ely and economic heresy,

Wisconsin State Journal (*cont.*): 139; libel suit of La Follette, 186-187

Wisconsin Win the War for Permanent Peace Convention: 188

Woodworth, Leo Day: 203

Workingmen. *See* Labor

World as the Subject of Redemption, The, by Bishop Canon Fremantle: 62

World Politics at the End of the Nineteenth Century, by Paul Reinsch: 128

World's Parliament of Religions: 62

World War I. *See* Ely: World War I

Wright, Carroll: 141; defense of Ely, 148-149; and labor study, 167

Young, Allyn A.: 183; as author of *Outlines of Economics,* 161; on *Property and Contract,* 197

Young Men's Christian Association: at Johns Hopkins University, 18

BENJAMIN G. RADER, the author of this book, is a graduate of Southwest Missouri State College. He holds the M.A. degree from Oklahoma State University and the Ph.D. degree from the University of Maryland. Presently he is an assistant professor of history at the University of Montana.

The Academic Mind and Reform: The Influence of Richard T. Ely in American Life received honorable mention by the Frederick Jackson Turner Award Committee of the Organization of American Historians in 1966.